Homo Religiosus

Homo Religiosus

SOCIOLOGICAL PROBLEMS
IN THE STUDY OF RELIGION

ROBERT TOWLER

Lecturer in Sociology
The University of Leeds

ST. MARTIN'S PRESS
NEW YORK

AFFILIATED PUBLISHERS: Macmillan Limited, London
also at Bombay, Calcutta, Madras and Melbourne

O Tree of many branches! One thou hast
Thou bearest not, but grafted'st on thee. Now,
Should all men's thunders break on thee, and leave
Thee reft of bough and blossom, that one branch
Shall cling to thee, my Father, Brother, Friend,
Shall cling to thee, until the end of end.

Francis Thompson

Preface

This book is addressed, I suppose, to students of sociology. Certainly I have had in mind while writing it those students at the University of Leeds who have attended a course of lectures on the sociology of religion which I have given for the past five years. But just as students of subjects other than sociology have strayed into the lecture room, so I hope that people other than sociologists will find something of interest here.

At a time when religion is supposed to be dying fast if not actually dead, it seems to have an uncanny fascination for many people. Perhaps it is the fascination of the corpse just before it is lost for ever to the grave, or perhaps that of the chrysalis just before it disintegrates to release a new unlooked-for creature, the butterfly. Who can tell? What is certain is that people of all ages talk of religion with undiminished interest. I have tried here to discuss a few questions of perennial concern from the standpoint of the sociologist, but one question in particular runs through the book: What is religion? This question is important for the student of religion and for the religious believer alike. But it is of wider importance than that: like Pilate's question, 'What is truth?', it is important for every man as well. 'Where there is no vision the people perish', said one of the prophets. If that is true, as I believe it is, we must use every insight we possess to learn more about the vision, and that includes the insights of sociology. And within sociology the study of religion must be the central concern just because religion is the vision by which people, and peoples, live.

I should like to thank all those who have helped me in various ways to make this book, especially Dr Anthony Coxon, Mrs Elizabeth Smith, Dr and Mrs Iain Richardson, and my friend the Revd Hugh Bishop.

R.T.

Drummin, Inverness-shire
December 1973

Contents

1. Sociology and Religion

The expression 'sociology of religion' is not a satisfactory one. It is commonly taken to imply a discipline which studies an institutional area within societies in the same way as do the sociology of industry and the sociology of medicine in their respective areas. This is very far from the truth and although the confusion is understandable, it is none the less unfortunate for that. It has arisen because the West, at least since the Renaissance, has remained insulated from cultures outside the main thrust of its own development. By and large we in the West have chosen to ignore foreign cultures; we have sought to conquer them instead. We have ignored the cultures of our own past; they have been superseded. We have ignored even the contemporary cultures of those areas in the West which are not in the mainstream of progress; we are still trying to modernize them. The form of progress which we have chosen to pursue has been that which has been determined by the working out of the internal logic of our own culture, rather than what might have been achieved by confrontation and contact with other cultures.[1]* One not insignificant result of this insularity has been that religion, if it is to count as religion at all, is assumed always and everywhere to have been broadly similar to what it is in the industrializing countries in the West: a fairly distinct, and not particularly important, institution in society. In fact the place of the formal Christian institutions within the pattern of western industrial societies constitutes a very special case within the general study of religion and society.[2]

If it is properly and seriously undertaken, the sociology of religion exposes a scholar to the beliefs which are regarded as precious and inviolate by a people other than his own, and to aspects of their lives which are of crucial importance to them. It involves exploring the ideas and practical attitudes by which people make sense of their society and of the world as they experience it. The discipline is thus

* Notes and References begin on p. 183

1

fundamentally hermeneutical – that is, it seeks to understand the lives of other people as they experience them themselves; it aims to grasp the meanings attached to various situations strictly in terms of the components of the respective people's own mental worlds. In other words, it is concerned with interpretation.

This first aspect of the sociological study of religion – and it is prior both temporally and methodologically – has an important quality which has been stressed by Mircea Eliade.[3] It forces a scholar to confront a view of the world which is foreign to him; it brings him into face-to-face contact with that which is entirely alien. In itself this is both dangerous and potentially rewarding, for it is a personal as well as an intellectual exercise. Safer, indeed, is the more widely favoured approach which bases itself on what has been termed 'method-ological atheism'. This methodological stance has been strongly supported by Peter Berger, and if, with him, we take the essential perspective of the sociological theory of religion as being that 'religion is to be understood as a human projection', then we are in the comfortable position of imagining ourselves to be detached scientific observers.[4] Our quasi-scientific working assumption will be that the beliefs we study are not true. And yet that would be to ally ourselves with precisely those sociologists who, Eliade says, 'conduct themselves, not as humanists, but as naturalists with respect to their object of study'.[5] In the first instance the sociologist's task, difficult and un-comfortable though it may be, is to take seriously the beliefs of those whom he studies and to seek to enter into the mentality which they bring to their ritual and to their everyday lives, even if in so doing he runs the risk of 'going native'. The task is comparatively easy for the field anthropologist studying peoples in far-off places but it is no less important for the sociologist of religion who studies less inaccessible peoples. Only thus will he be able to grasp the full significance of elements which constitute a radically alien world of meaning; only thus will a foreign symbolism retain its essential life while under study, and not be transformed into a sterile and inert specimen. Avowed methodological atheism is a fail-safe device which protects the sceptical researcher from taking the beliefs of others too seriously, and which protects also the religiously or ideologically committed researcher from allowing his own beliefs to pollute his research. The latter problem is of special interest and will be discussed briefly below, but it is clear that too high a price has to be paid for the safety of methodological atheism. It precludes the possibility of a serious confrontation with an alien set of beliefs, whereas that is in fact the first prerequisite for a worthwhile sociology of religion.

It should not be difficult to see in what sense this enterprise is both dangerous and also potentially rewarding. Concerning the dangers of studying an alien religion and the resistances which scholars experience in doing so, Eliade has written of those who

> ... defend themselves against the messages with which their documents are filled. This caution is understandable. One does not live with impunity in intimacy with 'foreign' religious forms, which are sometimes extravagant and often terrible. But many [scholars] end by no longer taking seriously the spiritual worlds they study; they fall back on their personal religious faith, or they take refuge in a materialism or behaviorism impervious to every spiritual shock.[5]

The potential rewards are no less real. If truly comprehended, a religion makes the same kind of impact as a great work of art, for it poses familiar existential problems in entirely novel forms and lays bare new ones; and, like a great work of art in any medium or *genre*, it has its own unique content for which no equivalent means of expression exists. While individual scholars may differ in the ease with which they are able to grasp a religious system, due perhaps to a deep-rooted sensibility in some, such as Max Weber referred to in speaking of those who are 'religiously musical',[6] the complexities of meaning even in a simple religion, or in one period of one of the great world religions, may take a very long time to appreciate. This constitutes a severe practical problem in the study of religions; but then the rewards may be proportionate to the difficulty of appreciation.

On the basis of a hermeneutical exercise of the kind just indicated, and only on such a basis, the sociologist proceeds beyond the exploration of a particular religion and examines it in relation to its general social context and in comparison with the religions of other cultures and sub-cultures. This comparative method is fundamental in sociology proper, but it is always comparison within a theoretical framework. Direct comparisons between two religions such as, say, between monasticism in Christianity and Buddhism, are ruled out as illegitimate, since they involve wrenching individual elements out of their proper contexts. It is the contexts alone which make individual elements meaningful, and direct comparisons violate the hermeneutical method. The theoretical framework, however, consists of propositions

about the relationship between abstractions which have been made
from hermeneutical interpretations of religion; it does not consist
simply of propositions about concrete religious phenomena. Thus if
we use a concept of monasticism in a theoretical context, it is not the
concept of monasticism as used in a specific religion; it is a sociological
concept derived from the concept which a group of religious persons
uses to talk about an aspect of their own behaviour and ideas. It is
a concept of a concept, twice removed from the religious persons
about whom we are trying to make meaningful generalizations.
General relationships involving aspects of religious systems are
proposed at a theoretical level, and the viability of these proposals is
examined by returning to a hermeneutic study of actual religions.

This and much more will be only too obvious to the reader at all
familiar with problems of sociological methodology, as will be also
the oversimplification involved in these few remarks and the evasion
of some significant problems.[7] A cursory examination of recent
research in the sociology of religion, however, would suffice to show
that methodological sophistication has not been one of its notable
characteristics, and this is a point to which we shall return. Although
the illustrations used by those who have discussed methodological
problems have frequently been drawn from the area of religion, with
the exception of Ernest Gellner[8] they have not themselves been involved in substantive research in religion.

Emphasis is here placed on the problem of hermeneutics for two
reasons. In the first place it is in itself a type of analysis which has
been seriously undervalued although it has great humanistic potential.
In the second place the worst barbarisms committed in the name of
the sociology of religion could have been avoided if all research had
been based on sound hermeneutical studies. The importance of
hermeneutics has been argued in recent years by Eliade and his colleagues but, as Robert Bellah has pointed out, 'the full implications
of their work have been somewhat muted by the relatively exotic
material to which they have largely confined themselves'.[9] Much the
same criticism can be levelled at modern social anthropologists.
Evans-Pritchard, for example, can say 'I regard this problem of translation as being central to our discipline', and it is clear that he means
translation in its fullest sense, for in the same lectures he states:

For someone who has not made an intensive study of native
institutions, habits, and customs in the natives' own milieu (that is,

well away from administrative, missionary, and trading posts) at best there can emerge a sort of middle dialect in which it is possible to communicate about matters of common experience and interest.[10]

Translation is indeed involved when, from the hermeneutical study of a particular society, we move on to the area of analytical comparison. But more than mere translation is involved since the analytical concepts employed are of a different order. In their concern to make their discipline more rigorous, modern anthropologists have become specialized and particular almost to a fault. The work of an earlier generation may have been sadly erroneous, but at least it was addressed to a wide cross-section of the public of the day. There was some hope that the glimmer of interest being shown in other peoples, even if for ulterior reasons, might be fed with informed opinion. Now that anthropological opinion is so much better informed there seems to be a widespread reluctance to forgo 'that sweet sense of accomplishment which comes from parading habitual skills'.[11] Nor does the plea that public interest has waned stand up to examination, since the appearance of magazines like *Man, Myth and Magic,* in the mould of *Playboy* and *Mayfair,* attests to a popular concern in England, not to mention North America. It may not be such a bad thing if the contemporary imagination is caught by rather partial and superficial aspects of alien cultures. An untutored curiosity it may be, but it is a genuine curiosity for all that, and one which has respect for the ideas of others. As such it is more promising than the inquisitiveness which preceded it, which was interested almost exclusively in finding ammunition with which to advance fashionable opinions and lampoon unfashionable ones.

In practice the disciplines which study religion – the history of religion, comparative religion, anthropology, psychology and sociology – are inseparable, as is obvious from the fact that the scholars of earlier generations are acknowledged and invoked in all the above disciplines without discrimination. Certainly the disciplines developed in different ways, each concentrating on a different aspect of the totality of religious phenomena and each evolving an appropriate methodology. Religion is now ignored by all psychologists except a few who appear eccentric compared with the mood prevailing amongst their colleagues. Between the remaining disciplines a substantial convergence is discernible. Some problems, such as that of secularization, have come to be shared, but fruitful though this may be it is less significant than the move towards a common methodology. An anthropologist (Evans-Pritchard) and a sociologist (Bellah) have just been cited as supporting a methodology advocated by an historian of religions (Eliade), who designates it as hermeneutics.[12] This convergence is of the greatest importance for the future study of religion. It means that scholars from different disciplines can talk the same language, and the sharing of a common language is obviously of greater significance than the sharing of common problems. Given a methodology on which all can agree, the dispersion of interests becomes a positive advantage, since it facilitates the cross-fertilization of ideas from many sources and the consequent enrichment of theory. It bears repeating once more, however, that the discovery of a common hermeneutical methodology has an importance which transcends the useful expedient of a common language: it is also a more accurate manner in which to study alien cultures, and it is a timely challenge to cultural insularity as well.

There are other disciplines which study religion which have not been mentioned so far, and of these the most obvious is theology. To reserve a special category for it is less possible now than formerly it was, since the characteristic stances of both theology and social science have shifted so as to have become less incompatible with each other. In the latter part of the nineteenth century the relationship was clear; it was one of opposition. Theology was predominantly apologetical in tone, and defensively so. Acceptance of newer forms of biblical criticism, however, gradually led to the view that a valid exegesis of scriptural writings was possible only if they were located within the social context in which they had been written. This was a development made possible, particularly in the case of the Old Testament, by the accurate dating of materials and advances in archaeological knowledge. Hence arose the accepted role of hermeneutics in biblical scholarship, and the consequent possibility of studying Christian theology without necessarily having to accept as true for oneself the beliefs concerned.

Social science, for its part, has moved a long way from the dogmatic atheism which it began by espousing, although it must be admitted that the process of abandoning entrenched beliefs has been even slower and more reluctant among sociologists than it has among theologians. Of course there are still diehards in both camps. Kingsley Davis deserves to be pilloried for a passage in his sociology primer, a standard textbook for nearly twenty years after its publication in 1948, in which he asserts:

> Dependent as it is on subjective faith, religion withers like a leaf before a flame when the scientific attitude is brought to bear on it ... If the public in general undertook an analysis of religious behaviour, using systematic research tools, it would be the death of religion.[13]

Yet, despite the intransigence of some, it remains true that among an increasing proportion of both theologians and social scientists, there is greater concern with religious belief as it is held by believers than as it appears to the student.

A strange contrast is provided if we look at a field of study which is generally called religious sociology[14] although the name is unfortunately misleading, since it is not at all interchangeable with the sociology of religion in the way that political sociology, for example, is with the sociology of politics. It has grown up quite recently, and is concerned principally with aspects of ecclesiastical administration. It is a type of research which, as Louis Schneider has said, has 'a highly "practical" orientation and is designed to solve or help solve immediate and pressing church problems, but that is not particularly characterized by sociological imagination or theoretical vigor'.[15] Interest in practical problems need be no bad thing, and indeed religious sociology has provided a certain amount of valuable empirical material. The drawback, however, is that the problems studied are determined by organizational needs, and that evaluations derived from the organization enter into certain of the key conceptions used in the precise formulation of the problems and also affect the course of their solution.[16] A simple example might be that of the religious sociologist who is called in to study the effects of rehousing on church attendance, implicity charged with the tasks of explaining why attendance drops and suggesting how the situation might be remedied. He is unlikely to pursue any line of enquiry which will not help to fill the churches. The relationship between religious affiliation, attitude to work, and the decision to seek new housing, for example, all questions which might be suggested by the 'Affluent Worker' studies, would be almost certain to go unexplored.[17] The writings of even the best religious sociologists betray a kind of naïveté born of the technician's concern with solving a problem rather than the scientist's desire to trace it back to its sources. Thus Boulard, for example, has written:

Clearly religious practice is not the whole of religious vitality. Yet it is a sign the importance of which is not to be underestimated; the canons make attendance at Mass and performance of Easter duties obligatory, so that a man is not, in a strict sense, a Christian, unless he practises his religion. In addition, the sign has the great advantage of being objective.[18]

Similarly Gabriel le Bras, whom Birnbaum and Lenzer have described as a '*doyen* of contemporary scholars in the field',[19] has suggested that 'research should progress gradually from the most concrete aspects to the heights of abstraction', clarifying his notion of the concrete by saying that, in the initial stages of his research, the sociologist 'will observe what can be counted, weighed and measured only taking care to be accurate and exhaustive'.[20]

The clergymen who take up religious sociology, for clergy they usually are,[21] have turned to sociology for a set of practical skills which will render them valued technicians, effective in solving problems where their uninitiated colleagues have proved powerless, and at the same time acquiring an aura of professionalism which will make them the envy of their fellow clergy. Clergymen they remain, however, and it is the aims and interests of their churches which are uppermost in their minds. Organic chemistry and civil engineering are divisions within larger disciplines, whose special principles must be consonant with the general principles of the parent disciplines. Religious art and religious sociology, by contrast, have their own special principles which, in the final analysis, must be consonant not with the general principles of art or sociology, but with those of religion.

Implicit in what has been said of sociology and its relationship to religion as an object of study is the idea that it cannot impugn the validity of religious belief. Not to put too fine a point on it, Kingsley Davis was talking nonsense. And yet there is a sense in which the religious person who undertakes to study religion in a rigorous and scientific manner must expect to find his own beliefs changing. When the student of theology stops plundering the Bible for a text with which to confound the infidel, and starts to look instead at what meaning the text had for the writer and the readers who were the writer's contemporaries, he thereby grasps the meaning at second hand. A text or a rite speaks to him, not as he is, but as he would have been in another place or at another time. When the readers of the text or the participants in the rite are here and now, this involves standing back from the group and distancing oneself from the action, not in order to become a detached observer, but in order to understand indirectly through the participants: not directly. Where only texts or carvings or wall-paintings survive from a culture, this is an extremely difficult thing to do, since it requires an imaginative reconstruction. Where the culture observed is alive but foreign to the observer, it may require an equally great effort to take seriously what seems absurd; but for the observer who is also a believer it may be more difficult still to participate through others, when the accustomed mode of experience is direct.

It is this learning to experience a religious world through the medium of other people's experience which is likely to have an impact on the serious student's own religious belief. In the initial stages of study a kind of scepticism may arise which springs from the conviction that religion adds nothing to our understanding of life. Aspects of experience previously regarded as having an irreducibly religious meaning can now, it seems, be reduced to non-religious factors. The classic expression of such disbelief was the answer given by La Place when asked by Napoleon where God fitted into his explanation of the universe – 'Sir, I have no need of that hypothesis.' For those who persist in their study of religion a problem arises which is more radical still. No longer is one all-embracing truth exchanged for another,[22] but rather the simultaneous validity of a truth other than one's own becomes an inescapable fact. And if more than one account of 'the truth' is recognized, then no version of 'the truth' can claim a monopoly. This is shattering for some people and it is disturbing for everyone. The sociological study of religion, then, may lead the religious person to view his own faith as one amongst others, to believe that, in a profound sense, religious truth is plural rather than unitary. Such a possibility is recognized by Christian theologians, but this is not the place to discuss their ideas.[23]

The pluralism of religious truth of which we speak here is not to be confused with the religious pluralism which is characteristic of the u.s.a. The latter pluralism means no more than the co-existence of a number of religious organizations amongst which there is fair competition recruiting adherents.[24] Its primary characteristic is a plurality of religious organizations, rather than of belief systems; and it implies that people may choose the organization to which they attach themselves, rather than that they may have multiple attachments even at an organizational level. Nor should pluralism of religious truth be

confused with the idea that all religious truth is relative. Berger has
spoken of sociology's role in 'relativizing' religion. By this he means
that religion can never have the same absolute and autonomous
authority after it has been understood as being in a dynamic inter-
relationship with other social institutions.[25] No doubt such relativity
is an issue which confronts some scholars, and Berger's treatment of
it is sensitive and very suggestive for the layman. He argues that
there is nothing unduly disturbing about the ability of sociology to
show how religion is relative to other social institutions, since sociological propositions themselves may be shown to be no more than
relatively true. He then goes on to point out that there are, in any case,
certain universal human experiences which point to the existence of
realities which transcend the propositions of both sociology and of
any particular religious formulation.[26] But this is not what is meant
by the pluralism of religious truth. That term means, not that one
absolute is replaced or made relative by another, but that more than one
absolute is acknowledged. As Bellah has said, 'To put it bluntly, religion
is true.'[27] It is true as a reality *sui generis*. It is not to be reduced
to any other order of reality. The implications which this recognition
will have will be different for different people, as has been indicated.

We must now turn to two related questions. What is the precise
way in which religion is to be recognized as true, and what exactly
is meant by religion? The basic idea which needs, first, statement and
then explanation is the proposition that a religion is a system of symbols and that only when it is recognized as such can it be said to be
true. That is not to say that the truth of a religion lies in the reality
represented by symbols, but rather in the reality conveyed by the
symbols themselves. When we say that religion is a reality *sui generis*
we are saying that religious symbols may be comprehensible; and
indeed it is the first task of the sociologist to understand them. We
are also saying that religious symbols may be explicable, and it is the
sociologist's second task to unravel their relationship to the rest of
the culture in which the religion is found. But we are not saying that
they are either replaceable by other forms or reducible to another
symbolism. In *A Passage to India* E. M. Forster said of the India
he wrote about:

> ... 'white' has no more to do with a colour than 'God Save the
> King' has to do with a god, and it is the height of impropriety to
> consider what it does connote.[28]

It is that impropriety which must be recognized if the symbol is not to die on us. Of course not all symbolism has the same validity or vitality: it is not all equally true. Bellah suggests that the validity of religious symbolism varies just as the validity of scientific theory varies,[29] but that analogy is hardly helpful. Eliade is nearer the mark when he compares 'religious data' with works of art;[30] and yet even that will not do, for, we insist, religious symbolism is a reality *sui generis* for which no satisfactory analogue exists. The validity of religious symbols depends on their relationship to their cultural context, and so their truth may be assessed only by the test of whether or not they are used. In examining the truth of religious symbols, situations of social change are crucial. Monica Wilson, in her Scott Holland Lectures for 1969 on the subject of social change in Africa,[31] gives some important examples. She shows that the symbolic truth contained in rituals collapses at that point when there is a 'loss of certainty as to their necessity and appropriateness'. On the other hand, the same situation of social change can be the matrix for new religious symbolism, particularly when a conscious effort is made to find new forms of expression, as in the Independent Churches in Southern Africa. In the final analysis there is no test for the truth of a religious symbol other than whether or not it is used.

To grasp the way in which a religious statement may be understood as true it is usual to take simple examples. As a device this is fair enough, but it can be misleading, for beliefs rarely occur in isolation and generally they can be understood only in their ritual context. As Eliade says, 'a *living myth* is always connected with a cult, inspiring and justifying a religious behaviour'.[32] If a man says, 'I am a parakeet', or if another man says, 'I have been saved by the blood of the lamb', we cannot expect to judge the truth of either statement except by knowing both about the religious culture in which it is made, which forms the general context; and about the life of the man who makes the statement, which forms the particular context. Knowledge of the general context tells us the way in which the statement might be true; it gives us the information by which we can judge whether or not it could have a meaning which is valid for a group of people. Compare, for example, the statement, 'I am married to Christ' and 'I am married to the Virgin Mary'. Information about the consecration of a nun in some branches of the Christian religion and about the beliefs which surround the ritual make it clear in what sense the first statement could be true. On the other hand no information exists, to the author's knowledge, which suggests that there is any sense in which the second statement could be true. The first statement has a social context in which it is religiously meaningful and may therefore be judged to be true or false; the second has no social context in which it might have meaning and therefore cannot be true, or false for that matter. When a particular person makes the statement 'I am married to Christ', it may be judged as true or false on the basis of relevant biographical information about the person concerned, whereas no amount of particular biography will make the statement 'I am married to the Virgin Mary' true.[33]

The relationship of religious truth to common-sense or 'real' truth is defined by the social boundaries within which statements are made, and arguments as to which is the 'more real' lead in the end only to ritualized beating the bounds. Common-sense truth has the advantage of being accessible to all reasonable men when discussing matters of mundane experience; religious truth is accessible to a limited group of reasonable men, but it has the advantage of extending the discussion to supra-mundane matters. An extended quotation from Clifford Geertz will help to clarify the issue a little further. He is discussing the example, drawn from Percy,[34] of the statement by a man of the Bororo people, 'I am a parakeet':

. . . it is unsatisfactory to say either that the Bororo thinks he is literally a parakeet (for he does not try to mate with other parakeets), that his statement is false or nonsense (for, clearly, he is not offering – or at least not only offering – the sort of class-membership argument which can be confirmed or refuted as, say 'I am a Bororo' can be confirmed or refuted), nor again that it is false scientifically but true mythically (because that leads immediately to the pragmatic fiction notion which, as it denies the accolade of truth to 'myth' in the very act of bestowing it, is internally self-contradictory). More coherently it would seem to be necessary to see the sentence as having a different sense in the context of the 'finite province of meaning' which makes up the religious perspective, and of that which makes up the common-sensical. In the religious, our Bororo is 'really' a 'parakeet', and given the proper ritual context might well 'mate' with other 'parakeets' – with metaphysical ones like himself, not commonplace ones such as those which fly bodily about in ordinary trees. In the common-sensical perspective he is a parakeet in the sense – I assume – that he belongs to a class whose members regard the parakeet as their totem, a membership from which, given the fundamental nature of reality as the religious perspective reveals it, certain moral and practical consequences flow. A man who says he is a parakeet is, if he says it in normal conversation, saying that, as myth and ritual demonstrate, he is shot through with parakeetness and that this religious fact has some crucial social implications – we parakeets must stick together, not marry one another, not eat mundane parakeets, and so on, for to do otherwise is to act against the grain of the whole universe. It is this placing of proximate acts in ultimate contexts that makes religion, frequently at least, socially so powerful. It alters, often radically, the whole landscape presented to common sense, alters it in such a way that the moods and motivations induced by religious practice seem themselves supremely practical, the only sensible ones to adopt given the way that things 'really' are.[35]

There remains the problem of deciding on the nature of religious statements for those not themselves members of the religious group in question. For a solution we must return to the question of translation. Even at the elementary level of schoolboy French there often comes a point at which a simple phrase comes to life. It is not that *joie de vivre*, for example, has no English translation, but that there is no English phrase which packs as much meaning into a comparable sound. When one becomes thoroughly familiar with the expression one is alerted to the meaning which it conveys and the very fact of *joie de vivre* assumes a new lease of life. To learn a new language is to enter into a slightly different world of experience. One's previous world is not lost, but nor is it merely added to: it is extended and its structure is altered. If linguistic symbols have this effect, religious symbols, which are more highly charged with meaning, have it as well. And it is the system of symbols with which we are concerned, not dogmatic formulations of faith, for creeds are quite uniquely bad as guides to a religion. They arise solely as devices of exclusion, as shibboleths of the group, and religions which do not share Christianity's imperialist zeal are happily free of such symbolic decoys as the Westminster Confession, the thirty-nine Articles of Religion or, most confusing of all because of their sheer volume, papal pronouncements.

Leaving aside, then, credal formulations, a religion is first encountered and learned as something foreign, not unlike a foreign language. Statements made within the context of a particular religion obviously have truth for the people concerned, but other people have their own ways of expressing and conceptualizing the same things, ways which for them carry more conviction. With increased familiarity comes a growing sense of the appropriateness of the religious symbols within the culture to which they belong, leading to the point when the native account of native life seems more valid than one's own foreign account. To go native is not to be degraded, but to slip into another world. For the scholar such journeys across the culture border into the territory of another religion are temporary, but their effect is permanent. The religious symbolism is no longer foreign, but merely different; in its own context it may be a more valid form of expression. In general it is part of an expanded world into which the scholar has been admitted.

In his ecstatic review of Norman O. Brown's book, *Love's Body*, Robert Bellah sees the possibility of a symbolic world containing elements from many religions and claims that Brown's book is an important step in that direction. In one way such a vision is the logical conclusion of taking religion seriously; in another way it is the *reductio ad absurdam* of the enterprise. He is right to recognize the impact which a variety of religious symbols might have, and to celebrate their release from 'their idolators, those who take them literally, and from their embalmers, those who think of them only as historical but not as present realities'.[36] The interaction of different cultures and religions provides fertile ground for symbolic innovation. But has not a confusion arisen when he sees the symbolism of one tradition 'liberated from its ghetto location in a special group', and 'released to play its role in the general psychic life of man'?[37] What is this 'general psychic life of man'? At best, surely, it is the cultural world of an intellectual élite, and at worst a will-o'-the-wisp,[38] for it ignores the stubborn fact that a plurality of religions is the inheritance of a plurality of peoples. At the institutional level encounters between religions are possible, with consequent modifications and the possibility of new traditions emerging. The pooling of all traditions into a single religious tank, however, presupposes the idea of religion in general rather than religions in particular, and as Santayana says, 'Any attempt to speak without speaking any particular language is not more hopeless than the attempt to have a religion that shall be no religion in particular.'[39] Such conjunctions may, of course, occur in the mind of the individual where they produce work like that of Norman O. Brown, and they may find a sympathetic audience amongst similarly cosmopolitan intellectuals, but they will hardly warrant being called the 'general psychic life of man'. It would be a mistake to confuse the rich experience open to the student of religions with the imminent evolution of a universal religious symbolism. Hope lies in the recognition of a pluralism of religious truth rather than in the evolution of one syncretistic religion with the consequent loss of the plurality.

The insistence that religions are particular and proper to specific peoples implies something important about the nature of religion as it is understood here, and since it is necessary to have some idea about what shall count as religion, the problem of definition has to be faced. There is no need to review the very many definitions of religion which have been proposed, for exhaustive reviews already exist.[40] The definitions available are of two radically different types: the nominal and the real.

A nominal definition specifies a phenomenon by reference to other concepts and terms already understood, as you might define a tiglon as the offspring of a male tiger and a female lion.[41] It has the advantage of being unambiguous and easy to apply. Nominal definitions have generally stated that beliefs in objects of a certain category shall count as religious, as in Sir Edward Tylor's classic statement that religion is 'belief in Spiritual Beings'.[42] One of the best nominal definitions, advanced recently by Melford Spiro, defines religion as 'an institution consisting of culturally patterned interaction with culturally postulated superhuman beings'.[43] Spiro has thus ruled out of consideration as religious such things as an obsession with association football, folk music and similar activities, by specifying superhuman beings as the necessary objects of interest; and he has also avoided falling into the intellectualist trap by referring to interaction with such beings rather than simply to belief in them. It is as good a nominal definition as one could hope to find, and its only disadvantage, which is inherent in most definitions of this type, is that its demarcation of the realm of religion is arbitrary. Even if Spiro were correct in his insistence that belief in 'superhuman beings' is the 'core religious variable' the decision to delineate the whole phenomenon by the single core variable would still be stringent, since it leaves such things as witchcraft, magic and astrology to be defined separately as independent phenomena. The simplicity is bought at a price.

It is of the essence of a nominal definition of religion that it focuses on the content rather than on the nature of belief.[44] If we confine ourselves to a consideration of beliefs for a moment, it is possible to derive from Talcott Parsons a definition which combines a specific content with a specific nature of religious belief.[45] Parsons suggests that beliefs may be divided into those which refer to empirical objects and those which refer to non-empirical objects. Gods, spirits and all supra-natural powers are clearly beyond the scope of empirical investigation, as are the Platonic Forms and certain other objects of philosophical belief. Scientific and ideological beliefs, on the other hand, have empirical referents. A division may also be made between those beliefs which display a cognitive interest on the part of the believer and those which are predominantly evaluative. Both scientific and philosophical beliefs are concerned with seeking to understand the way the world is, even though they differ in that science deals with empirical aspects of the world and philosophy with non-empirical

		referent	
		empirical	*non-empirical*
dominant interest	*cognitive*	science	philosophy
	evaluative	ideology	religion

DIAGRAM 1.1: Construction of a typology of beliefs

aspects. Ideology and religion, however, are characterized by beliefs which evaluate the world; they distinguish not between true and false, but between good and bad, between right and wrong. These two distinctions make possible the construction of a typology of beliefs as shown in Diagram 1.1.

This provides another nominal definition, which can be stated formally as follows: religious beliefs are those beliefs whose referent is non-empirical, and whose significance is evaluative rather than cognitive. It is more restricted than Spiro's definition in that it is confined to beliefs and makes no mention of any social interaction, but it is wider in so far as it includes all beliefs of a magico-religious kind, rather than imposing an arbitrary restriction on their content. Even in this respect, however, it is less than satisfactory. In the first place it is entirely erroneous to suppose that religious beliefs are not cognitive. The parakeet illustration given above shows one example of religious cognition, although it has evaluative implications; and more generally we may say that religions which are not sharply differentiated as separate institutions have important cognitive functions. In the second place the distinction between the empirical and the non-empirical can be misleading, for some objects of religious belief are certainly thought to exist in an empirical sense. The Russian cosmonaut's jubilant announcement that he had reached the heavens and found that God was not there did not shatter every theist's faith, but many contemporary Christians would say that their belief would collapse if it could be shown conclusively that Jesus did not rise from the grave in a strictly empirical sense. At a more general level the distinction can be quite difficult to sustain when it is understood to mean the same thing as the distinction between natural and supernatural, since the concept of 'physical' has been extended step by step to cover anything we understand scientifically.

Real, as compared with nominal, definitions of religion, instead of provoking disputes because of their arbitrariness, present other difficulties of their own. They attempt to tease out from the complexity and diversity of various religions the essential general characteristics of religion. In comparison with nominal definitions they inevitably appear vague and imprecise, and, since they seek to be truly inclusive definitions, each contains within itself an implicit theory of religion. In view of the importance which has already been attached to religious symbolism it is natural that preference should be given here to a definition of religion which lays the major emphasis on symbolism. According to Clifford Geertz's definition, religion is:

> a system of symbols which acts to establish powerful, pervasive, and long-lasting moods and motivations in men by formulating conceptions of a general order of existence and clothing those conceptions with such an aura of factuality that the moods and motivations seem uniquely realistic.[46]

The paper in which Geertz sets forth this definition consists entirely of an elaboration of it and no résumé will be attempted. It is a definition rich in implications, some of which the rest of this volume will attempt to elaborate; for the problem of what shall count as religion is too complex to be limited to a discussion under that heading.

One aspect of Geertz's definition, however, requires initial discussion, and that is the phrase 'conception of a general order of existence'. The emphasis is on the word 'order', signifying orderliness, as opposed to chaos or confusion. This central element in Geertz's interpretation of religion is one which he shares with other contemporary scholars, and most notably with Peter Berger.[47] It marks a shift away from the idea that the function of religion is to solve, or at least to make bearable, the 'ultimate problems' which are said to confront all men, particularly the problem of death, towards the idea that religion is an integral component in the cognitive apparatus which a culture provides for making sense of the whole of a people's experience. It may be that religious ideas alone can make death a phenomenon which is less than horrifying, but religious ideas are never limited to concern with 'ultimate problems' and it is doubtful whether they would be efficacious in making sense of those extreme situations if they did not play a part in explaining much more everyday occurrences. Indeed the whole idea of a 'general order of existence' is that of a world-view, a *Weltanschauung*, which gives a coherent account of all experience. It is in this sense that we must expect the boundaries of 'religious' understanding and 'natural' understanding to be blurred, and to find that often the distinction is one which is employed by the social scientist for the convenience of his own analysis rather than because the world is perceived in such a way by the people whom he studies. Social scientists have themselves come to recognize the truth of this in the difficulty they experience in distinguishing the sociology of religion from the more general sociology of knowledge.[48]

In an important sense religion may be regarded as belief in a 'god of the gaps' – the gaps left by the limits of other types of understanding and explanation. But it would be entirely wrong to suppose that the gaps are only those which are left by 'ultimate' problems. As Evans-Pritchard has shown, a Zande understands that a granary will fall down after a period of years because the termites eat the wooden supports on which it stands, but if people who are sitting in its shade at the time when it falls are hurt by the collapse, then the Zande further wants to know why those particular people should have been sitting beneath it when it fell, and why it fell when they and not some others were sitting there.[49]

Because the answers they give involve ideas of witchcraft they are studied by those interested in religion; if the answers given were in terms of chance and probability they would fall within the realm of science. And yet the notion of chance is as much a residual category as is any religious notion. To say that something happened as a result of chance is to say that there is no *particular* reason for its happening, simply that it fits into an order of events in such-and-such a way. Although there is variation between cultures, as there is between individual men, a significant proportion of each appear to be made uneasy by experiences for which no *particular* reasons can be adduced. Gaps in our understanding of the reasonableness of experience, whether they are due to ignorance or scientific reasons or because no particular reasons exist, play a part in the maintenance of religious belief. In some instances religion does not fulfil this function, and in other instances no reasons are sought. But very frequently religious accounts provide a meaningful order of existence into which experiences which would otherwise appear random and chaotic can be fitted. It must, however, be repeated that for some individuals, and in some cultures, gaps in the meaningfulness and order of experience are tolerated. Such tolerance may be interpreted as stupidity or insensitivity by those less tolerant, but it exists none the less.

Bearing in mind Geertz's definition of religion, which sets the so-called problem of meaning at the centre of a complex of problems which are characteristically coloured by religion, we can go on to examine some of the more important aspects of religion as it is studied sociologically, and to compare some of the different sociological attempts to investigate particular religious phenomena.

2. The First Inheritance

The ideas of those who first tried to analyse the relationship of religion to society have been treated in a way not unlike that in which the inheritance left by the first generation of a family which has recently acquired great wealth is often treated. The second generation lives on it, the third generation affects to despise it and reviles it as ill-gotten gains; in the fourth generation the wheel comes full circle and it is again revered as the source of all good things. The fourth-generation complex is apparent in the study of religion at the present time. Those who subscribe to what has been called the 'adumbrationist fallacy' seem anxious to show that every step forward which is made today can be found in the work of the first generation of sociologists who studied religion, if only we look hard enough. Perhaps fallacy is too strong a word, for this complex certainly has things on the credit as well as on the debit side. When carried to an extreme it all too easily leads to petty carping criticism of the work of subsequent scholars. Used carefully, however, it keeps us mindful of the debt we owe to the founding fathers and respectful of their insights.

The history of the theoretical developments in the sociology of religion is a story in itself, and one which has often been told.[1] Nevertheless, while avoiding a vain repetition of its *Heilsgeschichte*, it is necessary to consider briefly the origins of the discipline so that we may appreciate more fully the work which has followed. For the purpose of structuring a short review of theories it will be convenient to take the main types of inadequate or deficient theory outlined by Talcott Parsons.[2] It will suffice to consider only two groups of theory described by him. In the first place, there are those theories which are inadequate because they are rationalistic, assuming that religious ideas were the answers which men came up with when they consciously pondered on problems in their experience; and individualistic, supposing that religion originated with the speculations of isolated individuals. In the second place there are those theories which are anti-intellectual, assuming religious ideas to be contrary to sound reason and an escape from it; and positivistic, in that they suppose a valid theory must provide a complete and determining account of religious phenomena.

One of the earliest theories of religion was that of the naturist school, the best known representative of which is Max Müller, a German scholar who held a fellowship at Oxford. Naturist theory was concerned to show the connection between religious belief and the apprehension of awesome natural phenomena, a connection arising out of the confusion of meanings attached to names and studied philologically. They held that religion is fundamentally a product of a 'disease of language', to use Müller's infamous phrase. According to this theory man has always experienced a sense of awe in the presence of that which was infinitely greater and more powerful than man himself; and from such experiences is derived his sense of the Infinite. On watching a great river, for example,

> Without thinking as yet of all the benefits which rivers confer on those who settle on their banks, by fertilising their fields, feeding their flocks, and defending them, better than any fortress, against the assaults of their enemies, without thinking also of the fearful destruction wrought by an angry river, or of the sudden death of those who sink into its waves, the mere sight of the torrent or the stream, like a stranger coming they knew not whence, and going they knew not whither, would have been enough to call forth in the hearts of the early dwellers on earth, a feeling that there must be something beyond the small speck of earth that they called their own or their home, that they were surrounded on all sides by powers invisible, infinite, or divine.[3]

Many other things, maintained Müller, filled man with this sense of wonder and awe: trees, mountains, fire, the sun, the dawn, thunder, wind and rain. All gave man the feeling that he was confronted by the Infinite, which is the universal characteristic of religion for Müller. The names by which men called these fearsome natural phenomena all conveyed the sense of the Infinite as well as connoting the actual objects. The naturist theory went on to suggest that in time a natural phenomenon became not just an occasion of encountering the Infinite, but itself an example of the Infinite, the name of which was the name of something supernatural, and hence it became the name of a god. By these several stages, it was suggested, a generalized sense of

the Infinite was transformed into personalized superhuman beings,
and the principal link in this transformation was the mistaken meaning
attached to a name. But if names were so important some examples of
there mistakes should be traceable, and indeed the naturists found
many. So, for example, the idea of a soul comes from the name given
to the principle of life, as opposed to body, the metaphor and name of
'breath'. In time the name is detached from the metaphor and becomes
the name of a specific supernatural entity.

Two other early theories held religion to have originated in the
belief in ghosts and in souls. In the *Principles of Sociology*[4] Herbert
Spencer propounded the idea that the encounter in dreams with those
who have died gives rise to the notion of ghosts. It is confirmed by
many other experiences. The sun and moon come and go, so they
must have ghosts as well as their apparently substantial realities which
are visible only at certain times; the chrysalis is the ghost of the butterfly; and so, as examples multiply, the dual nature of everything is
established. Everything which is mysterious or difficult to account for
is understood in terms of the hypothetical existence of ghosts.
According to Spencer this explains why ancestor worship is the most
primitive form of religious cult known to us, being a simple propitiation
offered to the ghosts of those who have died but who remain tied by
kinship to the living.

Sir Edward Tylor's theory of animism, set out in his *Primitive
Culture*,[5] put the emphasis on the soul rather than on ghosts, and,
drawing more generally on the experience of dreams and trances, proposed that the earliest form of religious belief was belief in the 'soul'
which was thought of as that part of a person which could be detached
from the body and could lead a separate existence. From its original
application to human beings, the idea of a soul is extended to animals,
plants and even inanimate objects, all of which are then thought to
have souls. The theories of Spencer and Tylor are very similar to each
other although they were elaborated independently.[6] Both posit a
double world of reality for primitive man, in which everything seen
and known has its unseen equivalent which is no less active, but
which is essentially unknown and unpredictable.

Many other theories besides these three were proposed, of course,
many of them seeking to correct earlier theories and trying to account
more adequately for what was known of primitive religion. All are
now subject to specific and detailed criticism, much of it arising from
the more complete data than that to which the original theorists had

access. Some of the specific work of the naturist school has been corrected by later philology, but it was wrong in more obvious ways as well. The divinization of awe-inspiring natural spectacles was argued to be the most elementary form of religious belief, and yet the evidence was drawn from those ancient religious sources which have left a literature, which is hardly encouraging as an indication of how primitive they were. At the time when Müller was writing quite enough was known to indicate that peoples whose way of life was much more primitive treated humble objects like rabbits and stones with reverence, as well as mountains and floods. It would seem that the naturists have left accurate explanations of the names of many deities, but there is no way of knowing whether there is any connection at all between these names and the origins of the beliefs themselves. Similarly, the idea that religion originates with beliefs in ghosts or souls implies that ancestor worship commonly existed amongst the most primitive peoples, whereas no such general pattern has been observed, and ancestor cults have been known principally in complex cultures such as those of China and imperial Rome.

More generally these theories are unsatisfactory because they are of the 'if I were a horse' variety, as Evans-Pritchard has expressed it.[7] Knowing a little, and often very little, of a primitive religion, the theorist has settled down in his armchair to ask himself, 'Now if I were a native how could I come to believe that?' Whatever answer he gives results in a primitive theory of religion rather than a theory of primitive religion. In other words, these are all rationalistic theories. They assume that religion originates in the beliefs formulated by people who thought about problems to the best of their ability, as a nineteenth-century rationalist would have done, and drew the wrong conclusions. As Tylor said of magic, it is an 'elaborate and systematic pseudo-science. It is, in fact, a sincere but fallacious system of philosophy.'[8] The rationalistic theory is wrong on two counts. It is wrong because it assumes that beliefs must have arisen as a result of a rational attempt to solve a problem, and for this there is no evidence at all, nor can there be. It is wrong also because it assumes that a religious explanation is intended to be like a natural explanation, and this too is contrary to the evidence. Reacting against the rationalism of a previous generation, Marrett said vividly that 'savage religion is something not so much thought out as danced out'.[9] It would be comforting if we could plead that Tylor would not have been so rationalistic had he had the chance to observe primitive peoples for himself, but

B

that is not possible, for it is characteristic of his own manner of thought that rationalistic explanations should seem to be the right ones. It derives from the narrowly scientific explanations which were thought to be the only kind of explanation a reasonable man could possibly entertain, despite ample evidence to the contrary. The obsessive concern of these early scholars with discovering the origins of religion is also a source of error. It constantly directed their attention to a problem which admits of no solution. Indeed it is characteristic of all the rationalistic theories that they can be neither sustained nor refuted because evidence about the origins of religious belief is not available.

This same group of theories is defective also on the grounds that they all assume religions to have originated in the minds of individual men. Again, the hypothesis is basically worthless since it cannot be tested; it is improbable as well, for without exception the religions found among simple peoples are essentially social. It is difficult to see how the origins of so intrinsically social a phenomenon could be ascribed to the rational thought of the individual unless the mode of reasoning is of the 'if I were a horse' variety. None the less those theories have had a considerable value. In a negative way, it is obvious that more refined theories were provoked by absurdities in the early attempts to understand religion, but the absurdities should not blind us to positive advances which were made. Two of their contributions are of particular value. While it is erroneous to think of religious ideas as the product of faulty efforts to reach a rational understanding of the world, it is correct to recognize a cognitive element in religion. Previous scholars had tended to think of religion in animistic terms, as an entirely separate domain which was objectively either there or not there. Early anthropologists went too far in assuming all thought to be rational thought, at any rate in intention, but at least they introduced the idea that religious symbols could be part of an attempt to understand the world. While this innovation needed much refining it was still a new and valuable way of viewing religion which was to mark a fresh point of departure for students. The second contribution which was to prove of permanent value was the recognition that certain patterns of belief and practice are common to many religions. Religion was no longer conceived of as either a single universal phenomenon or as a series of independent and unrelated mythologies. Instead, the autonomy of religious traditions was recognized, and the search began for regular patterns running through the immense diversity.

The developments from these earliest theories were not always fruitful, and a complete account would include many theories which proved to be false starts. The understanding of religious thought as an attempt to explain human experience was ill served by Sir James Frazer's hypothesis that magic, religion and science represent three progressively more accurate forms of thought.[10] Similar errors continued down to Lévy-Bruhl's theory of a peculiarly primitive mentality.[11] The understanding of the relationship between different religions was also to have a chequered history, much of the unproductive theorizing being the result of determined efforts to make various religious traditions fit into an evolutionary sequence.

The second group of theories which have been important in contributing to the understanding of religion is quite different from those just discussed. The two outstanding figures in this category have been Marx and Freud, who will be treated together because the type of theories they proposed were very similar although they wrote almost a century apart. They are strikingly alike in two major respects. Neither's understanding of the origin of religion was rationalistic. Indeed they were quite the opposite, supposing religion to provide a radical alternative to scientific thought, an alternative which is accepted because the scientific truth is so unpalatable. Both were individualistic up to a point, but the origins of religion interested them less than did its persisting strength, although both of them believed that religion was about to collapse as the truth inevitably emerged.

Sigmund Freud's theory of religion evolved, with the whole corpus of his psychoanalytic theory, from his experience of clinical practice, and the explanation which he proposed traces religion back, with other aspects of adult life, to infantile experience. In crude outline, his theory starts from the child's earliest dependence on his mother. Relying completely on her for the gratification of his every need, the child develops the most intimate and intense relationship with her, from which all the basic emotions grow. Love and hate, security and fear, intimacy and estrangement, all stem from the relationship in which the child's needs and wishes can be gratified or thwarted by a single person. It is this earliest experience of total dependence which is crucial. The initial relationship is extended to the father in course of time, but the experience of dependence is only elaborated by such things as toilet training and other early disciplines which involve the father; it is not radically altered. Just as total dependence is crucial to the child, so is the discovery that his parents are not omnipotent.

According to Freud the early feelings of helplessness and fear, dependence and trust, are too firmly established to wane significantly, and when the child learns that he no longer stands in such a relationship to his parents these emotions are repressed; but they do not disappear. Religion, however, provides the child with a substitute which he is encouraged to believe has all the attributes which he has learned for himself that his parents do not possess. So in his attitude to God all the repressed and frustrated emotions are released, thus conferring on the idea of God the reality of a lost parent. This relationship with God comes to have all the intensity and intimacy which is elsewhere denied him. The idea of God provides an explanation for otherwise mysterious experiences of both frustration and good fortune; it provides an infallible sanction against the disobedience of conscience; it enables ultimate questions of the meaningfulness of life and death to be left in the hands of an ultimate authority. The price paid for this 'gift from heaven' is that the man never grows into a full maturity, for maturity comes from facing heroically the void which his departure from childhood should have left. The belief in an omnipotent God keeps alive a sense of dependence and helplessness and so hampers the continuing growth which is possible only when a man can match himself against the forces which really threaten to frustrate his ambitions. So in its developed form, Freud says, religion for the adult is:

> that system of doctrines and pledges which on the one hand explains the riddle of the world to him with an enviable completeness, and on the other assures him that a solicitous Providence is watching over him and will make up to him in a future existence for any shortcomings in this life. The ordinary man cannot imagine this Providence in any other form but that of a greatly exalted Father, for only such a one could understand the needs of the sons of men, or be softened by their prayers and placated by the signs of their remorse.[12]

Further than this Freud's original theory did not go. The Oedipus complex, for example, has no part in explaining how the individual comes to hold religious beliefs.

Superficially this appears to be even more individualistic a theory than those already mentioned, since it is couched in terms of the biography of an individual person, but on closer inspection we see some crucial differences. In the first place, it is a process repeated for every human being, not something which is discovered or invented and then handed on to later generations. In the second place, the creation of a religious need takes place, not in isolation, but in the social context of the family. Only in the sense that his explanation is social-psychological can Freud's theory be said to be individualistic.

What remains unaccounted for is the growth of religious institutions from the religiousness of individual people. Freud was aware of this, and since he could be content with nothing less than a complete theory he developed an anthropological extension from his account of the Oedipus complex. According to this theory, in the oedipal stage of development the boy becomes jealous of his father, and wishes to kill him in order that he may have his father's wife as his own. As a stage of individual development this has little or no effect on a child's religious ideas since the infantile sentiments of a relationship of dependence have already been projected on to the image of a Father-God. The father the boy wishes to kill, however, is the same as the father whose image was projected on to God who is now worshipped, and this suggests a connection between Him whom the child worships and Him whom the child wishes to murder. So while religious belief is already established, resolution of the Oedipus complex awakens in the child a racial memory, the drama of which is re-enacted in every religious institution. To quote Freud again:

> God the Father once walked upon the earth in bodily form and exercised his sovereignty as chieftain of the primal human horde until his sons united to slay him. It emerged further that this crime of liberation and the reactions to it had as their result the appearance of the first social ties, the basic moral restrictions and the oldest form of religion – totemism. But the later religions too have the same content, and on the one hand they are concerned with obliterating the traces of that crime or with expiating it by bringing forward other solutions of the struggle between father and sons, while on the other hand they cannot avoid repeating once more the elimination of the father.[13]

It is all disconcertingly reminiscent of stags in the rutting season, but in fact Freud got the idea from a paper by the anthropologist J. J. Atkinson, which was published in 1903.[14] This theory, which Freud elaborated at a later stage in his work, attempted to account for the origin of religious rites and explain their continued appeal to succeeding generations, thus complementing his psychological discussion of the origin of a religious predisposition in each individual person. But it is difficult to know in what sense the story of the primal horde is to be taken. Some take it to be no more than an aetiological myth which illuminates our understanding of the genesis of religion by means of an allegory. Others understand Freud to have meant it as an imaginative reconstruction of actual events which is supported by anthropological material and by inferences drawn from clinical experience. There is no doubt that Freud himself intended it to have historical meaning, and his authoritative English biographer, Ernest Jones, lends support to a generally historical interpretation when he writes:

> About these happenings there can be little doubt: fathers, gods and kings have been slain innumerable times in the tragic history of mankind.[15]

So we may assume that Freud's account is intended to be interpreted historically, and whether the events referred to were specific or general certain consequences should follow. Totemism should be the form of religion found among the most simple societies; known examples of totemism should display elements of a ceremonial killing and eating of the totem; pre-totemic societies should be cannibalistic and they should display group marriage or general promiscuity. In fact anthropologists and ethnologists almost universally have found these propositions to be unsupported by the evidence.[16] The later elaboration of Freud's theory must, therefore, be discarded. There is no possible way of validating it, and it does not help to make sense of the ethnographic data we possess.

The earlier, psychological part of the theory, on the other hand, has continued to influence students of religion. In the first place, when Freud said that religious beliefs are held in response to 'the oldest, strongest, and most urgent wishes of mankind',[17] although he was intending to dismiss them as wishful thinking, he was also pointing out that there are persistent elements in the universal condition of human beings which predispose men to look for accounts of the world of their experience which go beyond those which natural science can furnish. Müller's idea of man's universal tendency to be aware of an Infinite, for example, is slightly less fanciful when a psychological mechanism is postulated which explains the generation of such an awareness. Nor is the specific application of Freud's theory to western bourgeois culture a serious handicap since the basic elements of infantile dependence, followed by a traumatic loss of dependence, are at least arguably capable of universal application. Secondly, Freud emphasized the role of religion in coping with questions like, 'Why am I alive?' and 'Why must I die?' to which no answers except religious answers are possible.

Freud's general attitude to religion is not easy to assess. As his work progressed it seems to have become more hostile, and yet at the same time it was a subject which concerned him more and more.[18] In a letter of 1920, to a clergyman, he seemed to be almost impartial:

> In itself psychoanalysis is neither religious nor the opposite, but an impartial instrument which can serve the clergy as well as the laity when it is used only to free suffering people.[19]

And yet it is difficult to square such impartiality with what he wrote only a short time after:

> The whole thing is so patently infantile, so incongruous with reality, that to one whose attitude to humanity is friendly it is painful to think that the great majority of mortals will never be able to rise above this view of the world. It is even more humiliating to discover that a large number of those alive today, who must see that this religion is not tenable, yet try to defend it inch by inch, as if with a series of pitiable rearguard actions.[20]

The apparent dilemma is that of a practising clinician, not that of a scholar. If religion were really 'so patently infantile' then it is hard to see the way in which psychoanalysis, dedicated to helping people to become freer and more mature individuals, could be other than its sworn enemy. The encumbering religion is regarded as an additional shackle borne by those who are already weighed down with emotional problems and disabilities. The difficulty arises when it is supposed that the religion of those who are so sick that they need help, or at least that they ask for help, can be taken as a valid model for generalized statements about religion *per se*. It may be true that all religion is universally stunting and debilitating, but that is an empirical question which requires massive evidence, and it certainly cannot be answered by any amount of clinical experience, let alone by Freud's own limited case material. Had Freud, or his co-workers, or even latter-day Freudians, made use of anthropological material as serious data, rather than merely as a source from which to derive stories to illustrate a theory, their critique of religion might be better founded, although their presupposition of its falsity is hardly an auspicious premise on which to base the investigation. Psychoanalytic theory remains a clinical theory, and its extension to explain non-pathological experience, in which must be included religious belief, is rendered dangerous by the fact that all the evidence is drawn from patients whose experiences are pathological.

The tendency in Freud's thought is for all behaviour to be treated as pathological, and this extreme position has given rise to the exactly opposite view, advanced by the followers of R. D. Laing, that all behaviour is normal and that the category of the pathological is wholly unhelpful. Both extremes may shed new light on everyday life and have desirable clinical implications, but neither is productive of a theory which helps directly to understand a phenomenon such as religion. The inadequacy of psychoanalytic theory for explaining religion because of its basis in clinical material is aggravated by a further factor. Freud was not only a clinician but also a man with his own private problems and anxieties. Religion was not the least of these, as may be supposed from the increasing fascination it exercised over his later years. What he described as his 'estrangement from the religion of his fathers as well as from every other religion'[21] seems to have had some part in his theoretical formulations on the subject. Precisely what part is unimportant. What matters is the recognition that Freud's account of the origin and functions of religion was derived from his experience of patients who were mentally disturbed, and coloured by his own troubled and anxious relationship to Judaism and religion in general.

The Freudian theory of religion, even more than the entire corpus of psychoanalytic theory, is nearer to being a positivistic ideology than a scientific theory, but its impact on scholarship has been none the less profound for that. Two lasting contributions in particular deserve to be mentioned. First, Freud broke with the preceding rationalism in so decisive and radical a way that no subsequent return to it was possible. It is true that anthropologists had, for the most part, already given up the idea that religion, having arisen from a cognitive mistake, continued to exist as a series of erroneous answers to essentially scientific questions. But Freud's proposal, that religion began and continued as an emotional mistake, was so fundamentally anti-rationalistic that subsequent scholars had to argue very convincingly if they wished to secure a hearing for the claim that thinking, rational men played any part at all in the emergence of religion. Therein lies the importance of Freud in the historical development of the study of religion.

Freud's introduction of the idea of the unconscious, which is a related legacy, represents another substantive advance. The unconscious is a notion which has influenced almost every branch of humanistic learning, but for students of religion it meant that it was no longer necessary to demonstrate that symbolism was recognized and understood by believers before it could be considered potent. On the contrary, Freud's general theory made it arguable that covert symbols which are apprehended unconsciously have greater power than those which are consciously recognized as such. The significance of this innovation does not lie in the possibility of interpreting symbols, although the wholesale explanation of candles, crosses, pulpits, spires and towers in European Christianity as phallic symbols certainly followed, as well as the imputation of appealingly salacious hidden meanings to every other religious word, thought and gesture. For students of religion the significance of the unconscious lies rather in making possible the hermeneutical study of a religion without having first to check the validity of every single symbolic element against the criterion of how many people understand it. Once the unconscious is accepted as a mental mechanism, then religious symbols may be viewed not only as highly condensed symbols which are not easily susceptible to translation, but also as being powerful and effective independently of conscious thought. The dangers, of course, are enormous. It becomes possible for theoretical accounts to be treated seriously when they have no basis outside the mind of the student. The value remains, however, in the recognition that an autonomous realm of religious symbolism may be comprehensible in terms of its unconscious meaning to a people. It becomes possible to understand what previously was known only as an obvious fact: that religious symbols can be important to people and powerful in their effect without being recognized or understood.

Freud's contribution to the study of religion, then, has been very positive, even though much of his influence has come indirectly through his general psychology. His own personal view that religion is always a pathological illusion remained unchanged. Philip Rieff has expressed it well:

Religion may have been the original cure; Freud reminds us that it was also the original disease. And the cure is doubtful. Appeasement

feeds what needs to be fought. Were it not for religious encourage-
ment of anxiety, the individual would feel less anxious; and the
effect of this palliative is to remind the patient that he is ill.[22]

This summary of Freud's view of religion bears a striking and accurate similarity to the *locus classicus* on religion in Karl Marx's
writings:

> Religious suffering is at the same time an expression of real suffering
> and a protest against real suffering. Religion is the sigh of the
> oppressed creature, the sentiment of a heartless world, and the soul
> of soulless conditions. It is the opium of the people. The abolition
> of religion as the illusory happiness of men is a demand for their
> real happiness. The call to abandon their illusions about their
> condition is a call to abandon a condition which requires illusions.[23]

For both writers religion is an illusion. Both diagnose religion as a
disease, the one as a psychological disease and the other as a social
disease, which at the same time symptomizes an underlying disorder
and also sustains and aggravates it. Both see men as caught in the
clutches of a dementia against which they are powerless but which
must be shaken off if they are to grow to maturity and freedom. Both,
being immediate pessimists but ultimate optimists, saw the end of
religion in sight. Freud foresaw the collapse of the blatantly false;
Marx, the obsolescence of a substitute for action.

Marx's writings on religion, a subject which interested him much
less than it did Freud, date mostly from 1844 in the period when
philosophical considerations in his thought had not yet been entirely
superseded by his social and economic theory. Although he wrote
more than half a century before Freud their general way of viewing
religion was the same. The difference lies in the different diseases they
diagnosed as underlying religion, and the greater importance of
Marx's contribution arises out of his understanding of the fundamentally social nature of the disease. Whereas Freud had to extend his
theory in order to embrace the social context in which religion is
found, thereby causing his account to lose credibility in the process,
Marx started from religion's social context, which he saw as the sole
reason for its power over men.

Two concepts in particular are central to Marx's analysis of religion:
inverted world consciousness and alienation. The first of these concepts he uses to explain what religion is, while the second explains the

dynamic which keeps it alive. Marx was a simple materialist and he therefore assumed all religious statements to be fallacious. Consequently his first task was to explain why religion existed at all. He saw, as many later scholars failed to see, the futility of trying to reconstruct an imaginary account of the origins of religion, preferring to ground his theory on more immediately accessible evidence. As he wrote when discussing the origins of economic institutions:

> Let us not begin our explanation, as does the economist, from a legendary primordial condition. Such a primordial condition does not explain anything; it merely removes the question into a grey and nebulous distance . . . We shall begin from a contemporary economic fact.[24]

The most immediately relevant fact for him was that religion had already ceased to be plausible:

> Man, who has found in the fantastic reality of heaven, where he sought a supernatural being, only his own reflection, will no longer be tempted to find only the semblance of himself – a non-human being – where he seeks and must seek his true reality.[25]

So, then, religion is to be understood as a phase of his development which man has outgrown, but so long as religion still persists in some places there remains the possibility of examining what gave rise to it. Marx gave to it the highest interpretation possible for a materialist. He regarded it as a comprehensive framework within which men had seen and understood their relationship to the world about them. It was a mode of self-awareness; a total *Weltanschauung*. His understanding of religion was indeed hermeneutical, as was that of Bruno Bauer and F. D. Strauss, the two contemporary theologians who shared with Marx a philosophical background in Hegel; so also was that of the wider German tradition from Herder and Schleiermacher.[26] For Marx the problem was to show the relationship between the world as it appeared to people and the world as it really is. The essential contrast lay, he believed, in the religious assumption that God, or the gods, had created the world, including man and the social order, as compared with the real truth that man has created much of his physical world, his social order, and the gods who preside over it. According to Marx men have reversed the order of creation. The religious world-view conceives of God as ruling over a divinely appointed order of princes, rulers and states which are answerable to him and dependent upon him, and it conceives of men as similarly dependent upon and answerable to God's appointed rulers. This religious world-view, which found its fullest expression in the medieval notion of the 'great chain of being',[27] Marx insisted, is worthy of Alice in Wonderland, for it is completely topsy-turvy and sees everything upside-down. The truth, for Marx, is that men have created their own rulers and social organizations which remain dependent on them for their continued existence. Rulers, in their turn, invented a heavenly authority so that they might claim that their own authority is derived from above, not from below, as it is in reality. So the world presented to men in this religious world-view is a reversal of the world as it is. Men see themselves, in this religious scheme of things, as being on the lowest rung of a ladder of authority, and as possessing only such rights and freedom as their natural and supernatural superiors graciously choose to give them. Marx saw his task as exposing all the fallacies and lies in this: he was to be the small boy who pointed out that the emperor had no clothes. Once this so-called natural order was seen to be the reverse of the truth, it would be recognised, so Marx believed, that religion is simply a systematic statement of this untruth.

> Man is the human world, the state, society. This state, this society, produces religion which is an inverted world-consciousness, because they are an inverted world . . . The struggle against religion is, therefore, indirectly a struggle against that world whose spiritual aroma is religion.[28]

Marx's meaning is clear, although his language is political prose, not precise scientific terminology. He provided little further clarification of his ideas on the subject, for the understanding of religion concerned him less than did the task of abolishing it.

In order to pursue the 'struggle against religion' it was necessary to understand why men should ever have believed so monstrous a lie and accepted such a blatantly unjust world. The key concept which he uses in his explanation is that of alienation. Marx's theory of alienation does not so much precede his theory of the nature of religion as run parallel to it. According to Marx religion, which is an inverted world-consciousness, both grew out of the inverted world-order and also, as a form of self-consciousness, helped in no small way to sustain it. So we often find Marx comparing man's alienation in the world with his alienated consciousness in religion, and he argues that the abolition of religion will reduce alienation in the social and economic world almost as often as he puts the argument the other way round.

Stated in greatly simplified terms, Marx's thesis was that man in his unalienated state lived by the work of his own hands in simple communities. With the development of specialized techniques in hunting and agriculture, co-operation became necessary and some division of labour took place. Although all those who co-operated were dependent upon one another, it nevertheless seemed that some were of greater importance than others just because their work was more essential to the community's livelihood. Further specialization made such differences in labour assume greater significance, and the groups which performed the more important functions took for themselves greater rewards which, once achieved, were jealously guarded. Differences in wealth meant that further specialization was under the control of the more powerful group within the community, who thus came to own the means of the entire community's livelihood, whether in land, cattle, tools or factories. The concentration of the means of production, to use Marx's phrase, in the hands of a few disrupted entirely the orderly pattern whereby men had originally worked for themselves and lived in equitable communities. Instead of this the division of labour had established a pattern of social differentiation into unequal groups, or classes, which are necessarily opposed to each other. The members of the subordinate groups worked for the members of the superordinate groups, neither for their own greater good nor for the greater good of the community, but for the further enrichment of those who were wealthy and powerful already.

This development reaches its zenith in advanced capitalist societies, which are divided into two opposed groups defined by the ownership or non-ownership of the means of production: capital wealth. As a result of this development the great majority of men who do not possess wealth live in a world which has become strange, foreign, alien, to them. The society in which they live is no longer a community of equals, but a society divided into the oppressed and the oppressors, in which they are aliens. Just as the majority of men are alienated from society, so they are alienated also from their work. The things they make, the products of their labour, are no longer their own but the property of their employers; their work is no longer their own activity, but that of their employers who hire the workers to work on their behalf, under their orders, and for their profit. Marx draws the comparison between religious alienation and economic alienation as follows:

> Just as in religion the spontaneous activity of human fantasy, of the human brain and heart, reacts independently as an alien activity of gods or devils upon the individual, so the activity of the worker is not his own spontaneous activity. It is another's activity and a loss of his own spontaneity.[29]

This separation of the worker from the process of production, which should be inalienably his own, results in a general alienation of man: from his material environment, from his own active life, from his nature as an autonomous worker, and from other men, to whom he should be related as an independent member of a community, but to whom he is now related either as a slave or as a fellow-slave.[30] The alienation is complete when the worker is not only a slave, but a happy slave, convinced that it is his true calling. He has become, in Wright Mills's phrase, a 'cheerful robot'.[31]

Religion, then, in Marx's view, is the justification and legitimation of a system of slavery which results in alienated labour. Man's alienation from his work and from his world is set within the context of his alienation from God. Since the world is not his home he looks forward to 'a better country, that is, an heavenly'. His relationship to God is a 'cosmization', to use Eliade's phrase, of his relationship to society.[32] His experience of life is reflected in his experience of God; the experience of God as 'totally other' assures him that his experience of the world as alien is in accordance with the facts and just what he would expect within the divine scheme.

Furthermore, man's alienation from God on the one hand, and his alienation from work and society on the other hand, are both self-sustaining:

> ... the more the worker expends himself in work the more powerful becomes the world of objects which he creates in face of himself, the poorer he becomes in his inner life, and the less he belongs to himself. It is just the same as in religion. The more of himself man attributes to God the less he has left in himself. The worker puts life into the object, and the life then belongs no longer to himself but to the object.[33]

Here, again, Marx expresses his view that religion and society are twin phenomena, the obverse and reverse of the same coin.

The difficulty we encounter in the above quotation is that of Marx's concept of labour. If in alienated labour, 'the more the worker expends himself in work the more powerful becomes the world of objects which he creates in face of himself', why should not the same hold true for unalienated labour? Berger and Luckmann have taken this point and made labour, in this very general sense, the first element in their sociology of knowledge.[34] Clearly, Marx means to argue that man is poorer 'in his inner life' only as a result of alienated labour; otherwise the begetting of children would be an infinitely belittling labour, albeit of love, and this it manifestly is not. The contradiction points to a basic weakness in the theory. It is true that Marx does not begin his analysis from a 'legendary primordial condition', but his use of the notions of alienation from society and alienation from work do presuppose some hypothetical unalienated condition which must be either primordial or utopian. Alienation may be portrayed as a positive condition, but it can carry conviction only if we have a lively sense of what it was like, or what it will be like, not to be alienated, and this can be derived solely from the imagination. So the notions of community and creative labour, which are only indirectly invoked by Marx, lie at the root of his analysis of alienation as romantic ideals. There is nothing wrong with romantic ideals, of course, but they make unhappy premises for a scientific analysis, especially when they are not directly confronted. The great weakness of his theory, therefore, lies in covertly postulating an unalienated condition which is not within reach of empirical discussion. Recent attempts to utilize the notion of alienation, in terms of such ideas as powerlessness, meaninglessness, and self-estrangement, have served to underline the negative character of the notion, and thereby to point yet again to the importance in Marx of the unelaborated contrary.[35]

While the concept of alienation is difficult to use, this does not immediately invalidate Marx's theory of religion. We still have his account of the nature of the relationship of religion to society even if his explanation of how the relationship arose is found to be unsatisfactory. But before evaluating this main component of his theory it is necessary to mention briefly the contribution made by Engels, since it had a significant effect on Marx's interpretation. The interest of Engels in the history of religion, and his concern with the interpretation of particular religious ideas, need not detain us. He drew on the work of contemporary anthropologists but added little of substance to them. In his work with Marx, however, he tended to stress the way in which religious ideas may sometimes express directly the class structure of a society. He approached the position, adopted without apology by later vulgar Marxists, of saying that religion is nothing but a reflection of the class interests in society. He was aware of the over-simplification involved in such a position and wrote in 1890 in a letter to Bloch:

> According to the materialist conception of history, the ultimately determining element in history is in production and reproduction of real life. More than this neither Marx nor I have ever asserted. Hence if someone twists this into saying that the economic element is the *only* determining one, he transforms that proposition into a meaningless, abstract, senseless phrase.[36]

Where religion was concerned, Marx had asserted rather less than this, allowing not only that factors other than economic ones influence the development of religious ideas, but also that religion has an autonomous role to play in influencing social development. Since religion constitutes a form of self-consciousness its strength is not to be underestimated. We may guess that even if the economic and political inequalities which underlie the conflicts of Ireland were to be eradicated completely, there would remain a religious conflict. Marx commented on a comparable case of conflict in his article on Bruno Bauer's paper, *Die Judenfrage* (The Jewish Question):

> The most stubborn form of opposition between Jew and Christian is the religious opposition. How is an opposition resolved? By making it impossible. And how is religious opposition made impossible? By abolishing religion. As soon as Jew and Christian come to see in their respective religions nothing more than stages in the development of the human mind – snake skins which have been cast off by history, and man as the snake who clothed himself in them – they will no longer find themselves in religious opposition . . .[37]

The sheer inanity to which Marx could sink in practical affairs is illustrated by his proposal to abolish religion. The frequent naïveté of his theory is seen in his designation of religion as 'nothing more than stages in the development of the human mind' which, in some mysterious way, can be 'cast off by history'; but there is no doubt that he grants to religion an autonomous role, distinct from social factors, in certain situations.

The core of Marx's account of religion lies in the twin theses that, on the one hand, religion is a complex system of self-awareness by which the members of a society express and make meaningful their experiences of the world; and that, on the other hand, a religion is specific to a society and expresses the experience of particular material circumstances. The first of these theses was taken up and developed by Max Weber; the second was the principal strand in Emile Durkheim's theory of religion.[38]

One of the most powerful vindications of Marx's interpretation of the relationship between religion and the material conditions of a society has been provided in a short monograph by Gouldner and Peterson.[39] In an analysis of available data on pre-literate societies they found, from a factor analysis of fifty-nine characteristics of seventy-one societies, that two important factors were related. One of these defined the level of technological development and division of labour, the other assessed the degree of religious and ritual elaboration in a society. Some details of their analysis will be referred to again below,[40] but their general conclusion is that the degree of technological sophistication of a society plays an important part in determining the strength and complexity of its magico-religious system. No empirical finding could come closer to corroborating Marx's general contention.

Writing of the world as experienced from a religious perspective, Marx said:

Religion is the general theory of this world, its encyclopaedic compendium, its logic in popular form, its spiritual *point d'honneur*, its enthusiasm, its moral sanction, its solemn complement, its general basis of consolation and justification.[41]

His diagnosis of religion, like Freud's, was that it is an illusion. Like Freud he believed that the effect of its abolition will be to disillusion man 'so that he will think, act, and fashion his reality as a man who has lost his illusions and regained his reason'. Unlike Freud, he saw religion, so long as it persists, as a true expression of a real social situation, not as an individual fantasy. The theories of both Freud and Marx are unsatisfactory in many details but between them they provided sufficient insights to enable later scholars to pursue their serious study of religion more intelligently.

3. Science, Magic and Religion

One of the important questions left unanswered by the early students of religion concerns the nature of religious knowledge and its relationship to scientific and common-sense knowledge as these latter are understood in modern western culture. They were concerned with the origins of religion and they proposed different explanations, all of which, as we have seen, were unsatisfactory in one way or another. These early students fall into two main groups with respect to their attitudes to the nature of religious knowledge. On the one hand the rationalists saw it as a crude and faulty attempt at scientific knowledge, while on the other hand the anti-intellectualists Freud and Marx saw it as a substitute for scientific knowledge. There the problem remained until it was taken up again by another generation, notably by Weber, Durkheim and Malinowski. Although that was the order in which they wrote they will be considered here in the reverse order. Weber, who was influenced by neither of the other two to any significant degree and who occupies a unique place in the study of religion, will be left till the last. Malinowski's contribution will be considered first because he held a more simplified conception of religious knowledge than did Durkheim and, taking the long-term view, his ideas have exercised less influence on subsequent thought than have the contributions of either of the other two.

Dealing with them in this order has one obvious disadvantage for, notwithstanding the assertion of Talcott Parsons to the contrary,[1] Malinowski was influenced by the work of Durkheim and he saw his own formulation as a corrective to it. Thus he writes:

> What I am trying to contribute is a reinterpretation of Durkheimianism in empirical terms. Durkheim's basic conception that a great many phenomena in cultures, belief and emotional attitude have to be accounted for by the fact that man is dependent on his fellow-beings and that this dependence produces certain attitudes and leads

to certain beliefs, is in my opinion, fundamentally sound. Where Durkheim 'goes off the rails . . .'[2]

It is precisely in his brilliant empirical work that Malinowski made advances. The theoretical conclusions which he drew from his field-work, however, are over-simplifications compared with the work of Durkheim and they are distorted by the limited scope of the data from which he was able to draw. His main contribution to the theory of religious knowledge is in the distinction which he drew between magic and science on the one hand, and between magic and religion on the other hand. Although neither of these distinctions in its original form now commands support, further progress would have been difficult without Malinowski's clearly formulated ideas as a starting-point.

The mental processes of primitive peoples had traditionally been treated as confused. They were said not to distinguish between scientific and religious accounts of their environment. This school of thought reached its most sophisticated development in the comparatively recent work of Lucien Lévy-Bruhl. In his books, *How Natives Think* and *Primitive Mentality,* which appeared in 1910 and 1922,[3] he put forward the view that primitive thought was altogether more mystical than modern thought, with the important implication that religion is simply one component of a different way of seeing the world. Religious and scientific knowledge are thus not to be sharply distinguished, since they are mingled in a distinct pre-logical mentality. Malinowski disagreed totally with views such as these:

> There are no peoples, however primitive, without religion and magic. Nor are there, it must be added at once, any savage races lacking either in the scientific attitude or in science, though this lack has been frequently attributed to them.[4]

He maintained that primitive peoples have a clear distinction in their own minds between what is done for magical purposes and what has a purely practical effect. The Trobriand Islanders, whom he studied, understood that in their agriculture the ground must be cleared of stones, seeds must be planted deeper in dry seasons, weeds must be prevented from choking the growing plants, and so on. All these things were recognised as necessary means for achieving a successful crop. On the other hand they were aware that a crop is dependent on other things as well. They knew that adverse weather conditions or a blight of insects might destroy growing plants, and there were no practical precautions known to them by which they could prevent their efforts from being thus wasted. It was to ensure propitious conditions, Malinowski argued, that the Trobrianders resorted to the use of magic, but they did not confuse the two forms of activity. They did not imagine that magic could compensate for failure to till the soil properly, nor did they think that extra effort put into weeding would render the magic to ward off drought any less necessary. Magic, he concluded, occurs when people are confronted with a threat to their safety or their livelihood, in the face of which they feel themselves to be powerless. When practical means are at their disposal, the primitives will work hard to ensure success in any enterprise; when their efforts are threatened by circumstances beyond their control, however, they will also use magic to manipulate them to their advantage.

Magic arises, according to Malinowski, out of the anxiety which is produced by uncertainty; an uncertainty which would be paralysing if it were not controlled. Knowing that all practical efforts could be ruined by one serious rainstorm, a man would not work hard. But the function of magic is to 'ritualize man's optimism', and, thus reassured that his efforts will not be frustrated, he applies himself diligently to all the practical tasks he knows to be necessary in order to obtain good results. It should follow from this theory that in tasks which involve no risk of failure from the intervention of outside forces, no magic will be involved. The celebrated case of two forms of fishing found among the Trobrianders provided what Malinowski believed to be an 'interesting and crucial test' of his theory.[5] Fishing in the lagoons was done by a traditional method of poisoning; the technique was reliable and the catch predictable. No magic was associated with this activity, either in the preparation of the poison to be used, or in the fishing itself. On the other hand villages situated on shores facing the open sea used more dangerous methods. They fished from boats which were at the mercy of the weather, and the presence of shoals of fish was very far from certain. This type of fishing was accompanied by magical activities, and the contrast certainly confirms Malinowski's theory. He gives many similar accounts of ways in which magic is found in association with dangerous and unpredictable activities but absent when man is able to control his environment, thus showing that primitive people are themselves aware of the appropriate times to use or refrain from using magic. In so far as magic is used when scientific methods are not available, Malinowski regarded it as a precursor of science. Indeed he said that, 'with Sir James Frazer, we can appropriately call magic a pseudo-science'.[6] Elsewhere he spelt this out:

In the measure as humanity, through developing technique, conquers one realm of activity after another, magic disappears and is replaced by science and technique.[7]

So scientific knowledge is exactly the same among primitive peoples as it is in modern western culture. Magic, on the other hand, is pseudo-scientific knowledge which enables men to believe they control forces which are unpredictable and which fill them with anxiety.

The idea that magic originates in personal anxiety is an important aspect of Malinowski's theory. He believed that the attempt to 'ignore completely the individual and to eliminate the biological element from the functional analysis of culture' had to be 'overcome'.[8] The influence of the element of personal anxiety in determining when magical explanations will be invoked is illustrated by the attitude of the Trobriand Islanders to death. In common with many other peoples, they believed that death may be a result of either natural or magical causes, though the great majority of deaths were attributed to the latter. The distinction is clearly drawn and is significant because different types of post-mortem rite are appropriate in the respective cases; departed souls are believed to travel to the island of the dead by different routes according to the manner in which their deaths occurred. The mechanism by which death occurs naturally is conceived of in quite various ways in different cultures. Thus among some people in south-east Asia the death of some men was thought to be caused by the retraction of the penis into the abdomen. Among the Trobrianders it was thought that the closing of the oesophagus was the cause. It was quite usual for there to be disagreement over the cause of death of a particular Trobriander, and in such cases those most closely involved, and especially the person himself facing death, was usually more inclined to attribute the malady to magical causes.

The more closely a case has to do with the person who considers it, the less it will be 'natural', and the more it will be 'magical'. Thus a very old man, whose pending death will be considered natural by the other members of the community, will be afraid only of sorcery and never think of his natural fate. A fairly sick person will diagnose sorcery in his own case, while all the others might speak of too much betel nut or overeating or some other indulgence.[9]

To be involved personally with sickness or impending death is to be anxious and afraid, and rather than declare oneself impotent in the face of a natural inevitability, the illness is regarded as magical so that magical cures may be used.

The fact of differing diagnoses according to individual perspective underlined for Malinowski the irreducible element of personal anxiety in the origins and use of magic. This idea was challenged by Radcliffe-Brown, however, who argued that magic, far from being caused by anxiety, was often itself responsible for generating anxiety.[10] When rites are prescribed for a certain situation and safety is said to depend on the proper execution of the rites, it may be their non-performance which gives rise to anxiety, while no fear had been experienced prior to the time appointed for their execution. Malinowski was surely right in arguing that even modern seamen, for example, remain highly superstitious owing to the hazardous nature of their life; only some of their superstitions, however, can be traced to situations of danger. The sailor will insist on a bottle being broken over the bows of a ship before it is launched, and the Highland Scot will plant rowan trees on either side of his gate, but the sailor becomes anxious only if the bottle fails to smash and the Highlander only if his rowans die. Neither practice fits into Malinowski's framework which needs expanding to include practices such as these, which are partly magical and partly auguries or oracles. Neat as his theory is in distinguishing between the fear of frustration which may be averted by methodical scientific efforts and the fear of essentially uncontrollable conditions which threaten the individual, and neatly as it may fit the experience of the Trobriand Islanders, it is just too neat to accommodate the diversity of situations in which magic is known to be invoked.

More seriously, we have to question Malinowski's conclusion that primitive people are able to distinguish between magic and science. 'To the natives', he says, 'the aims of magic are quite different from the aims of work.'[11] But are they? All are aimed, surely, at a successful outcome of the project in hand. A plant is trained to grow up sticks in order that its fruit shall not be crowded and die; the ground is cleared of stones so that the roots shall get nourishment; a particular magic is used to keep away some grub. All are means used to achieve the one aim, and the means are different as the hazards differ. It is playing with words to distinguish, as he does, between means for achieving a goal and conditions which can affect the achievement. Every known hazard is a condition of success, and every technique employed is a means of meeting such conditions. The only difference is that some means are capable of being understood and explained while others are traditional techniques for which no explanation can be given. But the explanation provided need not necessarily be a scientific one, although it may seem quite straightforward, unmagical and 'scientific' to the person concerned. The kinsmen of a man in south-east Asia, believing retraction of the penis to be the natural cause of death, gather round to take turns in holding it to prevent it from disappearing into the body, and thereby to prevent the man from dying. To the western observer this is not science but magic. In other cases the observer might judge to be scientific what the participant regards as magic, as with the Zande method of catching termites described by Evans-Pritchard:

A man burns a piece of barkcloth and, holding some magic plant in one hand, blows the smoke into the opening through which termites come out of their mounds when they swarm after rain. This is said to encourage them to come out. Azande say that the barkcloth is a termite-medicine, but they are probably speaking metaphorically.[12]

The happy mixture of science and magic by general practitioners of modern medicine, obvious in the use of placeboes, but no less real in other medications, provides a more familiar example of the difficulty with which people judge between various means of achieving the desired end.

Malinowski's distinction between science and magic was useful, but overdrawn. He applied a timely corrective to those who had argued for a primitive, pre-logical mentality which sees no difference between watering a tree and shouting at it. In his eagerness to establish the distinction, however, he failed to examine its utility in a sufficient range of circumstances. Evans-Pritchard was probably much nearer the truth when he pointed to gaps in man's understanding of the connection between an action and its result as the loci of magical beliefs. Failure to grasp the scientific link between sexual intercourse and the bearing of a child, for example, may result in magical beliefs just as readily as may the performance of a fertility rite from fear of barrenness. We may conclude, then, that Malinowski was correct in saying that scientific accounts and magical accounts, scientific activities and magical activites, are similar but distinct. When we look outside the Trobriand Islands, however, we find that the distinction is sometimes blurred, and it is, rather, 'the number of steps in an activity which are, or are not, subject to observation and control that is the important differentiating factor' between magic and science.[13] The difference is quantitative, not qualitative. Malinowski was right to attack the notion of a coherent and unified world-view characterized throughout by a pre-logical mentality; but having demonstrated the existence of scientific as well as magical activities he was being more Durkheimian than Durkheim in denying that sacred and profane activites all blend together into a world-view which is essentially one to the people concerned. Worsley has emphasized this point:

> The two kinds of activity – which we analyse out into two separate compartments – are thus abstractions from the social behaviour of men, which is of a piece until analytically broken down by the observer.[14]

Worsley notes parenthetically that the distinction can become apparent to the person concerned if he self-consciously observes his own behaviour, counterposing, in Meadian terms, the 'I' to the 'me' in himself.[15] Although this problem will be discussed later,[16] we should note that Malinowski asked questions, in his field research, in terms which may not have been native to his respondents, and thus may have received answers within his own frame of reference rather than theirs. He writes, for example:

> I was always able to ask whether it was the way of magic or of gardening, and received unambiguous answers early in my work.[17]

One is left wondering whether he deserves praise for skilful field-work or for having so rapidly educated his respondents into the intelligent use of western categories of thought. To anticipate the later discussion, it must be added in all fairness that direct questioning of this sort is sometimes unavoidable unless the field-worker is prepared to spend years patiently waiting to hear the answer to a question he has wanted to ask from the very outset. Even Evans-Pritchard says:

> A Zande once told me that Ngbitimo of Rikita's province possessed powerful magic to kill leopards. When I asked him what medicine

Ngbitimo employed, he said that he did not know but he must possess medicines or he would not be so successful in killing leopards.[18]

Having asked the question, Evans-Pritchard can never know whether it would have occurred to Ngbitimo to have asked it of himself.

To modern western man the difference between magic and science is axiomatic. Magic deals with souls and spirits, sorceries and witches, whereas science is concerned with what we can see and touch, measure and weigh. Or so it seems to the layman. The scientist knows better. His theories postulate entities and powers which are very far from being directly observable, whose existence is often postulated on very indirect evidence or on their logical place within a theory whose predictions conform to observations. The difference between an outmoded or untested scientific theory and a magical theory is one only of degree, and indeed the remote history of science is effectively indistinguishable from the history of magic. Magic differs little from scientific knowledge which is accepted unquestioningly.

If Malinowski distinguished too clearly between magic and science, he made the same error with respect to magic and religion. Magic he defined as 'a practical art consisting of acts which are only a means to a definite end expected to follow later on', whereas religion, according to him, consisted of 'a body of self-contained acts being themselves the fulfilment of their purpose'.[19] The distinction had been made by Frazer and Durkheim, but it was Malinowski's formulation which influenced later scholars, such as William Goode, in the importance which they continued to place upon it. His influence was due mainly to his demonstration of the quite distinct social functions which each performed. As we have seen, he argued that the function of magic was to enable man 'to maintain his poise and mental integrity' in those situations where, without the aid of magic, he might be tempted to despair or might be paralysed by anxiety; it expresses 'the greater value for man of confidence over doubt, of steadfastness over vacillation, of optimism over pessimism'.[20] It serves as something like a crutch to help men, individually, whenever their own strength, knowledge or skill fails them.

Religion, on the other hand, serves society as a whole, rather than the individuals who compose it. This is seen most clearly in the rites of passage, of which initiation may be taken as an example. Initiation rites generally take place at the time when a child reaches puberty, and yet they are more than a solemn celebration of the physical changes. The physical transition is important to the child, and by marking it with ritual the society makes it a public event which is thereby easier for the child to accept and understand since he or she has the acceptance and understanding of the community to offset the anxiety which commonly ensues if the experience is private. In most societies the transition is more than merely physical, however, for it also signals the entry into adult status in the community. So the rites, taking place at the time of puberty which is already charged with emotional significance at the personal level, are used as the time when the child is re-educated out of childhood, with its dependence and privileged irresponsibility, into adult status marked by responsibilities and duties. He is initiated into the lore and traditions of the society, previously forbidden to him as the secret knowledge of the initiated; he undergoes physical rigours which may include circumcision or ritual marking of the skin, and in various ways is socialized into the attitudes and values of adult members of the society such as, for example, respect for tradition, bravery, love of cattle, or whatever. The rites, which may go on for many months and involve the separation of the child from his family and the rest of the community, are thus a period of re-education and socialization into a new status. Nor is it only the child who is socialized by the rites. They serve also to educate his family and the whole community to the idea of the new person who will emerge from the ceremonies, marking a break from the past and preparing the community to treat the newly initiated person no longer as a child but as a man whom they must expect to behave as other men do. Initiation rites fulfil the additional function of reinforcing, for the adult group, the values by which they order their own behaviour, for in instructing and initiating a new adult those who are adult already are made more forcibly aware of the duties and responsibilities into which they were themselves initiated.

Rites of passage, then, as pre-eminently religious events, serve to educate the initiate in his new status, to educate the community in the attitudes and behaviour towards the initiate which will henceforth be expected of them, and to reinforce in the community as a whole the values conveyed by the rite. The mixture of these three functions, with different emphases, is found in all religious rites from celebrations of the summer solstice to funerals. Since the characteristic of religion, according to Malinowski, is the establishment and reinforcement of socially valuable attitudes, religious rites are performed for their own sake (cryptically, for the sake of society), in conformity with the demands of tradition (cryptically, the demands of society), for the well-being of the community as a whole. While they are quite distinct from magical rites the similarity of the two is obvious: births, deaths, and changes in social status within the group provoke a general anxiety about the good order and stability of the group as a whole. In Malinowski's words:

> Both magic and religion arise and function in situations of emotional stress: crises of life, lacunae in important pursuits, death and initiation into tribal mysteries, unhappy love and unsatisfied hate.[21]

The difference, for the actors concerned, lies in the practical purpose of magic compared to the self-justifying and self-authenticating character of religion; for the observer, on the other hand, it is seen in the way in which magic functions to allay specific anxieties and make possible practical work, while religion serves to dispel generalized anxiety and to reinforce values useful and functional for the good order of the society.

It was soon realized that even if this clear distinction held good for the Trobriand Islands it could not be applied elsewhere without forcing the facts to fit the theory; and yet many scholars were apparently wedded to the distinction. In a recent discussion of the problem, Milton Yinger starts by saying that magic and religion are almost always found together, and may be distinguished only for purposes of analysis, like the atoms of hydrogen and oxygen in a molecule of water; he ends rather lamely, however, by quoting Middleton as saying that, 'None the less, in general the distinction is fairly clear', and leaving the reader completely unsure as to whether it is clear or not.[22] The idea that magic and religion are analytical categories, and that pure examples of either exist only as extreme rarities, was made popular by William Goode. It is an attempt to reformulate the elegant distinction in such a way that it applies to phenomena which are not unambiguously either magical or religious, without losing the heart of Malinowski's functionalist analysis. He proposed that magic has eleven characteristics when compared with religion: (i) it has specific goals which are expected to materialize as a result of the magic; (ii) the attitude of those using magic will be manipulative, their main concern being with the precisely correct use of objects, words and gestures; (iii) the man with magical powers will adopt a professional

relationship towards clients who seek his assistance, providing them
with no affective support; (iv) the ends or goals of magic will serve
the wishes of an individual client rather than an entire community;
(v) magic is the personal possession of the individual magician, who is
in no way representative of the community; (vi) if one magic does not
achieve the desired end a substitute is used; (vii) performance of magic
is accompanied by a low degree of emotional involvement; (viii) magic
may be performed at any time chosen by a magician; (ix) precisely
which magic is appropriate is at the discretion of the magician and not
prescribed; (x) it is always, at least potentially, dangerous and liable
to go wrong; (xi) and finally the use of magic is always instrumental
rather than affective.[23] Goode provides what is intended to be a
reasonably comprehensive list of the characteristic differences between
magic and religion. He restricts himself to purely descriptive differences so that the differences in function between the two may be
used to understand a particular magico-religious phenomenon when
it has been allocated to one category or the other.

Even if it is granted that a particular rite may be treated as being at
the same time magical and religious, rather than having to be cate-
gorized as predominantly one or the other, Goode's reformulation is
useful only so long as the essential validity of the distinction is not
questioned. Many scholars now, however, tend to dismiss the distinction altogether. Robin Horton has suggested that magico-religious
beliefs cannot usefully be broken down, and that whether the emphasis
is placed on manipulative (magical) or on supplicative (religious)
aspects is simply a function of the prevailing tendency towards
manipulation or supplication in any particular society.[24] It is common
to dismiss the distinction on the grounds that religious beliefs generally
involve magical practices, while magical practices usually presuppose
something remarkably similar to religious beliefs,[25] and examples are
cited of practices which involve both elements and on which no useful
light is shed by distinguishing between the two elements. Theoretical
arguments against distinguishing carefully between magic and
religion are perfectly valid, but in a sense they are unnecessary, for the
distinction is based on the separate functions which each is said to
perform. In common with other functional definitions, Malinowski's
definitions of magic and religion impute functions and imply theories
about them. If the theories are disputed then the definitions are rendered
obsolete and the distinction must be abandoned. Hence we find that
it is those scholars who maintain a broadly functionalist approach to

religion who are the most reluctant to dispense with the distinction between magic and religion.

But a quite different way of criticizing this distinction is open to us. If we can find examples of what would normally be counted as magic and other examples of what would normally be counted as religion, and then demonstrate their essential similarity, the point of distinguishing between them will be questioned on purely practical grounds. The matter is worth taking a little trouble over, not because of the continuing debate, which has long since become tedious, but because it contributes in a small way to our understanding of what is meant by religion. The general trend of the argument presented here is that definitions which are based on excluding various beliefs and practices may be neat, but they are not helpful. We wish to criticize every definition of religion, on the grounds that particular religions are properly understood only as ways of acting in the light of a particular understanding of experience, and never as particular cases of some general category called 'religion'. The world-views with which we are dealing here are religious in the sense that they incorporate a belief, although it is not always explicit, in an authority which the actors perceive as being above natural authority. They are interesting because they are experienced as authoritative and compelling views of the world. If it can be shown that magic and religion are aspects of a single phenomenon then one restriction on our understanding of religion will have been overcome.

In order to compare a magical rite with a religious rite the method of analysis elaborated by Malinowski for the study of magical formulae will be adopted.[26] In his Melanesian field-work, Malinowski made a detailed study of the verbal magic used in many different situations, and he has left an exhaustive account of the magic associated with agriculture in one area, complete with transcriptions and translations of magical formulae. In his systematic analyses he considered each unit of magic according to the same procedure. First, the sociological context in which a formula is used is examined. The formula is spoken by a specific person whose place in the society is significant. It must be located in relation to the routine life of the community, and it must be clear whether, and to what degree, the use of the formula involves the knowledge or participation of other members of the community. Second, the ritual context of the formula must be specified. Under this heading must be detailed where it is said, what appurtenances are involved, what gestures accompany its recitation, how, if at all, it is related to the use of other formulae, and so on. Third, the linguistic structure of the formula is examined to show both the significance of the words used and the manner in which they fit together. Fourth, the dogmatic context of the formula is explained. References to people, places, objects or events, whether practical or mythical, must be explained to show the formula in relation to any wider corpus of belief and practice. The dogmatic context may do as much to show the intention behind the use of the formula, and the way in which it is thought to work, as the content of the formula itself or the sociological context of its use. Fifth, and finally, the manner in which the formula is employed is described, e.g., whether it is to be whispered, shouted from the house-top, or whatever.

The translation of one of the Trobriand gardening formulae runs thus:[27]

1 Here, this is our oblation, O old men, our ancestral spirits! I am laying it down for you, behold!

2 Here, this is our joint oblation, O Yowana, my father, behold!

3 Tomorrow we shall enter our gardens, take heed!

4 O Vikita, O Iyavata, fountain-head of our myth and magic,

5 banish the pests, the insects and grubs.

6 I shall open for you, O pests, the sea-passage of Kaulokoki, your sea-channel Kiya'u!

7 Drown, begone!

As so often in magico-religious rites, the text alone is not very informative, even, or perhaps especially, in translation. It is the first formula used in a series of magical rites at the beginning of the gardening season, at the time when men are starting to clear the undergrowth and prepare the ground for planting. It is used by the magician, who sits alone in his hut, on behalf of a group of men who are about to start work. Although he is alone, the magician's words are not secret. They may be heard by people standing outside his hut, and what he is doing and for whom he is doing it are general knowledge, although no one except the magician is involved in the rite itself. Only a magician, called a *towosi*, can perform the magic, and he is socially defined by his lineage, since the office of *towosi* is handed down by a man either to his younger brother or else to his matrilineal nephew. The ritual context will further clarify his activity. He has with him two things: a small portion of fish, and a mixture of herbs. The fish, called the *ula'ula*, has been obtained by the men for whom the magic is performed on two expeditions they have made to the coast, and it is given to the *towosi* as an offering, part being used as an offering to the spirits in the rite and the rest accepted by the *towosi* for his own personal use. The magician has himself collected the herbs which are used as a magical mixture, often referred to in other cultures as a medicine. With these preparations made, the rite consists in the recitation of the formula over the fish and the herbs which have been placed on the hearth-stone. The collection of the oblation, the giving of it to the *towosi*, and his offering of it, together with his own magical substance, to the spirits, establishes in ritual form the social relationship between the men, the *towosi* and the spirits.

The formula itself falls into three parts. The first is addressed to the spirits of dead persons who have power; the second to ancestors; the third to pests and grubs. Malinowski found this tripartite structure to be one commonly occurring form, the other being a simple and undifferentiated structure. The simple formulae, he found, are generally parts of a larger complex of formulae which are used in rites extending over a period of days, each unit having its own purpose which fits into the general scheme of the intentions underlying the rites as a whole. The formula with a tripartite structure, on the other hand, is used either on its own, as in the present case, or as the central section of a complex. As a rule the first part, being an invocation, is the most solemn while the two latter sections allude to magically significant characters and places and also state the intention of the magic. The language used in magic is of particular importance since it differs from everyday language in both vocabulary and grammar. As Malinowski frequently pointed out, the characteristic of magical language is the way in which it is at the same time both weird and also intelligible. The 'weirdness coefficient' in magic, as he termed it, stems from a number of things. The use of proper names not heard in everyday speech makes the vocabulary unfamiliar; words are addressed to objects which are treated as inanimate outside the context of magic; many of the phrases take the form of abrupt imperatives and expletives such as are normally addressed only to children or domesticated animals; objects and locations whose names are familiar appear in strange contexts and with unfamiliar associations. But it should be noticed that words, simply as words, take on a special significance when used in magic, for they have an immediate power over the objects to which they refer. Malinowski comments on the origin of this special use of words as being in the origin of language itself:

> From the very use of speech men develop the conviction that the knowledge of a name, the correct use of a verb, the right application of a particle, have a mystical power which transcends the mere utilitarian convenience of such words in communication from man to man.[28]

Of course names are only a special case of the general magical principle that what is done to part of a person affects the whole person. Thus the acquisition of a person's nail parings, some of his hair, or some other exuvia confers possession of the person himself, who can thereby be affected for good or ill. The use of wax models in voodoo similarly gives power over the person in whose image the model is made. A name is the verbal symbol for a person. The discussion of names between hobbits and an ent in J. R. R. Tolkien's *The Lord of the Rings* illustrates the point excellently in a fictitious cultural context not far removed from western tradition. In magic, associations and connections which are familiar enough when used in a sentimental context are taken seriously. A letter, a photograph, a ring, a lock of hair, which is commonly said to be of *only* sentimental value, is taken to have a *special* value in magic, just because the sentimental connection is taken seriously. Sentiment is the most important link in magic, and because words are peculiarly evocative of sentiments, the use of words is not merely convenient but powerfully effective.

In the two opening lines of this formula the magician summons, first, ancestral spirits to witness the offering; he then summons the man who initiated him into the magic, his magical father, addressed by his name, Yowana, as a further witness. In line three the occasion of the magic is stated, and in line four two women are addressed by their proper names, Vikita and Iyavata. The dogmatic context of the formula is illustrated by these references, for Vikita and Iyavata are the mythical ancestresses who are believed to have emerged from the ground at a particular geographical spot not unfamiliar to this group of Trobrianders, bringing with them, from their subterranean home, the system of magic used. They are invoked, as the powerful original agents of the magic, to banish a particular species of insect and a particular species of grub, both of which are mentioned by name in line five. The first three lines, which constitute the first part of the formula, solemnly call witnesses to the rite and set the scene; lines four and five, the second part, invoke magical power to drive away pests; in the last part, armed with the power which has been invoked in part two, and witnessed by those summoned in part one, the magician addresses the pests directly. He commands them to go by a route which he specifies by naming two sea-channels, and to be drowned. The specified route is significant because, passing between the shore of the main island and two offshore islands, one of which is uninhabited, and the other of which, called Tuma, is the island of the spirits, it is the route taken by the spirits of the dead on their way to the island of Tuma. The dogmatic context is further illuminated by this reference, and the offering of fish becomes meaningful when it is seen that pests are being consigned to a watery grave.

The dogmatic context in which the formula is used has become clear in considering the formula itself. It remains only to say that it is recited in a normal speaking voice.

Much greater detail could be given, but enough has been said to show that we are dealing with a fairly typical piece of magic. Taking Malinowski's main criteria, the magician and those on whose behalf the magic is performed clearly have very specific goals – i.e., they have a strictly instrumental orientation to the rite. The functions of the magic is to reduce anxiety about the agricultural work about to begin and to prevent the crop from being ruined by pests. On Goode's criteria it is not quite so pure a form of magic. Inasmuch as a group of men are involved the magic is not a completely personal affair, but this is not greatly significant; since the success of their gardening depends on a co-operative effort, the risk is a co-operative one too, and it is the wishes of the individual members of the group which are being served, rather than the wishes of the group *qua* group. It is not possible, from Malinowski's account, to say whether the rite used is arbitrary, or whether substitute techniques could be used if this one failed. His own field-work probably extended over too short a period for him to learn what happened when the magic failed, but it is unlikely that no extra magic was available if pests did in fact appear. This magic is atypical from the point of view of Goode's charac- terization only in so far as the need for it recurs each year at the same time, and its performance has therefore become as much a matter of

C

routine as the need. For Malinowski this is in no way atypical of magic, and so the slight disparity with Goode's elaborate characterization need not detain us.

As a comparison we may take a prayer from the Catholic liturgy. It suggests itself as a comparative case because it, too, is the first in a long series of prayers which make up the complete rite of the mass. Under the rubrics which governed the Catholic ritual for many centuries it was used at the principal service on each Sunday of the year, but recent revisions have restricted its use very considerably.[29] It will be treated here as it was until recently used traditionally Sunday by Sunday. Translated from the Latin, the prayer runs as follows:

I exorcize thee, O creature of salt,

by the living ✠ God, by the true ✠ God, by the holy ✠ God:
by God who commanded thee to be cast by the prophet
Elisha into the water to heal its barrenness:

that thou become salt from which the evil spirit has been cast out
for the healing of those who believe: and bring to all who partake
of thee wholeness of body and soul: and that there may be
banished from where thou shalt be sprinkled, every kind of hal-
lucination and wickedness, or craft of devilish deceit, and of
every unclean spirit, commanded

in the name of him who will come to judge the living and the dead,
and the world by fire.

The prayer is used by the minister who is to officiate at the rites which follow, either alone or accompanied by assistant ministers, who take no part even if they are present. It is used privately, either in a small chapel or in the sacristy where preparations are made for the subsequent rite. Although it is private, the prayer is available to the community in written form. While it is being used the whole com-munity is gathering for the public service which takes place in a church. The prayer can be used only by a priest, who has been given the authority to use it by the rite in which he has been made a priest.[30] His office is therefore held by ritual lineage and in deputed authority, not because of any personal qualifications; he is representative of the community indirectly, as the whole hierarchical ministry is repre-sentative of the people as well as of God in a ritual context.

To use the prayer the priest stands with a bowl of salt, which has been provided by the people, in front of him. In subsequent rites the salt is added to water, which is then sprinkled over the people. The significance of salt derives from the Judaic origins of the Christian tradition and was summarized by Alexander Cruden thus:

> This was even more indispensible to the Hebrews than to us, as they used it as an antidote to the effects of the heat of the climate on animal food, and it was also used in the sacrifices. They had an inexhaustible and ready supply of it on the southern shores of the Salt Sea, now called the Dead Sea. Salt symbolized hospitality, durability and purity. To eat the salt of the king was to owe him the utmost fidelity. To eat bread and salt together was to make an unbreakable league of friendship.[31]

The rite in which this prayer is used is only one part of the preparations for the mass, all of which follow a pattern which is ritually prescribed, down to the prayers which are to be said while hands are washed and while each article of ritual clothing is put on. The prayer itself is in four parts. The opening words form the first part, in which the physical object, salt, is addressed directly by name, and the intention of the prayer is immediately stated. The problems of hermeneutical interpretation are apparent in translating from the Latin text, which is given on page 59 below. 'Creature of salt' is an expression which portrays the salt, not as a common physical object in everyday use, but as something specifically created by God, and which has partaken in the general fall from the purity of creation which followed the original sin.[32] So both the physical object and the verbal reference appear strange in this ritual context. The verb 'to exorcize' is not a translation at all, but merely a transliteration; just what is being 'cast out' of the salt becomes clear later in the prayer.

   The second part invokes the name of God, the active agent in the rite, whose power effects the intention. The name, God, is repeated three times, with a different quality ascribed to him adjectivally each time, and each time the minister traces the form of a cross over the salt with his right hand. The weirdness of this repetition is clear, as is the power implied in the threefold repetition of the name of God and the sacred sign of the cross. There then follows a reference to the mythical hero, Elisha, who is mentioned by name.[33] The power of the minister is here implicitly claimed by precedent: he recalls that God commanded Elisha to use salt, thus implying that his own use of it should produce the desired result. The naming of the prophet also implicitly summons him as a witness to the rite. The third part of the prayer, addressed to the salt, states the intention of the rite and specifies what is to happen both immediately and in the subsequent rite when the salt is used. The intention is clearly stated, although it is entirely spiritual in its content. Translation is again problematic, since the things referred to are fearsome and spoken of only rarely in common speech: 'omnia phantasia, et nequitia, vel versutia diabolicae fraudis'. The fourth part invokes the power of Jesus Christ without mentioning him by name. It reinforces the invocation of the name of God, but serves two other purposes as well. In the Christian myth Jesus is believed to have told his followers to ask God in his name for whatever they wanted, and to have promised that such requests would be granted.[34] This last invocation is an almost invariable conclusion to Christian prayers and fulfils the instruction of Jesus. The reference to a final judgement also ties the prayer into the larger dogmatic context of the Christian myth, in which the world is believed to end with the return of Jesus to judge the world. But the 'world' which is to be judged, a translation of 'saeculum', refers to the whole creation, and the allusion to it here indicates that this particular prayer purifies the salt as a special event foreshadowing the day when everything will be made pure again by the judgement of Jesus at his second coming. The connection with the central theme of the Christian myth, sin and salvation, is intimate here but it is not necessary to explain the connection any more fully.

This prayer is not typical of Christian prayers, but the peculiarity of its structure in no way invalidates it for purposes of comparison. Indeed, as will be seen shortly, it is more purely 'religious' than many other Christian prayers. The common structure of a prayer in the Christian tradition is a four-part one: first, an address to God by name; second, a reference to some event or person in the sacred myth or to an attribute of God; third, a request which states the intention of the prayer; and, finally, the invariable invocation of the name of Jesus. An example taken at random will illustrate the common form and show the ways in which the example under consideration is typical and atypical. The 'collect', or proper prayer, for the third Sunday after Easter, in the Book of Common Prayer (1662) of the Church of England, runs:[35]

Almighty God,

who shewest to them that be in error the light of thy truth, to the intent that they may return into the way of righteousness:

Grant unto all them that are admitted into the fellowship of Christ's religion, that they may eschew those things that are contrary to their profession, and follow all such things as are agreeable to the same;

through our Lord Jesus Christ.

The standard form is clear, and it is plain that the example which is being analysed is exceptional only in that it is addressed to an inanimate object, rather than as the object being referred to in the course of a prayer addressed to the Divinity.

It is equally obvious that it is, by any criteria, religious. Using Malinowski's characteristics, the prayer has no specific goal to which it is orientated in an instrumental way. The intention is spiritual: 'wholeness of body and soul' (sanitas animae et corporis). The use is not confined to times when some sickness, either bodily or spiritual, is in evidence; it is not even restricted to a season of the year, such as Lent, when people are supposed to reflect on their own spiritual imperfection. It cannot, therefore, be said to function as a palliative for people's specific anxieties. Nor does it conform to any of Goode's characteristics of magic, except in so far as a particular minister may use the prayer in a matter-of-fact way, giving the impression that he is simply manipulating the salt according to an objective formula. Another minister may equally well treat the rite with great reverence and enter into it with considerable emotional involvement.

To clarify the comparison it may help to quote the formula and the prayer in their original languages, side by side.[36]

I Da vaku'ulu'ula-si tomwaya,   Exorcizo te, creatura salis,
       la-seyeli—kay!
   Da ka'ula'ula-ga Yowana—kay!
   Nabwoye ta-sunini da
       buyagu—kay!

II Vikita, Iyavata si libogwo   per Deum ✠ vivum, per
       daba-na.   Deum ✠ verum, per
   Ku-bili-se sigweleluwa*   Deum ✠ sanctum: per
       mwoytatana†;   Deum qui te per Eliseum
                                      prophetam in aquam mitti
                                      jussit, ut sanatetur
                                      sterilitas aquae:

* The proper name of an insect.
† The proper name of a grub.

III ba-vasasewo kam karikeda   ut efficiaris sal exorcizatum
    Kaulokoki, kam kovosasa   in salutem credentium: et
    Kiya'u.   sis omnibus sumentibus te
    Ku-vapulupulu, ku-waya.   sanitas animae et corporis:
                                     et effugiat atque discedat a
                                     loco, in quo aspersum
                                     fueris, omnia phantasia,
                                     et nequitia, vel versutia
                                     diabolicae fraudis,
                                     omnisque spiritus
                                     immundus adjuratus

IV   per eum, qui venturus est
                                     judicare vivos et mortuos,
                                     et saeculum per ignem.

If these two prayers are indeed of two different analytical families, they bear a striking resemblance to one another, to say the least. It is not possible to sustain the objection that, in many religious traditions, prayers are informal to the point of being made up spontaneously. Even slight experience of extempore prayer is enough to show that it is just as formalized in style as a traditional Latin or Greek collect. The language may be superficially more familiar, but the embarrassed discomfort of an outsider testifies to the weirdness apparent to anyone not steeped in the tradition.

When we come down to examples of 'practical religion', as Leach calls it, we see that 'magic' and 'religion' are sometimes so alike as to make the distinction redundant.[37] Some magic takes place in private, some in public. Some is little more than an attempt to obtain a material pay-off; some incorporates extensive and complex beliefs about an order of the universe which is acknowledged and venerated in the rite. Individual items of magic may function to allay anxieties about particular dangers and fears, but the existence of a magical system which is available to everyone in a society may also function to integrate that society and to inculcate a set of values associated with the recourse to magic. The same, *mutatis mutandis*, applies to religion. Leaving aside philosophical theologians (of whom there are few), and sophisticated mystics (of whom there are still fewer), religion consists of a way of looking at the world which includes quite as many prescriptions as to how to avert disaster as of how to understand it. Indeed the distinction between the two is a meaningful one only for the philosopher and the mystic. It may be helpful to distinguish between the mortuary rites of the Trobriand Islanders and their gardening magic. It is helpful also to distinguish between a cremation in Golders Green and the blessing of a Polaris submarine, but to superimpose on it the distinction between religion and magic makes the difference no clearer.

Religion and magic are of a piece. There are affective and instrumental moods in almost every magico-religious activity, but to isolate these two orientations and make them the basis of a fundamental analytical distinction is to lose sight of other orientations which are of no less significance. A woman may be distraught by the death of her son or by the loss of her daughter in marriage, and the appropriate 'religious' rites may put the world back into a meaningful order for her. A man may be frightened by the sickness of his son, and the 'magical' rites of prayer or the administration of a placebo may reassure him and make him feel better able to nurse the child. But the same man who believes magically on some occasions may behave religiously on other occasions: he may feel riddled with guilt at having failed to go to church on Sunday or he may be made uneasy if his lucky horse-shoe falls off its nail over the door of the gardening shed. And the same 'religious' woman may be 'magical' on occasions; she may feel impure and unsafe after the birth of her child until she has been 'churched'; she may want to know what it means if she finds a ring when she is walking through a field; she may be filled with wonder at the sight of a tropical night sky, or horror at the sight of a child who had been run over. All these responses demand, of some people and in some cultures, a significant and satisfactory place in the ordered meaning of life. Malinowski was right to point to gaps in one's understanding as sources of special explanation, but it is not only anxiety which blows gaping holes in our understanding. He was wrong in supposing that the special explanations can be separated, without difficulty, from a general understanding of a meaningfully ordered world.

4. The Durkheimian Tradition

Marx and Freud regarded any religious world-view as a cultural disease. Because the world is such a cruel and inhospitable place men prefer a comfortable illusion, and so they substitute an imaginary religious world for the real world and persist in this pathological way of interpreting the whole of their experience. For Malinowski religion is of some value in that it provides men with an explanation of their experience of the world, albeit a false one, at those points where science fails, thus saving men from the dangers of uncertainty and meaninglessness. Emile Durkheim united the positive elements from both these traditions. He followed Malinowski in treating religion as useful; and he followed Marx and Freud in treating it as providing men with a total world-view.[1] It is his distinction to have been the first sociologist to treat religion seriously as a total system of human knowledge from which all other systems of knowledge, more partial if more precise, have evolved. This point is illustrated in two passages from the beginning of *The Elementary Forms of the Religious Life*:

> There is no religion that is not a cosmology at the same time that it is a speculation upon divine things. If philosophy and the sciences were born of religion, it is because religion began by taking the place of the sciences and philosophy.

And

> In reality, then, there are no religions which are false. All are true in their own fashion; all answer, though in different ways, to the given conditions of human existence.[2]

Durkheim's sociology of religion was conceived as a special case within the sociology of knowledge, as is shown by the first sketches for a sociology of knowledge contained in the opening and concluding sections of the *Elementary Forms* which clearly provide the general framework for his substantive study.

Durkheim's general theory of religion contains two key concepts: the idea of the sacred, and the concept of moral community. His whole theory rests on the distinction between the sacred and the profane, and he uses this distinction both to demolish earlier theories and to form the basis of his own. Its importance lies in its universality, for it was Durkheim's aim to expound a theory of '*religion* in general' and to show how 'all religions can be compared to each other'. Belief in spirits, gods, magical powers and so on are found in different religions in various combinations, but none of these beliefs is common to every religion, not even belief in Tylor's rudimentary 'Spiritual Beings'.[3] What all these various elements have in common is their sacredness; they are all concerned with that which is set apart as special and extra-ordinary. Even the most philosophical form of Theravada Buddhism, which Durkheim was anxious not to exclude, contains precepts which are sacred. So he was led to regard the presence of sacred things, 'that is to say things set apart and forbidden', as a defining characteristic of religion. By 'the sacred' he understood not only those things which are worthy of worship, but everything that is not commonplace, ordinary or comparatively insignificant. It includes many categories which are generally differentiated from each other. The propitious and the unpropitious, the good and the evil, that which purifies and that which defiles, things connected with the powers of light and things connected with the powers of darkness: all these are subdivisions of the sacred. The divine and the diabolical are both alike set apart as having a special significance in comparison with everyday, ordinary, i.e. profane things. This distinction between the sacred and the profane is important, not only because it provides the starting-point for a universally valid definition of religion, but also because it points to a feature which may truly be said to be the most elementary religious form. Durkheim was concerned to discover the most primitive form of religion which could be explained 'without making use of any element borrowed from a previous religion', so that he could establish the 'first link' in the 'chain of scientific truths' and thereby present an accurate evolutionary model of religious development. But he was anxious to discover also the lowest common denominator in religions to enable him to analyse the 'permanent elements which constitute that which is permanent and human in religion', and thereby to analyse religion in general. So the distinction

between the sacred and the profane has three advantages for Durkheim: it makes the formulation of a universal definition of religion
possible; it is the first link in an evolutionary chain; and it is the
invariable and ineradicable characteristic of all religions.

Earlier scholars had given their several explanations of how in their
view the most primitive form of religious sentiment had been born,
but Durkheim was less interested, initially, in showing *how* religion
originated than in explaining *where* it originated. The animists and
naturists had suggested that religion was the divinization of some
experience which was imperfectly understood, but this approach
was unacceptable to Durkheim. If religion is based on a cognitive
mistake, he argued, it is unthinkable that it should have persisted
down the centuries. It must be founded on something more substantial than an error. Moreover many of the objects held to be
sacred in simple societies are neither awful nor mysterious. Thunder
and lightning are regarded as sacred by some peoples, but others
regard rabbits and beetles as sacred, together with a host of similarly
insignificant objects.

It was certainly true that the form of religion which, in his judgement, appeared to be the most elementary treated very ordinary
objects as sacred. With particular reference to the Arunta people of
central Australia, but using the totemism of North American Indians
as occasional cross-checks, Durkheim took totemism to be the most
rudimentary religious form.[4] The Arunta, or the Australian Black-
fellows as they used to be called, are 'hunters and collectors, wandering about in small hordes in their tribal territories seeking game,
roots, fruits, grubs, and so forth'.[5] The tribe is the inclusive social
unit, defining both the area in which they live and also the effective
limits of their social world. Within the tribe there are subdivisions,
first into phratries, of which there are usually two, and they, broadly
within phratries, into clans. The clan, which is seldom defined by
territory, consists of all those who share the same totem, or name,
which is inherited by children from their mother. In those few tribes
where the totem is transmitted through the paternal line, the clan
obviously has a territorial significance, but this is less common.[6]
The members of a clan gather together on various occasions, as will
presently be seen, but for most of the time the members of the tribe
are separated into small bands of hunters and the members of each
band will not all be of the same clan.

Each clan has a different totem, for example the lizard or the frog, and the various members of a clan are known by the name of their totem. Moreover it is not only the human members of the tribe who belong to these totemic clans, for within the tribe the whole known universe is divided among the various clans. Thus clouds will belong to one clan, the sun to another, a certain species of tree to yet another, and all known things are arranged in a sort of 'tableau or systematic classification embracing the whole of nature'. The totem of the kangaroo clan is not some particular kangaroo; it is not even the kangaroo species; it is the image of the kangaroo. The totem at its most explicit is the image carved on an oblong piece of wood or stone and known as a churinga. The species of animal or plant or whatever it may be whose image is the clan totem is sacred to the clan; but so also, by association, are all the other members of the clan, human and animal, animate and inanimate. All of them belong to the same 'family' and so have a common affinity with the totem and with each other.

According to Durkheim the sacred nature of the relationship between one member of a totemic clan and all the other members is the original religious sentiment. His account of totemism, which inevitably seems very incomplete to the scholars of totemism today, is much more complex than has so far been indicated. Not only are members of a clan associated with a totem, but the clans within a phratry are also associated with a phratry totem. Thus the universe is divided into two totemic groups corresponding to the two phratries, and each of these groups is divided in turn into clans. But there are also totems for sex groups, and individual totems. The theoretical implications of this complexity, as will presently be seen, have only recently been recognized by scholars. Durkheim himself was only concerned to demonstrate the isomorphous relationship between the social structure of the tribe and the structure of the sacred as it was perceived by members of the tribe. In the words of Fison, quoted by Durkheim:

> The South Australian savage looks upon the universe as the Great Tribe, to one of whose divisions he himself belongs; and all things, animate and inanimate, which belong to his class are parts of the body corporate whereof he himself is a member.[7]

It is this fact that the structure of the most primitive form of religious conception is so startlingly isomorphous with the structure of the society in which it occurs which is the main reason why Durkheim was led to see society not just as the matrix in which religion is shaped, but as itself the source of religion. If the totemic animal or whatever it may be is at the same time the outward and visible sign of the totem itself (i.e., of the abstract idea of the totem which he calls the 'totemic principle') and also the symbol which identifies the members of the clan, Durkheim concludes that the totem can be

> . . . nothing else than the clan itself, personified and represented to the imagination under the visible form of the animal or vegetable which serves as totem.[8]

The crude form in which this celebrated conclusion of Durkheim is often stated – namely that in religion society is worshipping itself – is clearly a gross misrepresentation. For one thing, the totemism of the Arunta is entirely devoid of worship. But, more importantly, Durkheim was not asking the simple question 'What do people really worship?'. Religion constitutes another world which has laws and customs, hopes and fears, of its own. Nature instructs men in the same way as it instructs animals, and religion is important because it represents the originally human:

> Animals know only one world, the one which they perceive by experience, internal as well as external. Men alone have the faculty of conceiving the ideal, of adding something to the real.[9]

But where does this other world, the religious world, come from? Since the religious world has such a compelling reality for men and, in more advanced societies, evolves into the manifold complexity of human institutions, this was the central question for Durkheim. The answer he gave was that religious authority derives from the authority of society. In answering thus he was locating the source of religious sentiment in an on-going reality of unquestionable power, but he was not reducing the sacred to the social. Men may worship a god, and the sentiments they feel towards their god may derive from their subordinate relationship to their society; but it is the god, not society, whom they worship. Indeed to worship society would seem to them meaningless. A crucial transformation of sentiments has to take place before the sacred can emerge as the object of such special significance – 'a synthesis *sui generis* of particular consciousness is required'.

Now this synthesis has the effect of disengaging a whole world of sentiments, ideas and images which, once born, obey laws all of their own. They attract each other, repel each other, unite, divide themselves, and multiply, though these combinations are not commanded and necessitated by the condition of the underlying reality. The life thus brought into being even enjoys so great an independence that it sometimes indulges in manifestations with no purpose or utility of any sort, for the mere pleasure of affirming itself. [0]

At the same time as the religious reality takes shape as a new, second world experienced by men as a factual part of their environment, a second set of imperatives is born. Danger evokes from the natural man the response of flight but from the same man, *qua* religious man, it evokes the response of resistance and courage. Just as the natural and religious worlds exist as two separate and opposed domains, so man is *homo duplex*, 'made up of two distinct parts, which are opposed to one another as the sacred to the profane'. We may say that, in a certain sense, 'there is divinity in us'.[11] This is a long way from the naïve statement that 'men worship their own society'. Certainly it sees social experience as the source of religious experience, but it also recognizes the reality and autonomy of religion.

If the morphology of the social and religious worlds of a people are originally one and the same, it must follow that the members of the society and the adherents of the religion are also identical. It is this other aspect of a society as the group which adheres to a set of religious beliefs and practices the rites connected with them which Durkheim designates as a moral communtiy. Men are confronted by the sacred and the profane; within themselves as individuals there is the natural man and the religious man; they live simultaneously in a society and in a moral community. Having thus shown the intimate connection between a society and a religion, it is inevitable that the religious aspect of a society, society regarded as a moral community, should be adopted by Durkheim as a defining characteristic of religion. Together with the distinction between the sacred and the profane it constitutes his formal definition:

A religion is a unified system of beliefs and practices relative to sacred things, that is to say, things set apart and forbidden – beliefs and practices which unite into one single moral community called a church, all those who adhere to them.[12]

Without a community of believers there can be no religion; but equally without a religion there can be no human society. The beliefs and rites of a religion are not 'merely received individually' by all the members of the society; they belong to the society and membership of the society involves embracing them. They therefore 'make its unity', as is so clearly seen in the example given of Australian totemism. It is the existence of this moral community which is chiefly responsible for giving to the religious world its objective character. The religion is received from earlier generations and passed on to future ones; it is shared by all members of the society and adherence is obligatory for every individual member of it.[13] Of course all this is much more easily recognizable in the small-scale societies of primitive peoples than in more complex societies, but perhaps Durkheim's Jewish background helped to make him especially sensitive to the communal basis of religion. As Evans-Pritchard has suggested, it alerted him to the religious significance of interdictions which exclude foreigners from religious membership.[14] It is in this insistence on the importance of the moral community that we see Durkheim's main advance on earlier scholarship for he argues not simply that religion originated in social experience but that the two are essentially and inseparably bound up together. The coercive and obligatory character of religion, which is implied in the notion of moral community, seemed so essential to Durkheim that he made it the sole basis of his earlier attempt at a definition.[15]

The concept of the moral community had a further significance for Durkheim which we need do no more than mention now. In his view it was the crucial factor distinguishing religion from magic, for he believed that there is no church in connection with magic.[16] The magic to which he referred was almost exclusively the black magic of modern times and the examples to which he refers in his footnotes are such practices as the profanation of the Host in black masses.[17] He ignored the implicitly communal nature of magic in many societies and, on the other hand, he exaggerated the communal basis of religion, in order to emphasize the distinction he wished to draw: 'It is difficult to imagine their not being opposed somewhere; and it is still more necessary for us to find where they are differentiated.'[18]

The concept of moral community has a further even more important consequence for, having explained that the source of religion lies in men's experience of their society, Durkheim is left with the problem of trying to account for how it originates. This he does by invoking the notion of collective effervescence to express the emotional excitement experienced by the members of a society when they gather together. Since the notion arises, at least initially, from the descriptive material about the Arunta, it will be useful to recall Durkheim's account.[19] As has been stated already, the Arunta spend most of the year in small bands, hunting game and collecting vegetable food-stuffs. These long periods are characterized by isolation, by hard and exhausting work, by an element of danger but also by a high degree of boredom. At certain seasons, however, they leave these small bands and gather into clans for celebrations of their totemic rites. These periods, by contrast with their life in the smaller groups, are marked by safety, by the absence of work, and by communal living. A high degree of excitement is experienced at such times and all the more so because of the contrast with the boredom of their normal daily routine. Some of this excitement Durkheim ascribes to the proximity of a large group of people, the result being that 'a sort of electricity is formed'. The excitement is still further heightened because the gatherings continue every day for weeks at a time, for the most part uninterrupted by sleep, so that a feeling of 'exaltation' steadily builds up.

The result of these gatherings, Durkheim argues, is that the people feel 'dominated and carried away by some sort of external power' to such a degree that the life spent wandering in small bands and the life spent in the clan gatherings seem to be two quite distinct lives. But the significant point for Durkheim, of course, is that the working life spent in small bands with members of other clans is profane, whereas the life encountered in the clan gatherings centres on the celebration of the totemic rites[20] and is pre-eminently sacred. Granted that the collective effervescence experienced in clan gatherings awakens within the members of the clan 'the idea of external forces which dominate them and exalt them', Durkheim suggests that these forces come to be identified with the totem by a process of association between the experience itself and the symbol under which the experience takes place. In order to emphasize the importance which we should attach to the symbol, he cites a colourful comparison which doubtless carried much weight at the time when he wrote, though it seems today merely picturesque:

The soldier who dies for his flag, dies for his country; but as a matter of fact in his own consciousness, it is the flag that has the first place. It sometimes happens that this even directly determines action. Whether one isolated standard remains in the hands of the enemy or not does not determine the fate of the country, yet the soldier allows himself to be killed to regain it. He loses sight of the fact that the flag is only a sign, and that it has no value in itself, but only brings to mind the reality that it represents; it is treated as if it were this reality itself. Now the totem is the flag of the clan.[21]

So Durkheim's account of the origin of religion discovers its genesis in those occasions when the society, *qua* moral community, is most aware of itself and of its power to transform the lives of its members. The example given is only a particular example of the more general phenomenon by which individuals experience society as a force superior to its members. From this phenomenon religious beliefs may be generated by any number of different mechanisms.[22] Once it has happened, socialization into the adult society is socialization into the religion; initiation rites exist to assist this process, and each new gathering serves to 'recharge the batteries' of belief for all.

It is ironic that the *Elementary Forms*, which has had such a profound influence on the sociology of religion and which has made a substantial contribution to the sociology of knowledge, should have been wrong in almost every particular with which it dealt. Subsequent anthropologists have not been slow to point this out. Apart from being motivated by the laudable desire to correct error, Durkheim continues to excite their displeasure by committing the twin offences of having failed to do any field-work of his own and of attempting to make statements about religion in general. There is no reason to suppose that field-work undertaken by Durkheim himself would have unearthed material which would have added significantly to what he obtained from the published work of Spencer and Gillen, and Strehlow, and it is even less likely that he would ever have repented of his concern with a general theory of religion. The sharp distinction which he drew between the sacred and the profane now seems difficult to sustain. Many societies are known in which the dividing line is extremely blurred, and in many more it is less apparent to the native than it is to the foreign visitor, especially if the latter is looking for it. Indeed the major difficulty lies in the fact that a specification of what is regarded as sacred by a people is generally derived 'not from the actor's but from the observer's assessment',[23] and where this is so the entire account of a people's world-view is called into question. Then again, within Durkheim's analysis it was crucial for his theory that the important religious rites should have taken place within the context of clan gatherings, since it was the clans which constituted the churches, or moral communities, of the Arunta. But later evidence tends to suggest that he greatly exaggerated the importance of the clan structure and this clearly puts a question mark against his whole exposition.[24]

If his application of the concept of a moral community is in some doubt, there is no doubt at all that he was mistaken in assigning so much importance to the derivative notion of collective effervescence. It may have been part of the structure of Aruntan religion, and he was careful to emphasize that it was but one mechanism by which social consciousness may be transformed into religious sentiments, but it remains confusing. It focuses attention on emotionally charged gatherings in such a way as to suggest that emotional arousal is necessary to sustain religious belief, and this is contrary to his general argument that religious conceptions have their source in the structure of routine social interaction, and are articulated and reinforced in ritual behaviour. Furthermore, his invocation of the idea of collective effervescence has caused confusion among scholars. Thus, on the one hand, we find Malinowski accusing him of thereby excluding from his analysis the fact that 'religion arises to a great extent from purely personal sources',[25] while on the other hand Evans-Pritchard says that Durkheim thereby offers 'a psychological explanation of social facts'.[26] That he appeared to these two distinguished scholars to be saying opposite things is a measure of the confusion he caused. While he was guilty on neither count, as Parsons has shown,[27] the introduction of the idea of collective effervescence has proved unhelpful and misleading.

Evans-Pritchard further criticizes Durkheim for producing no more than a 'just-so story' of the origins and nature of Australian totemism, and claims that there is no justification for the assertion that this is the most primitive religious form, since 'there is no means of knowing anything about the history of totemism in Australia or elsewhere'.[28] Now there is no doubt about what Durkheim, influenced by the model of biological evolution so popular in his day, was looking for: 'What we must find is a concrete reality, and historical and ethnological observation alone can reveal that to us.'[29] But that is precisely what Evans-Pritchard says Durkheim neither found, nor could have found. On the other hand there is no justification for speaking in a derogatory way about a 'just-so story', for that is precisely what a theoretical model is. Despite having been formulated from inadequate data and illustrated by inaccurate examples, the theory may still prove to be of value if propositions derived from it can be confirmed. It is not the theory itself which is tested by reference to historical materials, but propositions derived from the theory.

Durkheim's theory was far from perfect, but it did do justice to religious facts in a way in which no previous theory had done. The basic proposition which had been stated by Marx was deliberately extended by Durkheim: 'It is necessary to avoid seeing in this theory of religion a simple restatement of historical materialism.' It was extended by taking religious symbols seriously as an autonomous sphere of knowledge; and yet the precise way in which it was extended was patently unsatisfactory. He explained the origins of the totemic cosmology, marked by the radical division of nature into the sacred and the profane, with reference to social experience. All other religious conceptions, however, such as belief in spirits or gods or a single high god, are explained as having evolved from primitive beliefs. To a large extent this falsifies Durkheim's own position, for having argued that religious beliefs must be grounded in reality, which he identified as social reality, and having insisted that beliefs which are purely mistaken cannot persist, he now proposes that the beliefs of a society continue to live even though their connection with a social reality can be discovered only in their evolutionary past. It is true that established rites continue to vivify these evolved beliefs, but their connection with everyday social experience has become so attenuated as virtually to have disappeared. The moral community, moreover, becomes a church and nothing more. It is no longer the group which periodically recognizes its own sacred nature in re-creating the vital link between social experience and symbolic forms of the sacred. Durkheim proposed that religious beliefs are simply passed on to other peoples without losing any of their original strength. In describing the consequences of tribal interaction at rites of initiation, he says:

> Representatives from the neighbouring tribes are specially summoned to these celebrations, which thus become sorts of international fairs, at once religious and social. Beliefs elaborated in social environments thus constituted could not remain the exclusive patrimony of any special nationality. The stranger to whom they are revealed *carries them back to his own tribe* when he returns home; and as, sooner or later, he is forced to invite his former hosts, *there is a continual exchange of ideas from tribe to tribe*. It is thus that an international mythology was established.[30]

This would be entirely credible if the ideas thus transmitted were matters of technical innovation, such as a new type of hunting-spear. But it is a basic axiom of Durkheim's theory that a religious belief is the unique possession of a moral community – it *is* its 'exclusive patrimony'. Outside the moral community it is not religious at all, but profane, for one man's god is another man's vegetable. Yet Durkheim himself rides rough-shod over this axiom. If a religious belief is to be transferred from one people to another it is necessary, at the very least, that the supporting rites be transferred as well, for they are inseparable from the belief and symbolically prior to it.[31] But more than rites need to be transferred. If a religious conceptualization is convincing because it derives from the nature of social experience, then if one society wishes to adopt the religious beliefs of another, it must first adopt the structural characteristics which gave them significance. In the terminology used by Peter Berger, the social context in which a system of beliefs carries conviction is its 'plausibility structure', for beliefs are plausible only within the context to which they belong.[32]

So we are left with Durkheim's demonstration of the remarkable similarity between the morphology of a particular set of beliefs and the structure of the society in which they are held. At a more general level he has redirected our attention away from the problem of how religion originated, back towards the Marxian thesis that religion is an expression of social experience. The advance on Marx is to be found in Durkheim's refusal to treat religion as merely epiphenomenal. For Durkheim the religious world-view is an *essentially human* characteristic: it is an ideal world which takes its shape from the shape of the social structure in which it is located.

Taking this as his point of departure, and giving 'tentative acceptance to the spirit, if not to the details, of Durkheim's position', the American sociologist, Guy E. Swanson, has presented a more coherent account of why certain types of religious belief should be found in certain types of society.[33] Swanson accepts Durkheim's view that society is experienced, at least implicitly, as a source of power superior to men. But if religiously postulated entities, such as *Mana*, witchcraft, spirits, and gods are so diversified, how may we account for the diversity? Durkheim's explanation, as we have seen, was couched in terms of religious evolution. Swanson suggests that societies which provide different social experiences constitute the plausibility structures for different types of religious beliefs; but in order to perceive some pattern amidst the diversity of social experience it is necessary to be more precise about the dimensions of social structure which are relevant. Durkheim emphasized that society stands over against the individuals who compose it as something more durable, more long-lasting, and more powerful than they are. Society also commands respect and exercises authority, for often there are times when a man wishes to do one thing for his own gratification, but is bidden to do something else by the tradition of his people or for the general good of the society. Thus a man may wish to sit at home quietly minding his cattle, but if it is a time of conflict with neighbouring peoples the elders of his society may require him to take up arms and fight, leaving his cattle and his home. Or he may himself be an elder and be confronted directly by his wishes for his own contentment on the one hand, and his wishes for the contentment of the whole people on the other hand. In this sense he recognizes the interests of his society as distinct from his own personal wishes, and in bowing to the sovereign interests of society he acknowledges its authority over him. This deference to the superior authority of society is similar in kind to the deference he owes to religious obligations, and the similarity underlines the probability that the two are in some way connected. Further, when a man discharges his obligations to society by labouring or fighting or whatever it may be, he derives from the fulfilment of these duties a sense of satisfaction at having done the right thing; it makes him feel more secure, more confident and more content at having identified his own interests with those of a group which is larger, more permanent, and more significant than he is himself as an individual. Similarly the fulfilment of religious prescriptions yields a corresponding sense of rightness, making the man feel more confident and self-assured. Moreover what applies to one individual applies also to all the individuals who make up society, for the good of society is the good of a group with historical roots in the past and a future which has still to unfold; so to serve the good of society is to serve more than the common good of its present members. In these joint endeavours undertaken for the good of the community, and in the communal fulfilment of religious duties, the solidarity of the group is built up.

Now the structure of most simple societies is more complex than a mere aggregate of separate individuals who together constitute their tribe. Individuals owe allegiance to their families and to their villages as well as to their tribe. Often there are specialized groups within a society responsible for the exercise of some skill or for carrying out certain tasks. Some of these groups, in so far as they persist over the

course of time and are not created *ad hoc*, have purposes of their own
and exercise authority over their members in some department of
their lives. Others, of course, do not. They exist for only a few days to
perform some necessary task under the instruction of village headmen.
Some groups, however, form part of society's institutional structure,
and they will have sovereign authority within their own sphere of
competence. The notion of sovereignty is, of course, legal and political.
A body is sovereign in so far as it exercises independent jurisdiction
in some sphere, such that its decisions are not derived from above and
cannot be abrogated by any other body. Swanson suggests that the
experience of sovereignty is an important dimension of social experience
in general. It implies that society is not experienced as a mere col-
lectivity, nor as a single authoritative body. Durkheim spoke of society
being experienced by men as something superior to the individuals
who compose it and argued that originally religious conceptions
were derived from this. Swanson suggests that different societies
provide for their members radically different experiences of social life.
In the most simple society we can envisage each individual is free to
do as he wishes in some departments of his life while in others he is
beholden to the general will of the society as determined by the tribal
chief or the tribal council. In almost every known society, however,
the structure of authority is much more complex. The individual
retains some degree of freedom of action but he is also answerable to
various types of authority. His society may have a hierarchical structure such that some matters are the concern of the family, others of
the village chief, others of a council of several village chiefs; a group
of village men may tell him when he must join in communal agricultural activities; his maternal uncles may tell him whom he must take as
a wife. In each different society there is a different structure of authority
and each source of authority has sovereign control in a specific matter.
Sovereignty may reside with the individual holder of a particular
position, such as a chief or an elder brother, or it may reside with a
group, but each source of authority represents, in part, the will of
society as opposed to the will of the individual.

Durkheim argued that men are conscious of society as a will external
to the individual members of that society; Swanson argues that society
may assume various structures of authority, and each structure will
convey to individual members of the society a different impression of
the complex will which is external to them. It is not just 'society' which
is set over against the individual: groups and offices at various levels

and with various specific concerns, all of which are sovereign within defined limits, together compose that complex will which is external to the individual, and set over against him, which is called 'society'.

Although Swanson professes to be concerned with the origins of religion,[34] his theory is too involved with the immediate problem of establishing relationships between types of social structure and types of religious system to allow him to become over-concerned with intrinsically unascertainable matters. Durkheim's theory, as we have seen, supposed that the idea of the supernatural was born out of social experience, and that forms of religious belief more complex than his supposedly elementary totemism evolved over the course of time. His reasoning was guided in part by assumptions about the evolutionary development of religion from originally elementary forms; but it was also influenced by the wish to ascribe an independence to the sphere of religious knowledge. He showed no inclination to propose a theory which would enable us, given sufficient information about a society's economic and political structure, to read off the appropriate religious form, as Marx might have done if he had chosen to extend his studies of religion. Swanson, however, with his more complex social analysis, is prepared to move some way in this direction.

Monica Wilson has suggested that the prevalence of witchcraft and similar phenomena which imply a belief in somewhat generalized and non-specific supernatural powers is likely to be greater in small-scale societies which are 'dominated by personal relationships, societies in which people think in personal terms and seek personal causes for their misfortunes'.[35] Stated in this form we have a very interesting observation, but one which must be drastically reformulated if it is to be tested as a general proposition. Clyde Kluckhohn in his work on the North American Indians further suggested that witchcraft would be found to prevail in societies where people are dependent on the goodwill of others with whom they have to interact on strictly personal terms, without the guidance and sanction of established social conventions.[36] Such conditions are not uncommon, as in the situation, hypothesized by Swanson, in which people of one village have rules of exogamy:

> Let us suppose that these rules are present together with the condition that each village is the ultimately sovereign group for its members. The consequence is that men must obtain wives from groups to which they, themselves, do not belong. In these alien

groups they sometimes are not protected by laws or customary rules or public practices which define their rights and protect their interests.[37]

The reasons for such a lack of recognized practices may be various. Often competition for scarce resources may have caused the absence of customs of reciprocal interaction either between communities or within them, but in any case the causes are unimportant. What matters is that a definite hypothesis may be formulated to predict the social conditions which will predispose a society to belief in witchcraft. Some societies are so structured that their members are exposed as a matter of routine to social situations in which their well-being is dependent upon the successful management of personal, face-to-face relationships, and in which they are not guided by commonly accepted social rules and customs. Swanson puts forward the hypothesis that where personal success or failure can be attributed only to personal causes, and where social conventions are absent, we shall expect to find a prevalent belief in witchcraft. Using data culled from the ethnographic literature on a representative sample of fifty simple societies,[38] Swanson cross-tabulated the incidence of belief in witchcraft with the prevalence of necessary social interaction not generally legitimated or controlled by social conventions, and was able to show that a relationship exists with a probability beyond the 0.005 level of significance:

TABLE 4.I.

PREVALENCE OF WITCHCRAFT AND PRESENCE OF UNLEGITIMATED OR UNCONTROLLED RELATIONSHIPS[39]

Prevalence of witchcraft	Unlegitimated or uncontrolled relationships		
	none	within the society	with other societies
High	1	7	10
Intermediate	14	2	5
Low	9	0	1

Swanson claims for the relationship no more than a high degree of statistical probability, and the two cases which are directly at variance with his prediction are of obvious significance. It should be noticed, however, that he accepts the limitations of a statistical method such as he employs. Where only a limited number of discrete variables is used[40] it is inevitable that in many cases the categories cannot do justice to the ethnography. What is provided is a first approximation to a thorough test of the implications of his theory, and the results which he presents certainly justify more attention being given to his proposals than they have so far received.

One further example will clarify the positive significance which attaches to the notion of sovereignty. Monotheism, belief in a single high god, involves belief in a spiritual being who is the ultimate authority in the universe. Such a belief occurs only rarely, as arguably in Calvinistic Protestant Christianity, unaccompanied by belief in associated spiritual agencies such as angels, spirits and lesser gods. Whenever it does occur the character of the high god is one of absolute ruler or original creator. He differs from other supernatural beings principally in his singular status within a heavenly hierarchy, or pantheon, or 'historical' sequence. Since Swanson has proposed that personified spirits derive their significance for a particular people from that people's experiences of sovereign groups within society, it follows that belief in a high god may be anticipated where there is some hierarchy of sovereign groups, such that one group has answerable to it at least two other types of group, each of them sovereign within its own proper sphere. These conditions would be found, for example, where a tribe is divided into autonomous villages, each village being composed of independent family units. Swanson's data conform with the hypothesis that a high god will be found in societies which have a minimum of three types of sovereign group in a hierarchical structure, and are significant beyond the 0.005 level of probability:

TABLE 4.2.

NUMBER OF SOVEREIGN GROUPS AND PRESENCE OF HIGH GOD[41]

Presence of high god	Number of sovereign groups		
	one or two	three	four or more
Present	2	7	10
Absent	17	2	1

Again the findings require considerable commentary, but they are presented here to illustrate his method.

Swanson, it must be emphasized, does not present a series of tests of Durkheim's theory of religion. More important than his empirical findings – which are unavoidably contentious in many particulars because of the paucity of material and the limitations of his method – is the re-formulation of Durkheim's theory in order to elicit from different kinds of social experience the implications which they may be expected to hold for religious belief.[42] A particular religious belief always prompts the question, Why should this people find this belief credible? In other words one asks what it is about a plausibility structure which makes the belief plausible. The kind of general answer which Swanson's theory may suggest will never be more than a starting-point. The historical particularity of each case is important for a more complete account but, unless we are to limit ourselves solely to the particular circumstances in the study of a religion,[43] some general theoretical propositions are essential. In a later volume, to which reference will be made in the next chapter, Swanson has extended his theoretical approach to the analysis of religious change during the Protestant Reformation.[44] To make that analysis possible his notion of sovereignty, as experienced by the members of a particular society, is further refined. What he has provided already, however, is a more sophisticated method of attacking the problem which Durkheim identified. Given that the reality of religious symbols derives its potency from elements implicit in men's experience of social relations, then which dimensions of social interaction are significant for religious symbolization?

Mary Douglas, whose work lies within the Durkheim tradition, has approached the same problem, but has used different theoretical concepts and followed a more traditional anthropological method.[45] Avoiding a narrow concern with religious belief, she concentrates on ritual, and associated ideas for interpreting experience, as a mode of human knowledge. Like Swanson, she purges Durkheim's original theory of its evolutionary bias, particularly by calling into question the common assumption that a religious world view is characteristic of primitive societies whereas secularism is a phenomenon of modern complex society:

> Secularism is not essentially a product of the city. There are secular tribal cultures. Until he grasps this fact the anthropologist himself

is at a loss to interpret his own material. When he comes across an
irreligious tribe, he redoubles the vigour and subtlety of his en-
quiries. He tries to squeeze his information harder to make it yield
that overall superstructure of symbolism which his analysis can
relate all through the book to the social substructure, or he dredges
for at least something to put in a final chapter on religion.[46]

Mary Douglas does not enquire into the reasons why particular beliefs
and rites find a place in a society. She is more concerned to account for
the degree to which a society contains a ritualized world-view. She
works with an implicit single continuum of 'cosmization', a notion
akin to the secularization of which Weber wrote, characterizing it by
Schiller's expression 'the disenchantment of the world'. She takes the
view that it is equally problematic whether a society's world-view is
religious or secular. Both pose problems of interpretation and explanation, and this is emphasized by her demonstration that pygmies
can be quite as irreligious as people living in Basingstoke or Brooklyn.
The problem also comes into focus with particular clarity when we
observe the contrast between two neighbouring primitive peoples.

The pygmies represent the extreme case. So little ritual do they
perform that their first ethnographers assumed that they had, to all
intents and purposes, no religion, no culture even, of their own.
All that they had was borrowed from the Bantu. Turnbull's work
is inspired by the need to assert that their very lack of ritual is an
aspect of an independent culture of their own. He draws a picture
of pygmies, irreverently mocking solemn Bantu rites into which
they have been drawn, uncomprehending the magic for hunting and
fertility which their Bantu neighbours offer them, overcome with
giggling during Bantu attempts to divine for sorcerers, quite un-
concerned about incurring pollution of death. They perform no
cult of the dead, they reject the Bantu idea of sin. The whole
paraphernalia of Bantu religion is alien to them. Seen from the
Bantu point of view they are ignorant, and irreligious. But they
do not have any alternative set of paraphernalia, equally elaborate
and imposing, but different. Their religion is one of internal feeling,
not of external sign. The moods of the forest manifest the moods
of the deity, and the forest can be humoured by the same means as
the pygmies, by song and dance. Their religion is not concerned
with their correct orientation within elaborate cosmic categories
nor with acts of transgression, nor with rules of purity; it is concerned with joy.[47]

For Durkheim such contrasts would have been unmanageable within his theoretical framework, and, as Douglas points out, many contemporary anthropologists are little better prepared for the religious facts. The Durkheimian approach nevertheless contains the promise of an explanation – a promise which Mary Douglas realizes – for if a people's experience of their society can be the source of religious conceptions, then, surely, a different sort of social experience can just as well be unproductive of religion. Swanson, as we have seen, takes the sovereignty of groups as his principal social parameter. In keeping with the more general nature of the phenomenon to be explained, Douglas takes two variables which together determine the degree to which a person's place in society is defined and circumscribed, and these she calls group and grid. Each defines one way in which a person is locked into the structure of his society, and each is therefore a type of social control. This produces an angle on the problem rather different from that of both Swanson and Durkheim, and one more in line with the theoretical conceptions of sociologists of the structural functionalist school. If we start from the type of constraint which a society exercises over its members, we must then infer the nature of the subjective experience of persons living in that society; from those inferences we must construct a picture of the religious images which such a people will probably hold. The process is not as complicated in practice since the two stages are performed as a single intuition, but it is none the less methodologically less tidy than Swanson's approach.

Grid and group are parameters derived from the theoretical framework of Basil Bernstein's sociolinguistics,[48] but representing different ideas in this new context. The group parameter is high in a society when 'group allegiances' and 'experiences of inclusion and exclusion' are dominant. Of the line representing the continuum from low to high Professor Douglas says:

> It expresses the possible range from the lowest possible of associations to tightly knit, closed groups. A group essentially has a temporal dimension. It must endure through time to be recognisable. So this line also represents the permanence or temporary nature of people's associations with one another. A group must essentially have some corporate identity, some recognisable signs of inclusion and exclusion.[49]

To make the model easier to grasp it may be represented as a two-dimensional diagram:

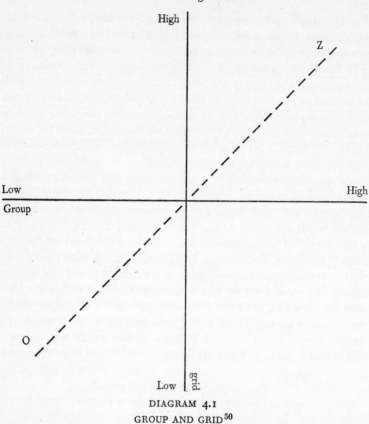

DIAGRAM 4.1
GROUP AND GRID[50]

The group continuum is shown as a horizontal axis, and the vertical axis represents grid. When a person's place in society is defined by many clearly articulated relationships, whereby he is identified as male with respect to females, young with respect to old, married with respect to unmarried and widowed, brother with respect to siblings, and so on, then to the extent that such ego-focused categories are salient in the society it will be said to be characterized by a high grid. Mary Douglas illustrates the two parameters thus:

> To the extent that the family is a bounded unit, contained in a set of rooms, known by a common name, sharing a common interest in some property, it is a group, however ephemeral. To the extent that roles within it are allocated on principles of age, sex and seniority, there is a grid controlling the flow of behaviour.[51]

The two continua are independent, as implied by the diagram, but they can be present and absent to the same degree as traced by the diagonal OZ.

The nearer to the point Z on the diagram that a society is located, i.e., the greater the strength of group and grid pressures, the greater will be the perceived importance of institutionalized social relations in influencing the course of a person's life and actions. In a society located near to point O, social relations are of minimal significance in comparison with natural aspects of the environment. Ritual will be a significant part of life, within a view of the world which populates it with supernatural powers, in proportion as life is dominated by strong social constraints deriving from a pervasive system of group and grid. *Mutatis mutandis,* religious conceptions will form an insignificant part of a way of life dominated by impersonal forces, whether they are natural phenomena like the seasons and the movement of animals, or man-made things like forms to complete in triplicate and parking meters. It is the degree to which personal, face-to-face relations, governed by established social rules, dominate the life of a people which determines the likelihood of its being religious, irrespective of whether the people live in the African bush or in Bootle.

Although Professor Douglas elaborates her thesis to include the important concomitant of body images associated with various types of social structure, the most rudimentary elements have been indicated above. We shall refer to it again to show its implications for more orthodox accounts of secularization,[52] but it will readily be seen as a significant advance on Durkheim's analysis while remaining in the same tradition. It shares a difficulty with Durkheim's own formulations, however, which Swanson has escaped. If we are to move from the description and interpretation of particular religions in their proper social contexts to propositions about religion in general, the elements which are to count as relevant to a theory must be stated in advance without ambiguity. The strategy of comparing two societies with respect to some common feature, maintaining *ceteris paribus,*[53] is not strikingly rigorous, especially when only partial descriptions of the societies are provided. The attempt to limit comparisons to within a 'given social environment' is, as she says, 'a matter of discretion'.[54] But whose discretion? Some of her anthropological colleagues will be certain to charge her with indiscretion, no matter how careful the comparison may be. And yet this method alone cannot begin to establish the validity of her own penetrating analysis, which is couched in the most general terms. Swanson has escaped this difficulty, though at enormous cost, for he makes no attempt to confine comparisons within a single type of social environment. But the price he pays seems worth it. Recognizing that other things are very far from equal, he has none the less established some relationships which are highly significant from a purely statistical point of view and these substantial relationships will not be wished away.

This chapter then may be summarized as follows. Durkheim maintained that our conceptions of the supernatural derive their strength and their form from men's experience of social life. The particular aspects of social life which are relevant to particular religious conceptions is a question tackled by both Swanson and Douglas with substantive results. The main problem for future investigation lies in choosing between the radically different methods which they have employed.

5. Religion and Social Change: Towards a Synthesis

Theories of religion, in common with other sociological theories, meet their most severe test when they try to account for the part which religion plays in social change. Durkheim's theory, as will presently be seen, is strained to its limits by this problem. On the other hand it is entirely in character with Max Weber's approach to the study of society that he chose to base the whole of his sociology of religion on this very factor. His comparative studies of Chinese, Indian and ancient Israelite religion, which will not be discussed here, contain the bulk of his theoretical formulations worked out in their applications to particular societies.[1] His essay, *The Protestant Ethic and the Spirit of Capitalism*, was an early work which, as Reinhard Bendix says, 'merely defined a problem for further investigation'.[2] The problem, as Weber saw it, was to account for the emergence of industrial capitalism as the economic form of the modern West, and in particular to show the role which religion has played in this process. In *The Protestant Ethic* he gives a first statement of his thesis that capitalism was linked with the rise of ascetic Protestantism, and the essay is of special interest since in it we may see the lines of enquiry that appeared promising to him. The thesis is worked out in his own comparative studies of the general historical relationship of religion and society, and in Ernst Troeltsch's writings on European religion and society which 'disposed of many of the things' Weber would have wished to discuss in a way which he, 'not being a theologian, could not have done'.[3] Although Weber's thesis is well known, it will be necessary to recall the main points in his argument, since they are so often misunderstood, not least by those who claim to support his general conclusions. This may be done most simply by focusing on the idea of 'the calling' as he uses it, and on the 'elective affinity' which, in his judgement, existed between the Protestant ethic and the spirit of capitalism.

It is often said that Weber's work was conducted as a lengthy debate with the ghost of Marx. Nowhere is this more apparent than in his writings on religion, or so it appears to a superficial observer. Marx, it is said, proposed that religion and religious change derive from the economic structure of a society, whereas Weber maintained the contrary position that religious change causes economic change. This representation distorts the ideas of both scholars. Within Marx's theoretical revolutionary programme the attack on religion, which he saw as an attack on men's systematic belief in an inversion of the real world, was the first item on the agenda: 'the criticism of religion is the premise of all criticism'.[4] As we have already noted, religion itself was of little importance for Marx. Its significance lay in the consciousness which it gives to men of the society in which they live. In a perfect world, religion, which is always symptomatic of a sick social order, would not exist. In an imperfect world, however, the very imperfection can find a religious expression and can evoke protest in religious terms. Marx viewed the German Reformation as just such a protest, although in the end it left men bound, not merely with chains, but in an 'iron cage' (the phrase is Weber's). This view is manifest in the following passage:

> Luther, without question, overcame servitude through devotion but only through substituting servitude through conviction. He shattered the faith in authority by restoring the authority of faith. He transformed the priests into laymen by turning laymen into priests. He liberated man from external religiosity by making religiosity the innermost essence of man. He liberated the body from its chains because he fettered the heart with chains. But if Protestantism was not the solution it did at least pose the problem correctly. It was no longer a question, thereafter, of the layman's struggle against the priest outside himself, but of his struggle against his own internal priest, against his own priestly nature.[5]

Economic determinist though he was at the end of the day, Marx's understanding of religion is far from the crude reductionism with which he is so often credited. It would be much nearer the truth to say that the tradition of ascribing every social phenomenon, including religion, to economic causes developed after Marx and originated with Engels. Within this tradition it was common enough to dismiss religion in historical analyses as irrelevant, and it was in opposition to this view that Weber wished to defend the role of religion as a factor which is highly relevant to the process of social changes. It was easy enough to show the influence of religion through historical studies of ecclesiastical politics and the exercise of the church's power, but Weber wished to go far beyond this and to show how the religious convictions of ordinary people might help to shape the institutional arrangements of their societies. The balanced modesty of his own proposals is clear in his comment that:

> ... we must free ourselves from the idea that it is possible to deduce the Reformation, as a historically necessary result, from certain economic changes ... On the other hand, however, we have no intention whatever of maintaining such a foolish and doctrinaire thesis as that the spirit of capitalism ... could only have arisen as the result of certain effects of the Reformation, or even that capitalism as an economic system is a creation of the Reformation.[6]

In spite of this clear statement, his intentions were none the less misrepresented even during his own lifetime, as a rather sour footnote in the revised edition of *The Protestant Ethic* testifies.[7] As someone wrote recently, 'The old serve as Aunt Sallies for their successors to shy at, and if Sally is erected crooked she falls the more easily.'[8]

The reaction against economic determinism was not the only feature of Weber's thesis. On the positive side he had been influenced by the work of Werner Sombart, who had examined the way in which modern capitalism is characterized by economic rationalism. The historical process whereby ever-increasing areas of life become subject to procedures of rational decision-making is, perhaps, the central theme running through all Weber's work. A general tendency such as rationalization cannot, however, account for specific features of social change, and Weber's task was to 'find out whose intellectual child the particular concrete form of rational thought was, from which the idea of a calling and devotion to labour in the calling has grown'.[9]

The idea of a 'calling' is central to Weber's thesis, and he attempted to show that it was born out of the Reformation. In pre-Reformation Catholic thought the idea of a vocation or a calling was used only with reference to a way of life which was considered to have higher religious value *per se* than any secular life could have. This in itself has to be seen against the background of the medieval idea of religious duty. A person's religious obligations were clearly defined and consisted in such things as attendance at mass on Sundays and holy days, prescribed fasting and confession, and so on. These observances admitted

D

of no choice on the part of the laity and salvation was thought to follow automatically from their fulfilment. Hence there was agonizing anxiety over the fate of a child who died before being baptized, and immense concern that the dying should make their confession and receive the last rites so that they might thereby be assured of salvation. People could ensure their eternal future by chalking up all the necessary good marks, which were recorded on the credit side in the heavenly ledger. Within narrow limits, the individual had some choice open to him in his conduct of secular affairs, but no amount of secular work or virtue would avail for his eternal salvation. It must be admitted that the wealthy and noble of birth are over-represented among those whose religious virtue the Church recognized by canonization, but this reflects more on the institution of canonization than on the Church's teaching.[10] The only direct road to salvation was to enter a religious order and forgo all worldly ambition. The contrast was stark. In the eyes of the Church, the only form of human effort which was supremely desirable was a life of monastic asceticism, to be followed as a calling from God. Worldly ambition was regarded as worthless; all that was asked of a man was patient acceptance of his lot in life.

The reformers introduced a new note. Instead of insisting on the fulfilment of numerous religious obligations, they stressed the importance of a subjective faith in God. This emphasized the choice which ordinary lay people have to make, and it makes Christian profession something essentially voluntary. It was taken for granted by Protestants no less than Catholics that all men would be Christian, but the Protestant was supposed to have made a conscious religious choice. Hence the life of the Protestant layman came to be seen in terms of a calling – a calling to be a Christian – and secular as well as religious duties became important. According to this new religious teaching all the vigorous effort which had been encouraged by the medieval Church when it was directed to a life of ascetism within a monastic context was now to be encouraged when it was directed to the right conduct of secular affairs. In short, effort became religiously desirable for the layman as well as for the monk. In a celebrated passage, Weber concluded that

... when asceticism was carried out of the monastic cells into everyday life, and began to dominate worldly morality, it did its part in building the tremendous cosmos of the modern economic order.[11]

This is not the whole story, however. It was understandable that monks should subject themselves to ascetic rigours if they hoped thereby to achieve deliverance from everlasting damnation. Similarly we can see why people should try to live upright lives if their salvation depends on that, rather than on the fulfilment of mechanical forms of devotion. But why should this have escalated into such ascetic concern with hard work?

To answer this question Weber turns to the teachings of John Calvin, for it was, he says, among the Calvinists that the devotion to labour was found at its strongest. Not only did Calvin emphasize the doctrine of *sola fide*, justification by faith alone, but he also preached a rigid doctrine of predestination. In the words of the Calvinistic Article XVII of the Articles of Religion of the Church of England: 'Predestination to Life is the everlasting purpose of God, whereby (before the foundations of the world were laid) he hath constantly decreed by his counsel secret to us, to deliver from curse and damnation those whom he hath chosen . . .' All the rest are predestined to damnation,[12] and since a man can do nothing to alter the divine judgement, which is passed at God's arbitrary pleasure, 'without any foresight of faith or good works, or perseverance in either of them, or any other thing in the creature as conditions, or causes moving Him',[13] a man was obviously concerned to discover whether or not he was predestined to salvation. The doctrine of predestination, when taught in its extreme form, places the believer in an agonizing position. He is required to believe that his eternal fate, be it salvation or damnation, is finally fixed. But as he is exhorted to live a godly life the exhortation serves only to remind him of the fact that his fate is fixed already, and so the question of whether he is numbered among the elect few who are predestined to salvation becomes a terrifying obsession: it provokes what Weber called the 'salvation panic'.

Now Luther taught that a man knows himself saved by the feeling of 'blessed assurance' and a sense of inner conviction. Calvin, on the other hand, taught that all feelings and emotions are to be distrusted; it was a sin to doubt that one was saved, he said, and *certitudo salutis*, the certainty of salvation, could only be strengthened in the Christian by knowing that his life proved him to be a member of the elect. Since only those who are saved can do anything pleasing to God, it was through the objective evidence of a good life that the Calvinist knew himself to be numbered among those predestined to salvation. As Weber says:

... It was through the consciousness that his conduct, at least in its fundamental character and constant ideal, rested on a power within himself working for the glory of God; that it is not only willed by God but rather done by God that he attained the highest good towards which this religion strove, the certainty of salvation ... Thus, however useless good works might be as a means of attaining salvation ... they are indispensible as a sign of election. They are the technical means, not of purchasing salvation, but of getting rid of the fear of damnation. In this sense they are occasionally referred to as directly necessary for salvation.[14]

So the 'salvation panic', that terrifying uncertainty which was left when the Catholic way of salvation was removed, was resolved for the Calvinist by recourse to hard work in his calling.

Weber did not suppose that the growth of Calvinism with its ethic of hard methodical work gave rise to industrial capitalism. The phrase Weber uses to describe the connection is *Wahlverwandtschaften* which comes from the title of a novel by Goethe. Parsons translates the phrase as 'certain correlations',[15] but this does not fully convey Weber's meaning, although it is causally neutral. Reinhard Bendix translates it as 'elective affinities' and this is much more satisfactory:[16] it gives the more accurate impression that there is some kind of natural affinity between the religious ideas and the economic interests, and that each modifies the other so that their affinity may be further strengthened. Weber suggests that there is a two-way relationship. The Protestant ethic forms a uniquely suitable legitimation for the spirit of capitalism, thereby encouraging and catalysing its growth. But equally the spirit of capitalism is singularly appropriate as an expression of the Protestant ethic, which is able to thrive when given a proper outlet and opportunity. They fit together, the former being, in Berger's terms, the legitimating belief of the latter, and the latter being an element in the plausibility structure of the former. The reciprocal nature of this connection is recognized and stressed by Weber.

All the ingredients of the Protestant ethic were present in medieval Catholic thought. The doctrine of predestination was fully developed by St Augustine of Hippo in the fifth century. The idea that the layman's calling to marriage and to secular work is of no less importance than the monastic calling had been taught by the German mystic, Johannes Tauler, in the fourteenth century,[18] although it was contrary to the teaching of St Thomas Aquinas, and was not held by Calvin.[19] Capitalism, too, was found before the Reformation. Whether it was confined to the capitalism of merchant adventurers, as Weber and Sombart supposed, or whether rational industrial capitalism already existed in embryonic form, its growth hampered by a lag in technical developments, is immaterial. What matters is that although both the Protestant ethic and the spirit of capitalism can be found in rudimentary form before the Reformation, the great efflorescence of capitalism took place at the time, and in the places of intense Calvinistic piety.[20] Weber hoped that his thesis would provide an adequate explanation of this historical connection between the two events.

The literature which has grown up round the thesis is enormous.[21] Much of it is not relevant to our purposes, but inasmuch as it affects the present status of Weber's thesis it must not go unmentioned. Subsequent work has fallen under roughly three headings: there are those critics who offer specific objections to Weber's thesis, those who consider that he used the wrong social variables, or too few of them, to account for the phenomenon, and those who have attempted empirical tests. Among the specific criticisms which have been offered, two may be picked out as especially important. The historian R. H. Tawney has expressed considerable doubt about Weber's evidence.[22] He points out that the picture which Weber presents of the Protestant ethic is based on 'not the conduct of Puritan capitalists, but the doctrines of Puritan divines',[23] and this is indeed so. Most of the illustrations which Weber uses are drawn from the writings of English Puritans at the end of the seventeenth century. As will be seen below, the implicit point of this criticism, which is that Weber was focusing his attention on the wrong group of people, has been repeated since Tawney first made it, and in a more positive form. It was also Tawney's contention that the thesis was over-subtle in places, 'ascribing to intellectual and moral influences developments which were the result of more prosaic and mundane forces, and which appeared, irrespective of the character of religious creeds, wherever external conditions offered them a congenial environment'.[24] Stated thus, it appears that Tawney wished to by-pass the role of religion altogether, although this was not so; but having dismissed a large part of Weber's evidence, and being unable to supply alternative support for his thesis, the possibility of having to fall back on a simple material explanation had to be faced.

Hugh Trevor-Roper in his more recent contribution to the discussion, proposes an alternative hypothesis.[25] Examining with great care the actual entrepreneurs of the period with which Weber dealt, and taking into account the European as well as the English literature on the subject, he agrees with Weber, that 'in Catholic as in Protestant countries, in the mid-seventeenth century, we find that the Calvinists are indeed the great entrepreneurs'.[26] But on the other hand he shows that their piety was less than exemplary, and that, in any case, their 'local origins were more constant than their religion'.[27] He concludes that:

> Analysing the entrepreneurial class of the new 'capitalist' cities of the seventeenth century, we find that the whole class is predominantly formed of immigrants, and these immigrants, whatever their religion, come predominantly from four areas. First, there are the Flemings . . . Secondly, there are the Jews from Lisbon and Seville . . . Thirdly, there are the south Germans, mainly from Augsburg. Fourthly, there are the Italians, mainly from Como, Locarno, Milan and Lucca.[28]

Trevor-Roper goes on to suggest that in the areas from which these immigrants came the sure beginnings of industrial capitalism were already in evidence, and furthermore that the men who were destined to emigrate had already become thoroughly acquainted with the idea of a religiously significant secular calling through the teachings of such Catholic divines as Erasmus. He maintains that 'in fact, the idea was a commonplace before Protestantism', and although 'there was a sense in which it was peculiarly the attitude of the *bourgeoisie*' it was 'an attitude which appealed to the educated laity in general'.[29] The cause of the emigration of these men with their already established skills in industrial capitalism was the hardening attitude of Counter-Reformation Catholicism. After the Reformation the Catholic Church no longer tolerated the liberal views which rising generations had come to regard as the proper expression of their religion. The Catholic Church's 'old elasticity had gone, intellectually and spiritually, as well as politically'.[30] Thus:

> It was not that Calvinism created a new type of man, who in turn created capitalism; it was rather that the old economic élite of Europe were driven into heresy because the attitude of mind which had been theirs for generations, was suddenly, and in some places, . . . declared heretical and intolerable.[31]

Hence the cause of the great upsurge of industrial capitalism among groups of Calvinists was not Calvinism at all, but Catholicism. It was a result of the expulsion of the proto-capitalists and proto-Protestants from their old Catholic homes by the counter-reformers.

Now Trevor-Roper's thesis has a particular attraction in that it explains why the blossoming of capitalism should have occurred some time after the Reformation itself. But it has weaknesses too. An obvious defect of *The Protestant Ethic* is that in it Weber advances a very specific historical application of his general thesis without accepting the constraints of what Roland Robertson has referred to as its 'contextual uniqueness'.[32] Weber did not examine the evidence relating to this particular case with sufficient thoroughness. But nor has Trevor-Roper done so. Both his criticism of Weber and his own alternative theory rest on the evidence of a small number of *great* entrepreneurs. It is better, to be sure, to cite the cases of several entrepreneurs rather than just one or two, as Weber did, but only if they are representative. And they are not. All the men to whom Trevor-Roper refers are Fuggers amongst seventeenth-century entrepreneurs. They are all big men, and as such they are far removed from the little men to whom Benjamin Franklin addressed his *Advice to a Young Tradesman* and *Necessary Hints to Those That Would Be Rich,* who were the men of whom Weber believed himself to have written. So Trevor-Roper's criticisms are fundamentally misplaced, and Weber's thesis is left untouched. This reflects little credit on Weber, however, for it is extremely doubtful whether the documentary material exists which could either confirm or refute his thesis. It must therefore stand as an account which is adequate as an 'ideal-typical' analysis.[33] So far as Trevor-Roper's own thesis is concerned, it seems to rest largely on his assertion that 'the religious attitude of those actively engaged in economic life in 1500' was 'Erasmeanism'.[34] Leaving aside the ambiguity which is involved when he uses the expression, 'those actively engaged in economic life', we still see no evidence presented, nor any other scholarly opinion cited. Unless he is simply referring to the great entrepreneurs again, it is not easy to see what evidence could be available, unless it were in the form of contemporary opinion or of the reported popularity with the *bourgeoisie* of preachers with known Erasmean proclivities.

Of the critics who suggest that variables other than those used by Weber should be considered, two in particular need to be mentioned. Michael Walzer shares Weber's interest in ascetic Protestantism, but he is less concerned with its specifically economic implications. He seeks to show the importance of Puritanism in stimulating the English

revolution and, like Trevor-Roper, judges the evidence which might
confirm Weber's thesis to be lacking:

> Neither Max Weber nor any of his followers have ever demon-
> strated that the Englishmen who actually became Puritans, who
> really believed in predestination and lived through the salvation
> panic, went on to become capitalist businessmen . . . it is possible . . .
> The weight of such diaries, letters and memoirs as we possess,
> however, suggests that the most significant expression of the new
> faith was cultural and political rather than economic.[35]

We see at once that Walzer is focusing his attention on that same group
of people who engaged Weber's attention. His distinct line of enquiry,
however, will enlarge our examination of the role of religion in a
period of social change, only one aspect of which is concerned with
the rise of modern industrial capitalism. He calls the Puritans, as
they often called themselves, the saints, and says that the two groups
of people who most readily adopted Calvinist beliefs were 'the clergy
and the new class of educated laymen'.[36] The effects of their new
religious beliefs were to be seen in the complete transformation of
their lives, which were henceforth marked by an extreme self-discipline,
frenetic activity and consciences hypersensitive to every possible
transgression. Their exaggerated activism found a natural outlet in
their calling to be Christian citizens who regarded themselves as
being responsible for building a Christian community as well as for
the transgressions of their fellow-men. As the new élite of an urban
society in which the middle class was emerging as the dominant
stratum, they were in a position to spread the newly found ideology
by which they themselves were activated.[37] They provided the answer
to the need, recognised by Lenin, 'to discover real organisers, people
with sober minds and a practical outlook, people who combine
loyalty to socialism, with ability without fuss (and in spite of fuss and
noise)'[38] if a successful revolution was to be launched. The saints
were precisely such men. Walzer portrays the Calvinists as men who
felt themselves compelled by their divine calling to act as they did
and so to press forward with the revolution. So his first implicit
criticism of Weber is that his concentration on economics led him to set
unwarranted limits to his use of the historical material. As a criticism
of Weber this is unfair, for he was, if anything, more interested in the
emergence of rational capitalism than in the role of religion, and his
thesis provides a theoretical outline which is adequate within the

methodology which he used. Walzer has nevertheless performed a useful service by pointing out some of the other implications of this syndrome of ascetic Protestant devotion.

His second main criticism is more substantial, and also serves to widen the analysis. Weber did not attempt to consider why men should have been attracted to a Calvinist faith: he was concerned only with the implications of their faith. Trevor-Roper suggests, rather lamely, that some were attracted to Calvinism because of the unwillingness of the Catholic Church to grant any degree of religious responsibility to the laity. Walzer suggests that men became Calvinists because:

> . . . they felt some need for the self-control and godly government that sainthood offered. This is to push Weber's explanation of Calvinism a step further back: he has argued that Calvinism was an anxiety-inducing ideology that drove its adherents to seek a sense of control and confidence in methodical work and worldly success . . . Now it is probably not true that Calvinism *induced* anxiety; more likely its effect was to confirm and explain in theological terms perceptions men already had of the dangers of the world and the self. But what made Calvinism an 'appropriate' option for anxiety-ridden individuals was not only this confirmation, but also that sainthood offered a way out of anxiety.[39]

The question of what it is that drew men to Calvinism could not be more pertinent. The almost incredible fact that men should feel themselves actually attracted by doctrines so monstrous as those taught by Calvin demands some form of explanation.

While Walzer has no specific explanation to offer, he has at least raised the question, and suggested that we should look to the disorder and confusion resulting from the break-up of medieval society for the source of the malady which drove men into the arms of Calvin. The confusion was all the greater because of the very stability of pre-Reformation society. It had been an unchanging and apparently unchangeable order in which, for all its bloody conflicts, disasters occurred within an immutable context in which everything could be understood and fitted into its proper place. This medieval world-view portrayed the world as a 'great allegory whose essential secret was its meaning, not its operation or its causes; it was a hierarchical order, extending from lowest to highest, from stones and trees through man to choirs upon choirs of angels, just as society ranged itself from serf through lord and king to pope; and it was inspired

throughout by the desire to fulfil its divine purpose.'[40] The slow
collapse of so magnificent an edifice through social and political
decay could not fail to be traumatic. As Johan Huizinga has written
of the fifteenth century:

> Is it surprising that the people could see their fate and that of the
> world only as an endless succession of evils? Bad governments,
> exactions, the cupidity and violence of the great, wars and brigand-
> age, scarcity, misery and pestilence – to this is contemporary history
> nearly reduced in the eyes of the people. The feeling of general
> insecurity which was caused by the chronic form wars were apt to
> take, by the constant menace of the dangerous classes, by the mis-
> trust of justice was further aggravated by the obsession of the
> coming end of the world, and by the fear of hell, of sorcerers and
> of devils.[41]

It is Walzer's suggestion that Calvinism offered the hope of creating
order out of chaos to those who were most exposed to the bleak and
tempestuous 'winds of change': to the clergy and the newly educated
laymen of the day. Such people saw the condition of their world as
being under the domination of omnipresent and uncontrollable evil,
a world about which Luther could declare with utter conviction:
'It is an article of faith that the Devil is *Princeps Mundi, Deus huius
seculi.*' It was this experience of a world in disarray which led the
bourgeoisie, made up of those who were neither above the turmoil,
nor sunk so low in it as to be insensible,[42] to embrace the Protestant
creeds with an alacrity which is otherwise incomprehensible.[43]

Once espoused, Calvinism was a powerful agent in dissolving what
remained of the old order. In a study which nicely complements
Walzer's, David Little has shown how Puritanism created a radical
sense of discontinuity between the old order and the new. The old
order was interpreted as sinful and of the devil; the order which replaced it was seen as a divine dispensation in which all things were made
new. Puritans saw the old medieval social and political traditions as
'robbed of all automatic sanctity' since they were 'subordinated to the
overriding claims of the coming order'.[44]

> The crucial distinction between past and future, old and new, is
> present in the Puritan system, thereby giving solid support to the
> devaluation of tradition and making possible a disciplined *re*-
> systematization of conduct in keeping with long-range, future-
> orientated goals.[45]

The picture which begins to emerge is one of Calvinism's role as the midwife of a new social order which was born from the wreckage of an earlier one. It is in the change-over from a society of one type to a society of an entirely different type that Puritanism played its crucial part. One aspect of the change-over – perhaps the most important aspect – is the emergence of modern capitalism, based on a business ethic marked by 'a duty of the individual towards the increase of his capital, which is assumed as an end in itself'.[46] Under the new dispensation a man is judged by what he has made of himself, not by the station to which he was born. In the new bourgeois ideal all citizens share responsibility for the state, as free men and equal. The new order is composed of new social, political and economic institutions, and it is crowned by the new religion of Protestantism.

But it was Protestantism, not Calvinistic Puritanism, which was the religion of the new order. Weber was clear that once modern capitalism was brought into existence it developed foundations of its own, and it no longer needed the support of Calvinism. The same is true of the wider social context. The disappearance of Puritanism from the English scene after a very short time suggests to Walzer that the need for it had gone, for this need had been limited to the 'period of breakdown and psychic and political reconstruction. When men stopped being afraid, or became less afraid, then Puritanism was suddenly irrelevant.'[47] The Protestantism which remained was no longer ascetic and frenetic; it was merely disciplined, earnest and dour. Calvinistic Puritanism became 'a remembered enthusiasm and a habitual self-control devoid, as Weber's capitalism is, of theological reason'.[48]

Had Durkheim turned his attention to the Reformation we might have been given a very different picture from that which Weber drew for, as Parsons says, 'he was always concerned, on the theoretical plane, with relatively simple, bold outlines and clear-cut alternatives'.[49] And that is precisely what Swanson has given us in his *Religion and Regime*. Disregarding the way in which the changes had taken place, Swanson examines European religions and political structures first before the Reformation, then in 1490, and lastly after it was all over, in 1780. A brief account of each Reformation settlement, as it was reached, is given to set it within its historical context.[50] The details of his analysis need not be spelt out. He develops the Durkheimian theory elaborated in his earlier book, concentrating on the notion of immanence as crucial to the difference between Catholic belief and the various Protestant creeds. In Catholicism, he points out, God is not only present in the world in the person of Jesus, but remains accessible through the Church. The sacraments, the relics of the saints, the priestly hierarchy, shrines, holy water and a hundred other things provide the faithful with tangible aspects of divinity which are ever present. The world of the Catholic is shot through with God, who is met at every turn, and who is no less immanent in the world than he is transcendent beyond it. Leaving aside various intermediate religions, such as Anglicanism and Lutheranism, at the other extreme we find that Calvinism presents a pattern which is in the sharpest contrast with Catholicism. According to extreme Protestant beliefs, when Jesus ascended into heaven the world was left without any trace of him. The disciples are simply the disciples of the Lord, not themselves sacred in their own right. The Lord's Supper is a memorial containing nothing sacred in itself apart from the memory which was recalled. God, for the Calvinists, is utterly transcendent, *Deus absconditus*.

Swanson sets himself the problem of explaining just what it is in men's experience of their social world that corresponds to this religious contrast. He points to differences among the political régimes which were emerging at about the same time as the Reformation, and makes use of the distinction, drawn by David Easton, between 'the polity of an organization as an association and its polity as a social system'.[51] Polity in the first sense involves decisions taken in the interests of the several parties concerned. The good of the organization or state is equated with the sum of the interests of the various members. Polity in the second sense concerns decisions taken in the interests of the organization or state *qua* institution.[52] Here the interests even of an overwhelming majority of the members may be disregarded in the interests of the organization itself. Decisions in matters of state include the authority 'to make war or conclude a peace, to create magistrates, to establish a system of judicial appeals, to pardon adjudged offenders, to coin money, to have allegiance or fealty or homage, to grant patents including those of monopoly, and to convoke and control the militia of the state'.[53] Following Easton's distinction we see that decisions such as these, which affect the interests of the state, may be thought of in two quite different ways. It will be clearer if we take as an example the decision as to whether or not war should be declared. On the one hand the decision may be taken so that the best interests of all the subjects of the state are followed. The landowners may want peace, while tradesmen, the army and the church want war. The decision will depend on the balance of power and the balance of interests between the various parties. On the other hand it may be that when all these various interests have been consulted a further consideration is introduced: what will most effectively preserve the integrity of the state as an autonomous community and advance its position vis-à-vis other states? This is an altogether separate matter, although in practice the long-term interests of the citizens may be best served by attending to the immediate interests of the state as a well ordered community. Bearing in mind these two types of consideration we can see that, at the extremes, there are two contrasting ways of deciding whether or not to go to war. At the one extreme the interests of the various constituent members are taken as together defining the good of the state. In such a society there will be appropriate political machinery for political representation. At the other extreme the interests of the citizens, as individuals and as diverse interest groups, are disregarded in favour of the interests of the state *qua* state. What advances the interests of the state may advance the interests of its several members too, but this will be fortuitous, for it will be the interests of the state as a continuing social system which are alone consulted. Again, appropriate political machinery, whether it be a monarch or a republican council, will exist to adjudge the interests of the state *qua* state, as opposed to the state *qua* its constituent parts.

In Swanson's view this distinction is crucial. On the one hand the state may be thought of solely as the composite of its members. On the other hand it may be thought of as an entity separate from its members and above them, with interests of its own which must be accorded primacy of place in all its decisions. He argues that experience of the respective types of political arrangement which enshrine these two contrasting conceptions of society will influence what kind of god will be found credible in the society.

In societies where the authority for matters of state[54] is clearly exercised as separate and independent of the interests of the subjects, this will predispose people to believe in a god who is immanent in the world. Just as the authority and purposes of the state are separate and visible, no matter how detestable they may happen to be, so the presence and purposes of god will be deemed to be visible and knowable. Conversely, the society in which there is no conception of the state as separate from, and above, its members, and has political machinery to adjudge no interests beyond the composite interests of its members, will predispose its members to belief in a god who is transcendent, invisible, and inaccessible. Just as there is no conception of the state as a separate and superior power with autonomous interests, so there will be no notion of a god who is accessible and visible.

Many of the political forms which emerged for the first time in the sixteenth century, Swanson points out, vested the authority for decisions in matters of state in representative assemblies. In such assemblies landowners, craft guilds, the professions, and so on were all represented, and their representatives exercised authority in the interests of their constituencies. The interests and authority of the state as such effectively disappeared from view, and while a distinction might still be drawn in theory, in practice the good of the state came to be equated with the good of the several constituent members. The authority of the state, *qua* state, had become an authority *absconditus*. So Swanson argues that the notion of a God immanent in the world has no social experience from which it might be rendered meaningful under such a political arrangement. Just as the state cannot be distinguished as a separate entity, so neither can God, who thus becomes totally transcendent and fundamentally unknowable and unapproachable. Swanson analysed the complexity of constitutional arrangements, and pointed out that the sovereign authority of the state is not dependent on monarchy. The Great Council of Venice, for example, which was the supreme authority in the state of Venice, was composed of all males who were full citizens; they conferred and legislated as Venetian citizens, not as representatives of particular interests. Moreover the officers of state held their positions for non-renewable periods of as little as two months, as temporary ministers of the Great Council to which all authority belonged.[55]

Swanson's thesis contains weaknesses, of course, and it must remain a moot point whether citizens in general are fully aware of constitutional arrangements, and experience their operation as immediately as Swanson assumes that they do:

> I have assumed that most members of a society's body politic will experience changes in the structure, power and moral force of such collective processes and that they will together seek a theology to define the source of their new experiences in order more adequately to cope with these basic changes in their world.[56]

It is entirely characteristic of Swanson's work that he thus draws our attention even to those assumptions which are most open to doubt.

There is, however, no doubt about the need to treat his theory seriously for, from the political arrangements of states, he is able to predict with a striking degree of success just what kind of Reformation settlement they might have been expected to reach. He is at least justified in proposing that 'religious conceptions symbolize men's experiences with the collective procedures by which their society reaches decisions'.[57]

So far as Swanson is concerned, exactly 'how such developments occur or in what sequence is unknown'.[58] That is to be expected from an account which works on so large a canvas; in any case it is with precisely those intermediate stages that the other studies under consideration deal.

Recent research which has attempted to test Weber's thesis in terms of the attitudes found in Catholic and Protestant communities today has generally been inconclusive. Too often it appears to have been undertaken for want of a more interesting subject for research. There is, however, one study which deserves attention. David McClelland's concept of the 'achievement motive' is a good approximation to the kind of zeal for industriousness on which both Weber and Walzer focused their attention.[59] Using standard procedures of experimental psychology, McClelland is able to demonstrate that some people have a greater need to do well and to put up an impressive performance than do other people, regardless of their particular circumstances or of the particular tasks on which they are engaged. These people, whom he designates as having a high need for achievement (nA), when they are set a task under laboratory conditions in which the only motive is achievement for achievement's sake, do significantly better than average, and much better than people with a low nA.

The test which he uses 'measures a critical ability – the ability to deal quickly and accurately with unfamiliar material. It is related to general intelligence . . . try to perform as well as possible.'[60] People with a low nA, on the other hand, are found to do better under test conditions which offer some reward or incentive for a good performance.[61]

Earlier work by Marion Winterbottom, whose findings were confirmed by McClelland,[62] suggested that the incidence of a high need for achievement was probably related to those particular forms of child-rearing in which great emphasis is placed on teaching children to be independent and self-reliant. McClelland suggests that these are precisely the values which one would expect to be instilled in their children by people who were themselves imbued with the 'Protestant ethic', with its emphasis on the need for hard work, for getting on, for never wasting time, and so on. If this is so, then it follows that his scheme provides a series of three causal links between the Protestant ethic and the spirit of capitalism. The Protestant ethic would dispose people to bring up their children to be self-controlled and self-reliant; children brought up in this way would have a high need for achievement; and,

> . . . if a number of people with high n Achievement happened to be present in a given culture at a given time, then things would start to hum. They might well start doing things better . . . or what is even more important, they might start doing them differently by trying to get achievement satisfaction out of what they were doing . . . it would not be at all surprising to imagine that an increase in n Achievement should promote economic or cultural growth.[63]

His theory may be represented in diagrammatic form thus:[64]

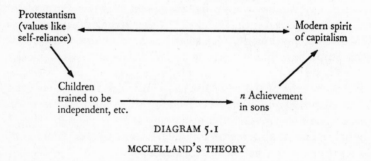

DIAGRAM 5.1

MCCLELLAND'S THEORY

McClelland goes on to show, with varying degrees of success, that a high level of n Achievement was present in many cultural contexts and historical periods which saw a flowering of some aspect, economic, political or cultural, of the society concerned. He calls this syndrome the Spirit of Hermes, since it manifests itself as a spirit of activity and liveliness.[65] It does indeed seem that McClelland's Spirit of Hermes is a general phenomenon of which the Protestant ethic may be a particular example. It need not always be tied to a religious derivation, but certainly some powerful stimulus will be required to awaken a spirit whose effects are so far-reaching.

But whence comes the Spirit of Hermes? This is not a question which

McClelland attempts to answer, but a similar question was posed in another study to which reference has already been made. Drawing on Nietzsche's celebrated distinction between Apollonianism and Dionysianism,[66] Gouldner and Peterson, using a methodology similar to Swanson's but relying on statistical techniques of greater sophistication, have concluded that their analysis of primitive societies suggests that 'the higher the level of technology, the higher the degree of demanded impulse control, or Apollonianism'.[67] The character of Apollonianism, and its similarity to the Spirit of Hermes, will be clearer if we contrast it, as Nietzsche did, with Dionysianism:[68]

The Apollonian model	*The Dionysian model*
1. freedom from all extravagant urges, no excess, 'nothing too much'	a sense of 'glorious transport', 'rapture', 'intoxication', 'demoniac'
2. rejection of all licence	'sexual promiscuity overriding . . . established tribal law'
3. stresses 'cognitive modes of experience', reason, knowledge and science	surrenders to intuition or instinct
4. hopeful, melioristic view of the world	tragic view of the world
5. activistic	'loath to act'
6. 'the *principium individuationis*', 'know thyself'	'the bond between man and man comes to be forged once more', the 'vision of mystical oneness', surrender thyself
7. emphasizes the plastic arts	emphasizes the 'non-visual art of music'
8. maintains a compensatory belief in gods that lived	(?) acceptance of the 'terrors and horrors of existence' without illusion
9. 'It was not unbecoming for even the greatest hero to yearn for an after-life'	acceptance of the dissolution of the self

If Apollonianism increases with the level of technology, it would be eminently reasonable to suppose that a conspicuous increase in the level of technology would precipitate the need for a dramatic increase in Apollonianism. There was certainly a spate of technical developments at the time of the Reformation,[70] though they were only one part of the much more general trend towards urbanization and of the loosening of the fabric of medieval society which Huizinga discusses. Gouldner and Peterson recognize that Apollonianism may perform precisely this function, and they note their concurrence with Swanson in their conclusion that 'the supernatural sanctioning of morality, implicated in Apollonianism, is associated with growing social and interpersonal strains', providing a way in which such strains may be met and turned to profit.[71] They agree that the Apollonian phase is likely to be relatively short-lived since its main function is to effect a transformation from one stable social system to another, by furnishing a provisional ideology which becomes redundant once the new equilibrium is attained:

> Apollonianism, in various forms, may be especially needed as a 'starting mechanism' at the beginning of a major technological spurt or reorganization, in so far as this entails a heightening of deprivations or an initial sacrifice of traditional gratifications. Under these conditions, a concentration of Apollonianism may serve in effect as a form of 'deficit-financing', providing social controls during a period when the new technology's rewards are not yet available to motivate the new demands for impulse control. When and in so far as the increased rewards of the new technology are distributed it may be that Apollonianism is a less necessary source of impulse control and may slacken.[71]

This same institutionalized enthusiasm may be seen at the present day within some sections of society, fulfilling much the same role. It plays a part, for example, in the systematic generation of an ideology of success among the salesmen of large corporations, of which International Business Machines is a fairly typical example. The salesmen of I.B.M., who are allotted individual sales targets at which to aim, all aspire to membership of the 'Hundred Percent Club', an élite status achieved by fulfilling their targets three times running, and rewarded with the enviable prizes of attendance at a self-congratulatory and morale-boosting jamboree, perhaps in Miami, together with an increased target the next time round.

If we now attempt to draw out the differences and the similarities between the studies which have been discussed, we can recognize three differences and three similarities between them. On the one hand they treat of different variables; they postulate different orders of causal priority; and they vary in the level of generality at which they aim. Closer examination shows that the first and second of these differences are largely a function of the third, for the more detailed studies fit into the framework of the more general and wide-ranging ones as intermediate stages and institutionally specific applications. On the other hand they also exhibit three similarities. They all deal with social change from one relatively stable social system to another; they are all concerned with the role of religious beliefs in the process of this large-scale change-over; and thirdly, four out of the five studies which we have been considering focus their attention on the

	STABLE	UNSTABLE			STABLE
	old I	decline II	transition III	growth IV	new V
1. Weber			Protestant ethic →	spirit of capitalism →	
2. Gouldner & Peterson		→ new technology →	Apolloni- anism		
3. McClelland			Spirit of Hermes →	economic growth →	
4. Walzer		social insecurity →	Puritanism →	social revolution →	
5. Swanson	S_1/B_1 —	—————————	—————————	——————→	S_2/B_2

DIAGRAM 5.2

THE PROCESS OF SOCIAL CHANGE

role of a crucial group of individuals within this process of change. This group is described by Weber as being imbued with the Protestant ethic, by Walzer as imbued with Puritan zeal, by McClelland as imbued with the Spirit of Hermes, and by Gouldner and Peterson as imbued with Apollonianism. All four studies are concerned with a similar group of people; in each case the group espouses and propagates a similar ideology and occupies a similar place in the process of social change. Swanson is the odd man out, but that is not surprising in view of his Durkheimian interpretation and the wide scope of his analysis which looks from one stable situation to the next, deliberately passing over the intermediate stages. Within this process of change, between the disappearance of the old order and the emergence of the new one, we can recognize three stages: a period of decline, a period of transition and finally a period of growth. Into these five periods the different variables used in the studies may be fitted, without needing to be forced, with ease.

Weber's analysis originates in the period of transition. The spirit of capitalism belongs to the period of growth, although the overlap is crucial; it leads to a stable economic order which rests on 'mechanical foundations'.

McClelland covers the same periods. He differs from Weber in so far as he intends the development from Protestantism to capitalism to be treated as a special case of the more universal effects of any manifestation of the Spirit of Hermes, and also in seeing direct causal links between transition and growth in the psychological mechanism which he has proposed. He, too, envisages a plateau of stability following on from the period of growth.

The development described by Walzer is more general than Weber's, but of greater significance is its origin in the period of decline, whence he traces it through transition and growth to the new stability.

The scheme proposed by Gouldner and Peterson pushes back the point of origin into an initial stability which, they argue, is shattered by material changes resulting in 'social and interpersonal strains'. While they envisage the emergence of a new stable state their concern effectively ends in the Apollonianism of the stage of transition.

Finally, Swanson leaps from stage I to stage V, focusing his attention on the elective affinities between the social structure and the structure of religious belief before and after the reformation period. He ignores, quite properly, 'how such developments occur or in what sequence'.

Each of these studies testifies to the importance of religious beliefs in social change, as do other studies which have been mentioned in passing. Whether a definition of what shall count as religion would have helped to elucidate the processes of social change at any point is to say the least, doubtful. It seems better to draw no hard-and-fast lines, but to keep implicit the idea that by religion we mean

> The whole area of individual motivation and social organization that transcends the utilitarian or rational and draws its vitality from what Weber called charisma and Simmel piety. What gives distinctiveness to sociology's incorporation of the religio-sacred is not the analytical and descriptive attention such men as Durkheim and Weber gave to religious phenomena. It is rather the utilization of

the religio-sacred as a perspective for the understanding of ostensibly non-religious phenomena.[72]

Nevertheless we must now return to consider some of the crucial distinctions which make the religio-sacred, especially in its organized forms, more easily intelligible.

6. Religious Orientations

The Christian religion has been organized in various ways in the course of its history. One classic confrontation between two forms of organization which have vied with each other down the centuries occurs in Dostoevsky's novel, *The Brothers Karamazov*, where the Grand Inquisitor of Seville concludes his peroration to Christ by declaring:

> But man seeks to worship what is beyond dispute, so that all men would at once agree to worship it. For these pitiful creatures are concerned not only with what one or the other can worship, but to find something that all would believe in and worship; what is essential is that all may be together in it. This craving for *community* of worship is the chief misery of each man individually and of all humanity from the beginning of time. . . . And so it will be to the end of the world, even when gods disappear from the earth they will fall down before idols just the same.

The Grand Inquisitor is a sad old man, sad with the realization that his fellow-men with whom he has dealt all his life, so far from being simple and heroic, are weak and stupid. He has come to this view regretfully, yet he is sufficiently sure of it to know that, as the official representative of the church, he must condemn Christ to be burnt at the stake. In so doing he claims that he is protecting the stupid and the weak from being excluded by the strong, who alone are capable of answering Christ's call to heroic devotion based on personal conviction. It is not physical or economic or even moral strength which is here involved, but religious strength; for in this confrontation we see two mutually exclusive religious orientations meeting head-on. The one regards religion as the whole community at worship, the other regards it as the way by which the select few chosen out of the community are led to salvation.

Max Weber made the distinction between these two religious

orientations crucial to his sociology of religion. For him, the fact that 'men are *differently qualified* in a religious way stands at the beginning of the history of religion'.[1] There have always been those who have responded naturally to a religious call by the passionate and devoted pursuit of religious values. They have been variously known as Shamans, ascetics or pneumatics or by some other name, but always the enthusiasm of their response has singled them out as being 'especially qualified in a religious way'. Weber contrasts this heroic religiosity of the few with the 'mass' religiosity of the many who are religiously 'unmusical'. The distinction can be drawn only in terms of those qualities which have religious significance; religious qualification, in this sense, bears no relation to a man's station in secular society. Now it is imperative that we grasp the distinction Weber draws between these two fundamentally different religious orientations. They recur throughout the study of religion, and although they invariably have consequences in the way in which different religions are organized they may often be discerned before the organizational implications have become explicit.

Heroic religiosity finds its natural expression in sects: 'that is, sociologically speaking, associations that accept only religiously qualified persons in their midst'.[2] While heroic religiosity is not restricted to members of such associations the sects nevertheless play a vital role in maintaining the tradition as the 'status carriers of a virtuoso religion'. A church, on the other hand, is 'a community organized by officials into an institution which bestows gifts of grace', and as such it must be, 'by its nature, "democratic" in the sense of making the sacred values generally accessible'. As the official representative of mass religiosity, a church tends to fight against heroic religiosity, both to defend the democratic rights of the majority and also to maintain its own monopoly over sacred values.

The specific formulation of the distinction between church and sect, as separate and opposed types of religious organization which are the 'carriers' of two equally distinct religious orientations, thus originates with Weber. It was not, however, developed substantially by him, because it was taken over and treated thoroughly by Ernst Troeltsch, who added 'mysticism' as a third type of religiosity, in his *The Social Teachings of the Christian Churches*.[3] Before spelling out the details of the systematic distinctions elaborated by Troeltsch, it is necessary to emphasize that he was elaborating ideal types in the Weberian manner. This point is important because, as will be seen, those who subsequently used and modified the distinction between church and sect departed from the Weberian and Troeltschian usage. Now an ideal type is 'a construction of elements abstracted from the concrete, and put together to form a unified conceptual pattern'.[4] It is an exaggeration of the characteristics of a particular sect, for example, as it is found historically, which serves to focus attention on the significance of each of them, and also to demonstrate the way in which they fit together as a coherent whole. An ideal type is constructed from the elements which are found to characterize many historical examples of the phenomenon, but it is in no sense a composite picture drawn from history. It is a theoretical construction which idealizes what is found in actual fact into a conceptually rounded entity. It carries to their logical conclusion characteristics often found in adulterated form, so that the important aspects of actual historical examples may be grasped the more easily, and the relationships between different phenomena may be examined without continual reference to historical instances. Thus *The Protestant Ethic* examines the relationship between the Protestant ethic and the spirit of capitalism as ideal types.

Most attempts to improve on Weber and Troeltsch have declared themselves to be using 'typologies', and it will be helpful to clarify this idea. A typology is normally a collection of types, not necessarily ideal types in the Weberian sense, arranged according to one or more theoretical parameters. Its purpose is not merely to illustrate a theory by reference to a number of examples; it is to bring out more clearly, in terms of the underlying theory, the nature of the constituent types. But a typology should serve a further purpose. From the gaps in a typology it should be possible to postulate the existence of types not yet found empirically or not correctly identified, and to explain why other types are unlikely to be found. A natural-science typology, for example, is seen in the periodic table of elements, and a social-science typology, albeit a very simple one, is seen in Merton's 'modes of adaptation'.[5] The simple arrangement of types on some continuum described by one property which, to varying degrees, they share in common is thus a typology in only a very limited sense.

The study which Troeltsch undertook examined, as the title of his book suggests, the social teachings of Christianity. What concerns us here is his finding that certain types of social teaching are almost invariably found in conjunction with certain types of church organization and certain emphases in doctrine. They form distinct complexes, each of which has a coherence and unity of its own. Furthermore, he pointed out that some of these complexes can be traced back to very early periods of church history, and each has its own justification in particular sayings of Jesus. Much church history, he claimed, can be explained as the assertion of one tendency over others for a period of time, only to be replaced later by the prominence of some other tendency, and so the process continues. The church and the sect, he held, represent two tendencies which have vied with each other throughout most of the church's history.

Troeltsch was indebted to Weber for the distinction between the two types and it may be useful to give the following brief summary of the way in which he elaborated it. According to Troeltsch, then, the church recruits its members from all strata of society, at least in theory, though in practice they are over-representative of the higher-status groups; the sect, on the other hand, recruits its members predominantly from lower-class groups and from those who have been dispossessed. Initiation into the church is by infant baptism, thus making membership automatic for the children of believers; initiation into the sect is through individual conversion and visible evidence of the possession of prescribed qualities. The church is a large, formal organization; the sect is built up of small groups, in each of which there are intimate face-to-face relationships. The church has a hierarchical structure with differences in status between the various grades of clergy, all of whom derive their authority from the office they hold, and all of whom are sharply divided from the laity who exercise no authority. The sect contains no power structure, but regards all its members as participating equally in the 'priesthood of all believers', and where the authority of an individual is acknowledged it is on the grounds of his pre-eminent religious qualities. Within the church every congregation is subject to higher jurisdiction, all authority being ultimately derived from a single centralized source; congregations of the sect, on the other hand, are autonomous, each consisting of a group of 'gathered saints'.

Doctrinal divergences between the two are equally sharp. The church sees itself as the guardian of the *depositum fidei* and as the dispenser of sacraments administered by priests who claim to have been ordained in a continuously valid line of succession from the apostles. The sect, on the other hand, sees itself as consisting of disciples of Jesus who seek simply to follow his commandments which are regarded as immediately accessible to every believer through the Bible. The church teaches that piety consists in simple obedience to the instructions and obligations which it lays on its members, through which 'grace' is dispensed; the sect, on the other hand, teaches the piety of subjective holiness. The church teaches that Christ has 'redeemed the world' and that the benefits of his 'atonement' are available to all men through their membership of the church; the sect teaches that its members suffer misery and contempt as a continuation of Christ's suffering and it looks forward to their vindication when Christ returns in glory to punish the wicked and to claim true followers as his own. The church teaches various ascetical methods of acquiring virtue in the world; the sect teaches detachment from everything worldly. The church seeks to embrace the whole world within its membership; the sect seeks to preserve undefiled those who have been called 'out of the world'. The church accepts and seeks to use secular institutions in order to extend its influence and sanctify the world. The sect is hostile to secular institutions or, at best, indifferent to them, seeking to avoid all involvement with them; in the more extreme sects this includes the refusal to swear oaths, to have recourse to law, to own property or to bear arms. The church seeks to strengthen, purify and stabilize society; the sect seeks to disrupt society by withdrawing from it and looks forward to its overthrow.

This brief résumé does not begin to do justice to the richness of Troeltsch's characterizations of the church and the sect as ideal types within the Christian tradition, but it should serve to illustrate their scope and complexity. His third type, mysticism, is not described in anything like the same detail. That is not because he regards it as being much less important, but because it is a particular form of heroic religiosity which eschews theological formulations, preferring poetical modes of expression, and avoids all forms of organization since its emphasis is strongly individualistic. If we were to characterize the church as accommodating itself to the world, and the sect as opposing the world, then we should have to characterize mysticism as retreating from it. Troeltsch's intention was to show that these three types are adequate as basic theoretical units from which all historical situations may be built up, and into which every empirical case may be broken down. Although the three types rarely, if ever, occur in the pure forms in which they are described, his analysis brings out the main elements of which they are composed and by reference to them we may see the predominant orientation within any particular organization. It should be noticed that the types, as he describes them, are quite discrete and they can be arranged in no kind of order. When

Troeltsch argued that the history of the church may be seen as the successive prominence of first one type and then another, he made no attempt to show what dynamic might be involved in these changes. It was precisely this feature of his account which proved to be the starting-point for further discussions about types of religious organization.

Richard Niebuhr made two particular contributions.[6] He argued that, historically, a sect tends to become more like a church in the course of time, and that there is an historically stable religious type which is somewhere between the two, namely the denomination. The dynamic of his thesis may be represented thus:

SECT → DENOMINATION ←→ CHURCH

Now it must be noticed how radically different are the concepts used by Niebuhr from those used by Troeltsch. When Niebuhr says that a sect tends to become like a church, he is referring to typical empirical examples of a sect which, he says, tend to behave in this way. This is quite different from the ideal type of a sect with which Troeltsch was dealing. That understood, we may examine his reasons for introducing into his theory the dynamic element and also the category of the denomination. It had been an element of Troeltsch's characterization of the sect that its members are drawn predominantly from the depressed classes in society. He showed how this feature is associated with a hostility towards secular society and a millenarian hope of the second coming of Christ to judge the world and vindicate the righteous. He pointed out that throughout most of the church's history it has been fairly easy to suppress deviations, with the result that the adherents of the various sects have been widely scattered and the sects have been forcibly kept down. Where a sect managed to persist, he said, the persecution to which it was subjected was sufficiently vigorous to ensure that its numbers remained small and its members depressed. The Catholic Church in Europe was strong enough to see to it that sects were either obliterated or domesticated, for it was sometimes more expedient to allow outlets for fervent devotion in new religious orders and organizations of lay piety under the control of the official religion. Immigrants to North America, however, found themselves in a different position altogether, for the absence of a dominant church allowed sects to flourish in a way which had no European precedent. The members of religious bodies who would have been regarded as outcasts in Europe often found themselves, in particular areas on American soil, to be the dominant majority with no outsiders to interfere with their religious freedom. Subsequent generations enjoyed an institutionalized religious freedom, and when new sects arose they were left alone. So the asceticism of many sects, which formed an essential component of their religious ethic, was effective in advancing the economic well-being of their members. This was a dilemma for the sect clearly recognized by John Wesley, who expressed it in a passage worth reproducing although so often quoted:

> I fear, wherever riches have increased, the essence of religion has decreased in the same proportion. Therefore I do not see how it is possible, in the nature of things, for any renewal of true religion to continue long. For religion must necessarily produce both industry and frugality, and these cannot but produce riches. But as riches increase, so will pride, anger and the love of the world in all its branches. How then is it possible that Methodism, that is, a religion of the heart, though it flourishes now as a green bay tree, should continue in this state? For the Methodists in every place grow diligent and frugal; consequently they increase in goods. Hence they proportionately increase in pride, in anger, in the desire of the flesh, the desire of the eyes, and the pride of life. So, although the form of religion remains, the spirit is swiftly vanishing away. Is there no way to prevent this – this continual decay of pure religion? We ought not to prevent people from being diligent and frugal; we must exhort all Christians to gain all they can, and to save all they can: that is, in effect, to grow rich.[7]

Wesley saw the result as the decline of 'true religion', but Niebuhr was more concerned to emphasize that a religious group composed initially of the poor and depressed would rapidly transform itself into a group whose members were comfortable and respectable citizens of the middle class. In fact it would rapidly cease to be a sect. The actual process of transformation was later described and analysed by Liston Pope, who showed that as the members of a religious organization became more affluent, so the sect would become organized more formally, employ a full-time preacher to whom it would pay a decent salary, and accept into fellowship those who were socially compatible, and its worship would become more passive and restrained.[8] The emphasis placed on doctrines which point to the sect's exclusiveness and suffering was played down, and in its place appeared a greater stress on Christ as the saviour of all men.

The other element in the tendency for a sect to approximate to a church to which Niebuhr pointed was the attenuation of fervour in the second generation. Those who had themselves experienced conversion in the context of a sect were likely to have altered their whole way of life to conform with the demands of the religious teaching which they had accepted, and their devotion remained undiluted throughout their lives. The children of such converts, however, were in a different position altogether. The teachings of the sect were familiar from earliest childhood, accepted as a natural part of the world around them, and even if the sect did not accept them into membership until they were old enough to make a conscious and responsible decision, their conversion could never be more than an emotional event. Their upbringing in a sectarian home had precluded the possibility of a radical break following their conversion, whereby they might have turned their backs upon the world: not having had the opportunity to experience the pleasures of sin they could be in no position to enjoy the thrills of virtue. For this reason alone, maintained Niebuhr, the sect is an essentially unstable form of religious organization.

The inherent dynamic which pushed sects in the direction of churches was matched by a similar tendency for what had been a church type of religious organization in Europe to become relatively more like a sect when it crossed the Atlantic. Many of the features which characterized a church in Europe were out of sympathy with the prevailing religious toleration in America. So while the same tendency which made sects more like churches continued to push them further in that direction, a corresponding pressure, derived from the legally supported plurality of religious organizations in America, prevented any advance towards a rigid church type of organization and modified the ethos of those religions which had arrived with that character stamped upon them. The form of religious organization which emerged within a pluralistic society as the most stable type was, therefore, the denomination. It has been argued that this is an autonomous type of religious organization which is specific to a pluralist society, and not theoretically conceivable within the constraints which were present during the periods of history dealt with by Troeltsch. This autonomy of the denomination has been underlined by David Martin, who has proposed that the denomination is a type, *sui generis*, which arises in this form without modification from what was initially a sect.[9]

Niebuhr transformed the sect and the church as ideal types of religious expression into the two extremes on a continuum of institutionalization. He explained why he believed the sect always to be unstable and the church unstable in a pluralist society, and proposed a stable intermediate type of religious organization in the form of the denomination. Much of the work which has followed on from Niebuhr has been a simple elaboration of his analysis. Becker proposed the addition of the cult as a type less formal even than the sect.[10] Pfautz substituted secularization for institutionalization as the basis of the continuum, thereby introducing the established sect as a further type and reversing the order of church and denomination.[11] Yinger expanded it yet further by introducing the idea of the 'class church' and elaborating the criteria on which the continuum rested.[12] The absurdity of this continual elaboration eventually became clear. It was recognized that little was being gained and almost all the insights of Troeltsch and Niebuhr, let alone Weber, were being lost.[13] Yet further elaborations of ever-increasing complexity continue to appear. Thus Yinger has now proposed eight types, arranged in relation to three variables, which he finds it necessary to distinguish, even though two of them 'are strongly inversely correlated'.[14]

Neither Weber nor Troeltsch related the church and the sect to each other according to key theoretical concepts, being content to distinguish them as ideal types. One of the few satisfactory attempts to establish typological relations between them is seen in Roland Robertson's recent proposal.[15] The first of the two criteria which he adopts is concerned with the principle on which the religious group recruits its members. At one extreme the group may aim at including the whole of society, and at the other extreme it may be preoccupied with excluding those whom it does not judge to be qualified for membership. The second criterion is concerned with the legitimacy which a group believes itself to have. On the one hand the group may consider itself to be the only and unique means to salvation, and on the other hand it may see itself as one among many roads, all of which lead to heaven. This enables him to construct a fourfold typology of types of religious organization (see Diagram 6.1).[16]

The advantage of Robertson's typology is its capacity to embrace religious organizations outside the narrow ambit of the Christian tradition, for although the names he uses to identify the constituent

DIAGRAM 6.1

FOURFOLD TYPOLOGY OF TYPES OF RELIGIOUS ORGANIZATION

membership principle	self-conceived basis of legitimacy	
	pluralistically legitimate	uniquely legitimate
exclusive	institutionalized sect	sect
inclusive	denomination	church

types are drawn from analyses of the Christian religion, they are not specific to it. The only constraint in using this formulation, as Robertson notes, is that we must be careful to locate an organization in its social context; it is not possible to speak of 'Catholicism' or 'Lutheranism', but only of Portuguese Catholicism or Chilean Lutheranism. Within these limits, however, it is possible to plot the life-history of a particular church as it assumes various institutional forms within the range of possibilities open to it.[17] This is an important use, for it greatly clarifies the theoretical significance of the vicissitudes experienced by a religious group in the course of its development. With the aid of such a formulation it is, however, too easy to portray the history of a church as a unique course of events having no significance for the study of religious development in general. Robertson's formulation in no way supersedes that of Troeltsch; it seeks only to provide a valuable complement to it. The richness of the distinguishing characteristics of church and sect which Troeltsch analysed are inevitably lost when we extract, as here, a single pair of criteria with which to distinguish them. Troeltsch pointed to no single difference which he regarded as crucial since he was concerned to demonstrate the coherence of each type in all its complexity.

An ideal type is not constructed for purely theoretical purposes, but as a methodological tool to assist the student in isolating the significant aspects of empirical material. So their use did not stop with Troeltsch, but is seen again, predictably enough, in the attempt to distinguish the important differences between the enormous variety of sects which now abound.

> Troeltsch's contrast of sect and church was no doubt an appropriate dichotomy in most European countries until relatively recent times. But in Britain, and more emphatically in America, the growth of tolerance permitted the development of religious pluralism. Many organisations grew up, and thus sects came to have some relationship to each other, a relationship of an ordered, systematic and recognised kind.[18]

So radically has religious pluralism transformed the setting in which religious groups operate that it has become necessary to reformulate the ideal type of the sect and to contrast it with the denomination, since there can no longer be any groups which approximate to a church, or which are especially illuminated by reference to the ideal type of the church.

Bryan Wilson has examined the distinctions between sect and denomination in a similar way to that in which Troeltsch analysed the distinctions between sect and church. It will be useful to give a brief summary of his findings, as was done above for those of Troeltsch. According to Wilson, the sect may be characterized as a voluntary association of people, whereas the denomination, though formally voluntary, is joined automatically at birth. The sect accepts as members only those whom it is satisfied display some personal merit, whereas the denomination grants membership on demand. The sect has rigid standards of orthodoxy, and expels those who deviate from them, whereas the denomination is tolerant of heterodoxy. The sect conceives of the elect as a clearly defined group, whereas the denomination has little sense of its own identity. The sect has clear and high expectations of personal conduct, whereas the denomination accepts the standards which prevail in the secular culture. The sect recognizes the equality of all its members, and in theory at least accepts the priesthood of all believers, whereas the denomination has a trained ministry. The sect encourages the spontaneous participation in worship of all those who are present, whereas the denomination has a formalized worship in which the laity's role is passive. The sect is hostile or indifferent to secular society, whereas the denomination accepts the values of the society and of the state.[19]

The study of sects has produced some interesting work in recent years. It has added significance for this present volume because the specifically religious character of many sects is open to some doubt, and in any case the striking similarities between sects with religious ideologies and those with secular ideologies makes it plain that if we limit ourselves to a consideration of religious sects, we do so for reasons of convenience only. Despite the relevance of evidence concerning sects in such areas as Japan, Africa and South America, it will not be considered here. The literature on them is voluminous, and it would need a lengthy and detailed discussion to bring out their significance. Two questions, however, which have been constant themes in this literature require mention here because of their theoretical implications. The first is the question of how sects emerge in the first place, and the second is the question of how we may attempt to distinguish some sort of order amidst the apparently infinite diversity of sects. A number of theories have been advanced to account for the rise of sects, but of more immediate concern than the problem of why sects are formed is the problem of how they are formed. In broad terms, there are three mechanisms involved in the formation of sects. In the first place a sect may originate as a group of followers around a person who offers some new teaching, or some new slant on old teachings, whose authority is based on his or her own personal gifts. Sects generated in this way may arise in almost every religious tradition and the feature they share in common is their dependence on the personality of the founder; for regardless of the particular doctrines of the sect the authority on which they are all based is ultimately the special charisma of the leader. This being so, the death of the founder is the crucial moment in the history of such a sect, and it cannot be said to be properly established until after that event. Generally the sect can continue after the founder's death only if two conditions are met: it must have grown sufficiently in size, and its teachings must be sufficiently distinctive. Unless both conditions are met the sect will either disappear or else merge with some other body whose teachings are similar. In the second place a sect may originate as a splinter-group which breaks off from another religious organization. The success of a sect so formed will depend largely on its relationship to the parent body, for it is unlikely to thrive unless it is markedly different. Many such religious groups enjoy only a short life, and end up by returning to the parent body. In the third place a sect may arise as the result of revivalist meetings. It often happens that revivalism seeks initially only to stimulate devotion in existing religious bodies, and that the formation of a new sect is an unintended consequence.

E

Indeed the organization set up to follow the progress of those people converted at a revivalist meeting and to prevent them from 'back-sliding' is almost a ready-made sect, for it requires considerably more complicated organization to commend those converted to the care of a suitable group already in existence than it does to form a new body. When revivalism is the work of a single celebrated preacher, it may at first appear to be a variety of the charismatic phenomenon, but this is not so. A sect so formed depends not on the preacher's gift, but on his function as a preacher. His appeal is to the emotional response of his followers to their own subjective religious experience rather than to his own powers, the importance of which he is usually anxious to minimize. It should be noticed that as this kind of sect is so dependent on the effective discharge of the preacher's function the need for specialized personnel is present from the beginning. Given the organization and training necessary for systematic evangelization through revivalist meetings, this kind of sect begins to take on denominational characteristics almost from its inception.

The question of why people should find themselves attracted to sect membership is complex, but two points may be noted. First, it would be wrong to reduce a phenomenon which is in many ways so manifestly psychological to social variables. This was clear to Weber when he pointed out that men are differently qualified in a religious way, some being religiously 'musical' and others religiously 'unmusical', and we have to bear this fact in mind. On the other hand it would be equally foolish to pretend that religious gifts are not more easily cultivated in a milieu in which they are valued and find ready acceptance. People who acquire the gift of *glossolalia* – speaking 'in tongues', or in languages unknown to the speaker – have rarely been known to possess the gift before they joined a pentecostalist group; contrariwise, it is a phenomenon known to spread with great speed when introduced into a group not pentecostalist in its foundation. The experience of conversion is similarly subject to social pressures. The unbeliever who attends a revivalist meeting, even if he is a confirmed agnostic, frequently reports having difficulty in resisting the blandishments of a preacher in the highly charged atmosphere of the meeting. Furthermore in those sectarian groups where a precisely dated conversion experience is deemed to be a necessary qualification for membership, people may retrospectively discover themselves to have had such an experience. A study of men preparing for the ordained ministry in an evangelical theological college recently showed that, on entry, sixteen of the twenty-three entrants had been 'converted' and could put a date to the experience. Twelve months later, twenty-one out of the group reported such an experience, the five additional men having discovered that they also had been converted prior to entry, but that previously they had not correctly identified the phenomenon as a conversion, exactly dated though it subsequently was.[20] However, although the social pressures which stimulate the development of religious gifts are so important, that does not deny the weight which should be given to purely individual qualities which predispose people to join sectarian religious groups.

The second thing we have to note in considering why people are attracted to sects is that we can discern certain broad similarities between sectarian devotees. Weber, Troeltsch and Niebuhr all remarked on the depressed social status of sectarians. It is in keeping with most of the theories of religion so far mentioned that the poor and the disinherited, to use Niebuhr's phrase, should seek religious affiliation. It provides a consolation for present misery and a promise of good things to come which, taken together, make temporary distress seem more bearable, and sometimes even desirable, as a price which is willingly paid for the future delights of celestial bliss. A great many sects are found to arise in areas of poverty and backwardness, tending to confirm this hypothesis. Others, however, appear to develop amongst people who are very far from destitution. California is an area of considerable affluence and yet it displays an almost unequalled proliferation of sects, by no means all of them patronized by the less opulent. The Christian Science sect is solidly middle class in its composition, and in some areas of the world sects which may be supported by the poor elsewhere are patronized by the well-to-do. These facts have led some writers to broaden the notion of the deprivation which may be significant.[21] It has been stressed that people may be relatively, rather than absolutely, deprived, on the grounds that privations are experienced in a social context and in comparison with how other people seem to fare. So a person might feel acutely deprived in California although he would count himself affluent in the Congo. Then again it has been argued that economic deprivation is not the only kind of deprivation to which people are exposed, and other things, such as physical disabilities, may give them a sense of deprivation and worthlessness for which religion is a palliative.

In many ways this attempt to expand the notion of deprivation is too simple. Affiliation to a sect provides a radical reconstruction of the world as it appears to the believer, together with a rejection of all his previous experience. Now the need to reinterpret one's experience may arise from many sources, of which economic depression is only one. More generally, rapid social change may acutely disorientate people. In a stable society the inequalities are generally made to appear normal, natural and legitimate because of their traditional character: they have always been there. In a period when rapid change has broken down the traditional legitimations, however, deprivation appears simply as deprivation. Moreover it is only one aspect of a disordered state in which social relationships and social processes lack any coherent meaning. The sect provides one way in which new circumstances, or circumstances newly perceived as strange, may be interpreted as being meaningful and explicable. The religious sect is, of course, only one way in which the world may be reconstructed. Secular ideologies may perform the same function, while political movements seek the social and political reconstruction of society, rather than a reinterpretation of the *status quo*. No account of why one option rather than another is selected is really convincing,[22] and part of the reason is undoubtedly that sects have their own dynamic and their own particular appeal. We return, eventually, to the inescapable facts of autonomous religious movements, and the differences between religious propensities of different individuals.

The second question to which some attention must be given is that of how we are to distinguish some order among the wide varieties of sect which exist. Bryan Wilson's work in this area has been seminal, and he has suggested two ways in which the question may be tackled, each of them leading to a slightly different categorization. His more recent suggestion is that we should focus attention on the types of answer which different sects might give to the question, 'What shall we do to be saved?' As he says:

> In settling this question, sectarians necessarily establish their conception of the world and of the supernatural, and how to behave towards them. Their response to conditions reflects their response to this ultimate religious concern. Their doctrine, social ethic, relationships within the group, posture to the outside world, and their conception of what it is expedient to do in their meeting together reveal what sectarians think is the way to be saved.[23]

Wilson distinguishes seven types of answer which can be given to this question. Some of them overlap with the categories which he proposed in an earlier paper and it is these which will be preferred here. They are based upon the 'characterization of types of mission' which rest on 'the ideological and doctrinal character of the sects, and serve as useful indicators of the clusters of other characteristics to be found in each type'. What is crucial is 'the response of the sect to the values and relationships prevailing in society'.[24] The two criteria are strictly compatible, and if we prefer the earlier formulation it is only because it springs more obviously from his general specification of the sect as an organization and ideology both of which are in some sort of tension with the secular world. The mission of the sect indicates what form this tension takes, and it is thus more directly related to the specifically sectarian character of the movement than is its particular soteriology. All religious groups, not only sectarian ones, must have an answer to the question, 'What shall we do to be saved?' and it could be used more properly as the basis for a typology of religious organizations. But its relationship to the world is especially problematic for the sect; indeed the fact that it is a problem may almost be used as a criterion by which to identify a sect.

Four major types of sect emerge on the basis of this criterion. The *conversionist* sect seeks to 'alter men, and thereby to alter the world'; the ultimate aim of its extremely positive mission would be the conversion of every man and woman alive. This response is almost quintessentially Christian, although it is shared to some degree by other vigorously proselytizing religions like Islam. The *adventist* sect awaits the second coming of Christ who will then judge the world and set up his kingdom on earth for the duration of the millennium. The attitude of such sects to the world is hostile, for they believe that only those who are 'gathered in' to the elect will enjoy the privileges of the new dispensation, and that the rest – notably those who are 'rich' and 'powerful' and 'religious' in the present world – will receive their just deserts. Their hope is conspicuously defined in terms of the new world order which is to succeed this one, rather than simply in the hope of a life after death. By contrast the *introversionist* sects seek to cultivate in their members qualities which will fit them for a higher spiritual life reserved for those who follow the path of holiness. Their rejection of the world is not limited to a rejection of the present imperfect secular order, but tends to include a rejection of everything worldly. It has little concern with eschatology since it is much occupied with the idea of a future life in which those who have lived the holy life on earth will find fulfilment. Finally, the *gnostic* sects are those which impart to their members a special knowledge which radically changes worldly life. By these esoteric means life on earth is transformed, and eternity begins here and now.

All four types of sect may be found recurring in different forms throughout the history of Christianity, and each has its own unique dynamic. The principal purpose of Wilson's original article was to show that Niebuhr's proposition about the inevitable tendency of sects to become denominations was applicable to only one type of sect, and it demonstrated this with such clarity that the article has become a classic in the literature on sects. The conversionist sect, which generally recruits from the members of non-sectarian religious groups by means of revivalist preaching, has a strong propensity to take on the characteristics of a denomination. Such sects are numerous and, because of their active evangelism, they are extremely conspicuous. Because of the proliferation of conversionist sects in the United States it was possible for writers like Niebuhr to take their development as the norm. This mistake was further encouraged by the fact that Niebuhr wrote from a Christian point of view and conversionist sects are clearly in the mainstream of the Christian religious tradition, whereas sects like the adventist Jehovah's Witnesses are not recognized as Christian by the Protestant denominations, and so are ignored. The adventist sects are most unlikely to become more like denominations. The whole *raison d'être* of the adventist sect is separation from the world in the expectation of a new order which will vindicate this separation. Any compromise on this principle spells death for the adventist sect, and it would have to be compromised considerably if such a sect were to resemble a denomination. Similarly the introversionist sect has little tendency to become a denomination. The emphasis is not on gaining more members, but on perfecting the lives of the individuals who already belong to it. Groups remain small therefore, and if the teaching becomes somewhat attenuated in the course of time the emphasis on personal piety is likely to make the sect more like an ethical movement than a religious denomination. Gnostic sects, by virtue of their basis in esoteric teaching, inevitably remain sectarian. The evolution of complex authority structures and the acquisition of wealth only serve to underline the special nature of the teaching on which their existence rests.

These are four types of sect which, in their elaborated form, still do not amount to ideal types. Although we may recognize a coherence in the way in which a sect is organized, in its teaching, its relationship to the wider society and its central values, each of the four remains a sub-type within the more general reformulated characterization of a sect. This itself is very much within the Weberian tradition, however. The application of the types is primarily Christian, but Wilson has suggested a way in which they can be seen as being of rather more general application. The modification is effected by isolating two key variables which distinguish the four types in the manner shown in Diagram 2.[25]

	other-worldly	this-worldly
collectivist	traditional religion	millennialism
individualist	evangelicalism	gnosticism

DIAGRAM 6.2

The names used to describe the sect types are somewhat different: for millennialism we read adventism; for evangelicalism, conversionism, and for traditional religion, introversionism. The order in which the last two appear seems open to question. While it is true that the introversionist group is typically constituted as a tightly knit fellow-ship which is regarded as the locus of divine illumination, the very emphasis on holiness and piety necessarily gives the sect an orientation which is more individualist than collectivist in its approach to salvation. On the other hand the evangelical stress on personal conversion as a *sine qua non* of salvation is less individualist than superficially it appears to be. Conversion may have been an essentially solitary experience for men like St Paul and Martin Luther (to whom it came in that most lonely of places, the privy),[26] but in its institutional form it is a pre-eminently social phenomenon, as important to other fellow-worshippers as it is to the man who has been converted. Indeed it is misleading to focus attention on the act of conversion only, for the heart of conversionism lies in the collective celebration of their salvation by those who have been saved. Much of the significance attaching to a conversion lies in its function as a rite of passage, like any other initiation, thus reinforcing the boundary of the group and encouraging group solidarity. The reason for the juxtaposition in Wilson's scheme is possibly due to the peculiarly Christian character of conversionist religion, apparently disqualifying it from any claim to be a traditional religious orientation in a wider context. Introversionism, on the other hand, is far from being atypical among the world religions.

One feature of Wilson's typology which is of special interest is that, although it bears a close relationship to the designated types of sect, it is not itself a typology of sects. It represents the analytical relationship between four distinct religious orientations, and this draws attention to Wilson's slightly equivocal attitude to the twin notions of sect and sectarianism. Weber, as we have seen, started his discussion of sects by remarking on the varying intensity of religious responses, and by showing that the sect is a group of the religiously 'musical' who develop a form of religious association appropriate to their common religious qualities and their intense devotion. Now the difference between the religiously musical and the religiously unmusical is a difference in degree; the religious collectivities which arise out of this difference, however – the sect and the church – are different in kind. The sectarian person is one who is religiously musical but whose gifts have been shaped by an institution, exaggerating the difference between him and the religiously unmusical person whose lack of religious gifts has also been institutionalized. What is equivocal is whether the difference between the sectarian and the non-sectarian is one of degree, like their gifts, or one of kind, like their institutions. We would suggest that it is more properly understood as a difference in degree.

'The Seventh Day Adventists', Wilson tells us, 'are a respectable middle-class denomination in some Californian communities: they remain distinctly a sect in France, Italy and Britain.'[27] We must conclude that the person who sought intense religious commitment would look elsewhere than to the Seventh Day Adventists in 'some Californian communities', and that his sectarianism is therefore of primary significance. This problem is present in Wilson's earlier formulation, in which he characterizes both the sect and the sect member in terms of their quantitatively greater involvement: 'the commitment of the sectarian is always more total and more defined than that of the member of other religious organizations', and, 'sects have a totalitarian rather than a segmental hold over their members'.[28]

To the fact that a sect may be more or less sectarian in various social contexts may be added something further. Within denominations, individuals may be found whose commitment is sectarian, and even groups of individuals who form themselves into sects within denominations.[29] Their organizations are important, of course, for they foster and guide the sectarianism of the individuals. This discovery of sectarianism within churches and denominations should be in no way surprising, for these groups are little more than latter-day extensions of the monastic communities which have been found in churches down the ages, and which have always been recognized as sects. If pockets of enthusiasm appear in sectarian form within denominations they deserve to be taken seriously. It seems right, therefore, to extend the significance of Wilson's typology by interpreting his types as types of religious orientation, each one of which may establish itself in an appropriate institutional form; the clearest examples of these will be the autonomous sects. But religious orientations they remain: species of one genus, the religiously musical.

7. Dimensions of Institutional Religion

In the remaining chapters we shall consider some of the problems which are involved in understanding the place which religion occupies in contemporary western societies. The constantly recurring idea in this area of study is secularization: the idea that societies are becoming less religious, a fact dramatically announced by Nietzsche, probed by social scientists, and now celebrated by theologians who have re-appropriated Nietzsche's slogan, 'God is dead'. But secularization is a topic which will only indirectly be considered here. The evidence for secularization, and the precise meaning attached to the term by those who are convinced by this evidence, has already been ably presented many times.[1] It is a notion generally popular with those who are satisfied with a nominal definition of religion, i.e., one which isolates the phenomenon with reference to substantive criteria; since we have rejected such a definition here the notion will have little value, for reasons which will become clear. From the vantage point of a less restrictive definition we shall try instead to see the significance of secularization in a wider context.[2]

It was in an effort to gauge the degree to which religion is losing ground in the West that writers first discussed the various dimensions of religiosity. It had once been assumed that a person was either religious or he was not, but that either way all the evidence would point in the same direction. The religious man would go to church, say grace before meals, find himself a religious wife and religious friends, believe the doctrines taught by his church, and so on. Some of these criteria might be given greater weight than others in assessing a person's religiousness, but it was assumed that all would roughly agree. This opinion has now fallen into disrepute. Social scientists in particular tend to believe that different people may express their religiousness in a variety of ways and that a person who appears religious in one respect may appear irreligious in others. So in any attempt to assess religiousness it is necessary to take into account more than one criterion. The position was summarized by Charles Glock and Rodney Stark thus:

> A first and obvious requirement if religious commitment is to be comprehensively assessed is to establish the different ways in which individuals *can* be religious. . . . If we examine the religions of the world, it is evident that the details of religious expression are extremely various . . . there nevertheless exists considerable consensus as to the more general areas in which religiosity ought to be manifested. These general areas may be thought of as the core dimensions of religiosity.[3]

One of the earlier attempts to utilize this perspective in research, involving the relationships between religious commitment and other social variables, was that of Gerhard Lenski.[4] He proposed an initial distinction between a man's commitment to a socio-religious group on the one hand, and on the other hand his commitment to a type of religious orientation. Perhaps his most striking contribution was in proposing that people may belong to religious groups in two quite different ways.[5] They may belong to a church in much the same sort of way as they belong to a club, a trade union, or a parent-teacher association. It is only one commitment among many and it impinges on them only in so far as their religious activity is concerned. On the other hand their commitment may be a more total one, to the extent that, for example, not only do they take care to marry within it, but all their friends belong to the same socio-religious group. The first type he calls associational commitment; the second, communal commitment. A person is rated high on the first type of commitment if he attends church services regularly each Sunday and on at least two weekdays in the month and also attends some group related to the church once a month. He is given a high rating on the second type if his spouse and most of his close friends belong to the same socio-religious group. On the other hand Lenski also took account of two types of orientation to religion which he designates respectively doctrinal orthodoxy and devotionalism. The first is assessed in terms of how many of the doctrines taught by his church are accepted by an individual, and the second by reference to 'the frequency with which he prayed and the frequency with which he sought to determine God's will when he had important decisions to make'.[6]

It is clear enough that Lenski has tried to find four measures which will take account of various expressions of religiousness, but it is equally clear that some problems remain. The choice of doctrinal orthodoxy and devotionalism is arbitrary and was justified by Lenski thus: 'First, on *a priori* grounds, they *appeared* to contrast, or even conflict, with one another. Second, both *seemed* to be widely accepted by modern Americans. Third, both *seemed* to be potentially important.'[7] Even though the findings demonstrated that his dimensions have a discriminatory potential, their random selection without systematic justification is unsatisfactory from a theoretical point of view. The theoretical weakness is also apparent in the distinction drawn between types of religious belonging and types of religious orientation. As Lenski himself says, it would be perfectly possible to interpret associational involvement as commitment to a 'collectivist' religious orientation,[8] and to redesignate communal involvement as a communal orientation. However, it would be a mistake to focus only on the defects and limitations of his theory, for Lenski has shown the practical utility of an analysis which takes account of more than one form of religious expression. The members of his four subgroups (Jews, white Catholics, white Protestants, black Protestants) come out with typically different ratings on his four indicators, thus demonstrating the need for a variety of measures.

The dimensions which have been proposed by Glock and Stark are similar in some ways to those of Lenski, but they reached them less as a result of considering modes of religious practice than through considering what various religions regard as proper modes of religious expression.[9] They make no attempt to include types of religious affiliation. They suggest, simply, that five dimensions will account for all the prescriptions which are required by the various religious bodies: belief, practice, knowledge, experience and consequences. 'Belief' is self-explanatory; it embraces the doctrines and myths which a religion teaches and to which adherents are expected to subscribe, and it is clearly parallel to Lenski's doctrinal orthodoxy dimension. 'Practice' includes all acts of devotion, whether performed in public or in private. Attendance at church services and at informal religious meetings, the reception of sacraments, the saying of private prayers, fasting or following particular dietary rules, keeping the sabbath, going on pilgrimages, are all examples of the diverse forms which may be assumed by practical piety. Both devotionalism and also associational commitment in Lenski's scheme fall under the heading of this wide-ranging dimension. The 'experience' dimension takes account of the various feelings which are deemed to be religiously desirable.

It includes not only such things as seeing visions or experiencing ecstatic trances which involve a person's entire emotional capacities, but also commoner and more subdued experiences such as conversion, a sense of peace, or of quiet certainty. Obviously not all these experiences are common to all religious people but there are few religions which do not assume their followers to have some kind of immediate experience of the transcendent. The dimension of 'knowledge' embraces whatever knowledge a particular religion considers to be necessary for its members, whether it is a holy book, a body of teaching, or the sacred significance of apparently mundane matters. The fifth dimension, 'consequences', is intended to take into account behaviour and beliefs which are not inherently religious, but which nevertheless stem from religious motives. Concern with poverty or racial injustice, work done for charitable causes, or even social and political involvement may spring from religious conviction and may indicate the degree of a person's religious commitment.

The five dimensions of religiosity proposed by Glock and Stark were, like Lenski's, intended to be used as empirical measures of the degree to which an individual may be described as religiously committed. They have been operationalized in numerous items included in survey questionnaires and the results of the research which made use of them have added considerably to our knowledge of the differences between various religious groups, particularly in North America. Here we are less concerned with the substantive findings than with the conceptualization of religion which is implicit in this five-dimensional model of religious commitment; and so certain problems need to be discussed. Glock and Stark themselves recognize that there are problems in using the fifth dimension.[10] The 'good works' which a man performs may be a very equivocal indicator of his religiousness. The same selfless act may imply deep religious conviction when performed by one person while another may be motivated by an entirely agnostic altruism, convinced of the inherent rightness of his behaviour but sure that it has no metaphysical significance whatever. Indeed a person may undertake some charitable work motivated entirely by religious devotion and yet, having become immersed in it and convinced of its intrinsic worth, he may work with redoubled effort after he has renounced his religion. So what value can we attach to patterns of behaviour as 'objective' measures of religious commitment, unless we can see them within the context of a person's particular mosaic of meaning; unless, that is to say, we know his own subjective understanding of them? Nor is the problem restricted to this dimension only. All five dimensions represent components into which we can break down the complex phenomenon of a person's religiosity, but problems follow when they are transformed into objective measures, for the significance of each of them is unstable, varying from one person to another and in the same person at different times. It is not only practical work for an aid programme, but such statements as 'I have a firm belief in God', 'I made my confession last Saturday' or 'I have a vivid sense of being saved' which can take on a multitude of different meanings. They are shifting and unreliable criteria with which to assess religiousness, though in very broad terms they represent different ways in which religiousness can be expressed. Glock and Stark are able to show, as Lenski had done before them, that different religious groups have different dimensions in which religiosity finds typical expression, and it will be useful to trace out some illuminating parallels.

It is possible to dispense with one of the five dimensions, or rather to combine two of them into one, for the distinction between religious belief and religious knowledge is redundant. You cannot believe something you do not know, except in a purely trivial sense, and the danger of taking people's statements about what they believe at face value was emphasized by Will Herberg. As he pointed out, independent surveys of Americans conducted in 1952 and 1954 showed that 86 per cent said they believed the Bible to be the inspired 'word of God',[11] and this assertion is supported by the 140 per cent increase in the circulation of printed scriptures between 1949 and 1953;[12] but on the other hand a Gallup poll conducted in 1950 showed that 53 per cent of the same public were unable to name a single one of the gospels.[13] This kind of facile profession of belief is clearly worthless as a valid indication of religious commitment. Mere religious knowledge is no more significant. A detailed knowledge of Catholic dogmatic theology is no proof that the person possessing it is a devout Catholic; he may be a Catholic theologian, an anti-Catholic propagandist or a student of comparative religions, but he is most unlikely to be a pious Catholic layman. Belief without knowledge is trivial, and knowledge without belief is academic. Only when they are combined into informed belief do we have a meaningful dimension of religious commitment.

Taking the remaining four dimensions of Glock and Stark, it is possible to see some parallels between these dimensions and the types of religious orientation which Wilson showed to characterize four kinds of sect, thus:

Glock and Stark	Wilson
experience	conversionist
practice	introversionist
belief	gnostic
consequences	adventist

The comparison is drawn in an attempt to extend the significance both of the dimensions of religiosity and of the types of sect. It was argued in the last chapter that sects are religious organizations which enshrine and propagate extreme forms of religiosity, or 'heroic religiosity' to use Weber's term. They differ from denominations in degree, as sectarian religiosity differs from denominational religiosity in degree. Interpreted thus, Wilson's four types of sect become types of religiosity: religious orientations.

The central feature of the conversionist orientation is the experience of conversion. In this experience it is not only the single act of conversion which stands out as important, for some people are known to be converted repeatedly, but the experience of 'having been converted' or of 'being saved'. Evangelicalism is basically a religion of the heart and its characteristic expression is emotional. The introversionist orientation lays particular stress on devotion and on personal holiness, thus making religious practice, as the dimension is interpreted by Glock and Stark, more important than the other three dimensions. Clearly, the gnostic religious orientation emphasizes the importance of belief in esoteric knowledge. The adventist orientation has a peculiarly worldly emphasis, for although the distinction between the religious group and secular society is rigidly maintained, their hopes are very much concerned with worldly matters. This is seen in its most dramatic form in the millennarian cargo cults, where practical preparations are made for the imminent advent of the expected aeroplane or ship which have no intrinsic religious significance,[14] and the same emphasis is present in less extreme examples of adventism.

We are left, then, with a list of four distinct religious orientations, each of which lays special emphasis on one dimension of religious expression, but the orientations are without any internal structure to set them in a relationship to one another. It is quite possible to adapt Wilson's typology presented earlier, however, as a theoretical framework for ordering these four orientations. Thus as his first criterion he used the distinction between those groups whose religion is collectivist and those whose religion is individualist and, slightly reformulated, this criterion becomes the relationship of the individual to his religious group. At one extreme religion is intensely personal; what is important is individual devotion and the group is almost incidental. At the other extreme religion is social; the group commitment is all important and little attention is paid to individual piety. Wilson's second criterion distinguished between other-worldly and this-worldly groups and this is clearly concerned with the relationship of the particular religion to the world. At one extreme religion is fully integrated into society and defines its hope in worldly terms; at the other extreme religion is differentiated from society, which it regards as irredeemable. But it will help if the criterion is widened somewhat so that what becomes crucial is simply the integration of the religious group within the wider society or alternatively its differentiation from society. This wider distinction will, however, generally include the distinction between this-worldly and other-worldly concerns, but we shall focus here more explicitly on the degree to which religious interests are differentiated from the interests of society.

The relationship between the four orientations may be grasped more easily if it is represented diagrammatically (see Diagram 7.1):

DIAGRAM 7.1

RELATIONSHIP BETWEEN THE FOUR ORIENTATIONS

involvement of the individual with group	involvement of group with society	
	integrated	differentiated
personal	gnostic BELIEF	introversionist PRACTICE
social	adventist CONSEQUENCES	conversionist EXPERIENCE

We see that both criteria are based on a dichotomy between involvement and non-involvement. At the individual level a person may express his religion as an integrated member of the group or as a differentiated person. At the group level the religious organization may be integrated with the world or differentiated from it. Two features of this scheme should be immediately clear. We see, first, that Wilson's four types are not only sects but religious orientations. The organizational form which it assumes, whether it is that of a sect or a denomination, is a matter of degree and does not detract from the primary significance of each as a distinct religious orientation. But we see also that Glock and Stark's dimensions have acquired an additional significance and have become types of religious expression. We have, instead, two purely theoretical dimensions by which we may distinguish between types of religiosity. These two dimensions, the relationship between the individual and his religious group, and the relationship between the group and society, are fundamental to the quality of a religious institution. If we represent them differently, as graphical dimensions, we shall see that they have certain other properties (see Diagram 7.2).

So far the four religious orientations have been described simply as types of religious orientation, but it is necessary now to qualify the description, for the discussion so far has been limited to orientations as they are found in *institutional* religion. In complex societies, religion, like politics and economics, is the province of a specialized institution which may be distinguished from other institutions with ease. In simple societies this is not so. The religious group and the society are, by definition, coterminous; when Durkheim spoke of the moral community as a 'church' he was referring to one aspect of a society, which is distinguished only for purposes of analysis. It is, in fact, society 'wearing another hat'. Now the four orientations with which we are dealing here are found to typify religion only when it takes the form of an institution which has a large measure of autonomy and when it is differentiated from other social processes. Thomas Luckmann has discussed the circumstances under which an institutional form of religion will be stable, and we may see that some elements of his analysis are illustrated by the two dimensions of the above diagram. A religious institution which is differentiated from society remains viable only if there is intense participation by its members in the social organization of the group, a combination represented by the bottom right-hand quadrant. The crucial dimension is the horizontal one, so far as the autonomous existence of a religious institution is concerned. As it becomes more integrated with the world it tends to lose its separate identity. Conversely it degenerates into no more than a club or a clique with no social significance at all if it becomes more and more differentiated from the wider society. So long as the involvement of the members simultaneously becomes more

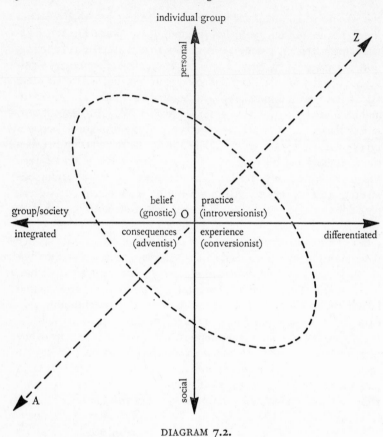

DIAGRAM 7.2.

DIMENSIONS OF INSTITUTIONAL RELIGION

social, however, it may remain viable even as it becomes more institutionally distinct. Similarly, the top left-hand quadrant contains the other stable tendency. The religious institution may become more concerned with worldly affairs, more integrated into society, without losing its separate identity only if the devotion of the members becomes more personalized at the same time.

The area within which religious institutions have a stable existence is enclosed within an ellipse, because the two remaining quadrants represent unstable circumstances. The diagonal designated AOZ plots the positions on the diagram of three forms of religion, only one of which is found as a stable institution. At point A, in the bottom left-hand quadrant, the religious group is integrated with society, defining its affairs as closely related to those of the world, and the members are highly involved in the religious group. To a limited degree this orientation finds institutional expression in adventist religion. As all the literature on millennialism testifies, however, adventism is unstable, at least in its extreme forms. Either it takes on a political form, thus ceasing to exist as a religious institution, or else it collapses. None the less religion of this variety is to be found. It occurs in simple societies in which there is no differentiated religious institution, but where religious ideas are those of the society as a whole, and are expressed socially in communal rites. Here we have religion without a clearly differentiated religious institution.

Similarly, in the top right-hand quadrant, we find a form of religion which is institutionally unstable. As a system of religious belief and practice becomes increasingly differentiated from a society, it ceases to be a recognizable institution if at the same time the devotion becomes more individualistic. It effectively splits up into a number of personal, privatized cults. People often overlook Durkheim's anticipation of just such an eventuality.

> Cults seem to be independent of all idea of the group. Not only are these individual religions very frequent in history, but nowadays many are asking if they are not destined to become the pre-eminent form of the religious life, and if the day will not come when there will be no other cult than that which each man will freely perform within himself.[15]

Durkheim's model of religion would need some radical revision to take into account such a development, as he himself realized; in particular, his definition of religion as being inherently a phenomenon of the group would have to undergo a modification. It becomes clear that his sharp distinction between magic and religion, which we have rejected above, must be treated as applying only to a particular type of culture, and this he himself recognizes when he says that 'we do not mean to establish a break of continuity between them. The frontiers between the two domains are frequently uncertain'.[16] This form of religion, if it exists, is clearly non-institutional. The tendency of religion to become specialized within an institutional framework, and to establish its primacy over the rest of social life, was an inevitable goal of the religious specialists who formed a priestly caste. In the middle ages they succeeded in securing the recognition of systematic, institutionalized religious knowledge as the 'queen of the sciences'. In the next chapter we shall argue that the institution never succeeded in capturing the religious sentiment of the whole of society, and the consequences of this reach down to the present day. But this institutional specialization – which represents a balance between a religion absorbed into the social framework and one totally autonomous, or between a form of devotion which is solely communal and one which is entirely private – must be recognized as only one form which religion may assume.

The notion of secularization, therefore, must be used with great circumspection. If, with Bryan Wilson, we define secularization as 'the process whereby religious thinking, practice and institutions lose social significance', *ipso facto* we define religion itself as the institution, for it is that which determines what shall count as 'religious' thinking and practice.[17] This is another point to which we shall return in the next chapter. If Wilson's analysis is not accepted, the thesis summarized by Thomas Luckmann in the following passage demands serious attention:

> The contemporary marginality of church religion and its 'inner secularization' appear as *one* aspect of a complex process in which the long-range consequences of institutional specialization of religion and the global transformations of the social order play a decisive role. What are usually taken as symptoms of the decline of traditional Christianity may be symptoms of a more revolutionary change: the replacement of the institutional specialization of religion by a new social form of religion.[18]

Such a suggestion simply poses the question whether a new form of religious devotion might not be emerging which is as different from the institutional religion of the churches and sects as that itself was from primitive religion.

Luckmann embraces William James's thesis, which is a psychological version of Durkheim's theory, that:

> As there thus seems to be no one elementary religious emotion, but only a common storehouse of emotion upon which religious objects may draw, so there might conceivably also prove to be no one specific and essential kind of religious object, no one specific and essential kind of religious act.[19]

This is not to propose some 'fund of "religiosity" in men', as Wilson fears.[20] It is simply to accept in principle that not every social process is one of decay and decline; some may be found to be emerging and evolving. Indeed the line AOZ in our diagram might be seen by Luckmann as tracing a continuous line of development. We noted above that nominal definitions of religion which define the phenomenon in substantive terms cannot avoid defining religion as it occurs at one point on the line. This procedure restricts us just as it would if we defined the economy of a society in terms of banks and paper money. So far as the economy is concerned the absurdity is blatant; it is clear that economics is concerned not just with the media of exchange and institutional arrangements for exchange, but with the function of exchange itself, whatever forms it may assume. So, too, with religion we reach a position summarized by Luckmann thus:

> Religious institutions are not universal; the phenomena underlying religious institutions or, to put it differently, performing analogous functions in the relations of the individual and the social order, presumably are universal. What are the general anthropological conditions for that which may become institutionalized as religion? What reality does it possess, as a social fact, even before it is institutionalized? How is it constituted before it assumes one of the variable historical forms of religious institutions?[21]

To answer these questions thoroughly would mean going back and re-examining in detail the way in which simple societies function, and that we shall not do. But the questions point us towards the sort of general definition of religion, implicit in the writings of Mircea Eliade and Robert Bellah, which has been favoured in this book. They also point us to Clifford Geertz's definition, adopted earlier,[22] in which a religion is seen as a symbolic universe. Luckmann is content with a simple formulation, for he sees religions as:

> Socially objectivated systems of meaning that refer, on the one hand, to the world of everyday life and point, on the other hand, to a world that is experienced as transcending everyday life.[23]

This definition is not substantially different from that proposed by Geertz.

Returning to Figure 7.2, we see that the symbolic universe, that is to say a religion, may be articulated in roughly three ways. At point O it is the only system of meaning available to the society and it is obligatory for every member of it. It 'permeates the various, more or less clearly differentiated, institutional areas such as kinship, the division of labour and the regulation of the exercise of power'. Furthermore, it 'determines directly the entire socialization of the individual and is relevant for the total individual biography. To put it differently, religious representations serve to legitimate conduct in the full range of social situations.'[24] As a society becomes more complex it is likely to develop 'distinct institutions supporting the objectivity and social validity' of the symbolic universe.[25] The institutions may assume different forms, but we have suggested that four orientations in particular are evident, and that these apply to all religions. Although the Christian religion has most typically been concerned with experience, and Islam with consequences, the other orientations have been found in both. In the religions of the East, religious beliefs and knowledge, implying a pervasive gnostic orientation, predominate but all four are found in them as well.

No matter which orientation predominates in a particular institutional religion, the very fact of its institutional separation tends to mean that 'an antithesis between "religion" and "society" develops'.[26] With this distinction between religious and secular affairs there emerges the idea that certain men are religiously more qualified than others and the 'tendency towards a sort of *status stratification*, in accordance with differences in the charismatic qualifications'.[27] In other words, some men have more immediate access than others to the symbolic universe of religion, and these specialists influence the development of the sacred cosmos[28] according to their own insights and in their own interests. The result of this specialization within religion (which is itself a consequence of the institutional specialization of religion), is that the majority in a society find that their religion does not have the same immediacy of meaning, or relevance, as it does for the religious specialists. This situation is problematical for institutional religion. If the 'official' religion of the church does not become too divorced from the everyday lives of a majority of the people, due to the watchfulness of some hypothetical Grand Inquisitor, the situation may continue for many generations.[29] So long as the divorce continues, however, the institution will remain unstable, and groups within a society who are particularly alienated from the religious symbols will be likely to split off into sects, for whom a revised system of symbols will have more immediate relevance.

If an 'official' religion is not continually adapted to the changing needs of a society, or if it is transplanted to another social context in which it has little meaning,[30] it will petrify. It will become marginal to the general life of society and will gradually decline. Judged from the standpoint of the official religion, using the outmoded criteria of religiosity derived from the dying orthodoxy, the society will be becoming secularized. If Luckmann's general premises are correct, however, we should expect to find another religious tradition in process of formation, for if the construction of a system of symbolic meaning really is an intrinsic part of the human condition, then we should expect to find men evolving a new religious system. Deserted by a moribund 'official' religion which has been killed by religious specialists who were mere 'embalmers' and 'idolaters',[31] men will seek new gods of their own making, meaningful to their condition and readily accessible. According to Luckmann, this is precisely what happens:

> The social form of religion emerging in modern industrial societies [point Z] is characterized by the direct accessibility of an assortment of religious representations to potential consumers. The sacred cosmos is mediated neither through a specialized domain of religious institutions nor through other primary public institutions. It is the direct accessibility of the sacred cosmos, more precisely, of an assortment of religious themes, which makes religion today essentially a phenomenon of the 'private order'. The emerging social form of religion thus differs significantly from older social forms of religion which were characterized either by the diffusion of the sacred cosmos through the institutional structure of society [point A] or through institutional specialization of religion [point O].[32]

The themes which Luckmann has in mind as symbols which give meaning to the life of western modern man are individual autonomy, self-expression, self-realization, the mobility ethos, sexuality, and family-centredness. To these we might add progress, meaning a steady annual rise in the Dow-Jones and FT Industrial Share indices. Religion has become, in Durkheim's words, the cult 'which each man will freely perform within himself'. It is a system of symbols which is entirely differentiated from the structure of society, celebrated by each man on his own.

The question which naturally arises with reference to Luckmann's proposal is whether there is anything sacred or religious about these themes, although it might be granted that they are important in giving a symbolic meaning to people's lives. The answer is simply that religious or sacred objects have no particular character which is intrinsic to them. Durkheim and William James were agreed on this point, and we have seen that the definitions used by Geertz and Luckmann do not depart from that tradition. It may be worth restating Geertz's definition, for although formulated with primitive religions in mind, a moment's reflection will show how applicable it is to the kind of symbolic universe described by Luckmann. A religion is, he said:

> A system of symbols which acts to establish powerful, pervasive, and long-lasting moods and motivations in men by formulating conceptions of a general order of existence and clothing these conceptions with such an aura of factuality that the moods and motivations seem uniquely realistic.[33]

We may add that if men do indeed make sense of their lives by reference to themes of the kind indicated by Luckmann, then who is to examine and analyse these systems of symbols if not sociologists of religion? It falls to their lot in the division of intellectual labour. But the recognition of contemporary religion in a form which omits all mention of God and the supernatural should need no such defence. As Mary Douglas has shown,[34] the ritual elaboration of a religion is not to be treated as evidence that it is primitive or underdeveloped. The symbolic universes of some exceedingly primitive peoples are very simple and entirely lacking in their expected quota of spirits and rituals.

A symbolic universe is to be taken on its own terms; all that is essential is that we should be able to identify the symbolic elements which may properly be termed sacred. For this we most emphatically do not need a definition. Durkheim qualified the term 'sacred' by the phrase, 'things set apart and forbidden', and that is enough. People are quite prepared to identify their neighbours' gods, with a small initial letter, and Jesus is not reported to have had any difficulty in making his meaning clear when he said that 'where your treasure is, there will your heart be also'. The sociologist must be content to seek precision in general observation, not to observe only what can precisely be defined and measured. The notion of 'the sacred' may not be precise, but it is clear. Luckmann interprets it as that which is 'experienced as transcending everyday life', and Geertz in terms of a 'factuality' which seems 'uniquely realistic'. For a more discursive statement we may turn to the eighteenth-century German writer, Johann Lavater:

What is man's interest? What constitutes his God, the ultimate of his wishes, the end of his existence? Either that which on every occasion he communicates with the most unrestrained cordiality, or hides from every profane eye and ear with mysterious awe; to which he makes every other thing a mere appendix; – the vortex, the centre, the comparative point from which he sets out, on which he fixes, to which he irresistibly returns; – that at the loss of which you may safely think him inconsolable; – that which he rescues from the gripe of danger with equal anxiety and boldness.[35]

Much of the uneasiness which people express at the notion of the sacred is based on their inability to identify it and count it like so many golf balls. Thus Wilson objects to the idea of religion as a constant element in the anthropological condition on the grounds that it is 'a hypothetical constant, *the means of measuring which* have not yet been discovered.'[36] Of course the objection is spurious. Ideal types cannot be *measured*, but the sociologist uses them none the less.

The institutional form assumed by symbolic universes of meaning will vary widely from one type of society to another, and within any one form we shall find a number of diverse orientations. Secularization only becomes a problem when we take a single institutional form of religion as normative. Where then, we may ask, does this leave the Weberian tradition, in which the notion of secularization seems to loom so large? Hans Gerth and C. Wright Mills summarize the position thus:

> The principle of rationalization is the most general element in Weber's philosophy of history. For the rise and fall of institutional structures, the ups and downs of classes, parties, and rulers implement the general drift of secular rationalization. In thinking of the change of human attitudes and mentalities that this process occasions, Weber liked to quote Friedrich Schiller's phrase, the 'disenchantment of the world'. The extent and direction of rationalization is thus measured negatively in terms of the degree to which magical elements of thought are displaced, or positively by the extent to which ideas gain in systematic coherence and naturalistic consistency.[37]

There is little doubt that Weber believed such a 'unilinear development' to be perceptible in history, and that his view was rooted in the conventional liberalism of his day. If it is understood in broad terms, the proposition has some validity, but only so long as it is also understood to be entirely descriptive. What must be rejected is the idea that secular rationalization is a mysterious force which somehow acts on societies, as if it were the hand of God. But even when it is understood descriptively, the idea must be handled with care, for there are many exceptions to the proposition. We may say that the symbolic universes by which peoples make sense of their experience of life show a general tendency to include fewer elements which refer to supernatural entities as societies become more complex. We must seek within the Durkheimian tradition for an explanation of why this is so, however, for it is the description of an effect, not the statement of a cause. Moreover we must not confuse the supernatural elements found in symbolic systems of meaning with the systems themselves. It is inevitable that the word 'secularization' will continue to be used to connote the diminishing frequency with which the supernatural will be invoked, but this need be no bad thing, so long as it does not distract attention from the study of the sacred. Belief in the supernatural is in itself a comparatively trivial phenomenon. What is significant is the implications which such a belief has for people's actions, and it is these implications which form the substance of religion, not the belief itself.

To break with the tradition of equating religion with the religion of the churches is easier said than done, and the next chapter will examine some of the theoretical and methodological problems which the attempt involves.

8. Common Religion[1]

When we cease to equate the religion of the churches with religion, *tout court*, a number of problems arise. In order to bring them into focus and examine whether there might be ways of overcoming them, it will be necessary to repeat some of the points made in the last chapter. The task in hand is that of studying the beliefs and practices found in a society which we may wish to designate as religious. This is a matter of intrinsic interest, but it is also a necessary task if we are to assess the claim that contemporary society is more secularized than it formerly was.

The first essential is to recognize how deeply embedded is the effect of the official teaching of the churches on popular ideas of religiousness. If we are to use the word 'religion' to connote something much wider than church religion, it almost becomes necessary to use it as a technical term, for its commonly restricted meaning is reflected not only in popular usage but in the social sciences as well, as may readily be seen. Lenski defines religion in a way which seems to be so all-embracing, that, according to his definition, 'every normal adult member of any human society is religious'.[2] And yet the dimensions on which he measures religious commitment are closely related to the expectations of a small number of religious organizations. Glock and Stark similarly announce their intention to take into account 'all the possible distinctions in what religiousness can mean',[3] and then proceed to use in their questionnaires only such items as are derived from the norms of various denominations. The same is true of other attempts to use a multidimensional model of religious commitment.[4] Despite the obvious intention to take into account all forms of religiosity, the construction of instruments for empirical measurement appears to force researchers into using items drawn from a wide range of conventional orthodoxies. The most that is achieved seems to be a measure which is biased towards no single denomination. Even the *Study of Values* test, devised by Allport, Vernon and Lindzey, falls far short of its aim. The R (religious interest) scale of that test, we are told, is 'primarily concerned with religious matters, and the person who scores high seeks to comprehend the universe as a totality, and to relate himself to the whole. The religious attitude is one of striving after that unity which comes from a divine principle.'[5] While this does not correspond to our definition of religion, none the less it takes a broader view than we should gain from the denominations. However, Richard Hunt has shown that in fact 'the R scale is primarily measuring an individual's active involvement in traditional religious institutions as a means of making life meaningful'.[6] So the *Study of Values*, too, must be discounted as a way of assessing religiousness generally.

Thomas Luckmann, as we have noted earlier, has drawn attention to the extent to which exclusive attention has been paid to the religion of the churches. He is most emphatic that, regardless of whether his analysis of a contemporary form of 'invisible' religion is found acceptable:

> One thing we may assert with confidence: The norms of traditional religious institutions – as congealed in an 'official' or formerly 'official' model of religion – cannot serve as a yardstick for assessing religion in contemporary society.[7]

The judgement seems to be entirely sound. The authors who admit several dimensions of religious commitment, or who assess secularization in terms of the 'independent' variables of belief, practice and institutions, always omit to mention that these are so many dimensions or variables of 'official' religion. We have seen that Luckmann contrasts 'official' religion with what he calls 'natural' religion, meaning a system of symbolic meaning in which there is no reference to the supernatural. The urgent need for a thorough investigation of the elements of natural religion requires no further discussion. The sweeping distinction between official and natural religion demands closer scrutiny, however, for it runs the risk of defining out of consideration some intermediate form of religiousness.

Official religion, as we have seen, is defined by institutional specialization. Because the symbolic universe constitutes an autonomous sphere of knowledge, there is a continual danger that it will lose touch with the majority of the people and, under the influence of a caste of religious specialists, will become a comparatively esoteric cult which fails to articulate the religious sentiments of the people. But we must notice that the very formation of an official religion means that only certain beliefs and practices are included within its sacred canon, for such an official religion, by definition, establishes a single and exclusive orthodoxy. Now this is a paradox, for an official religion comes into being only when a society has reached that degree of complexity which allows of institutional specialization. By its very nature it presupposes a uniform set of social experiences which will be expressed in the one orthodoxy, and yet at the same time it is a complex and differentiated society which contains disparate elements with diverse kinds of social experience. So, in one sense, institutionally specialized religion is doomed from its inception. It is viable only in a small-scale society, and yet it occurs only in large-scale societies. We shall look briefly at the ways in which an official religion accommodates itself to this situation a little later, but at this point we must ask whether any official religion ever successfully provides a symbolic universe for a society, as theological models assume they invariably do. Such a congruence between the need of a people for religious expression, and the provision of modes of religious articulation by an official religion, exists only as an ideal type, as a limiting case. Some European countries in the middle ages approximated to this ideal type, owing largely to the stability of the prevailing social order and to the wide-ranging authority of the church, which permitted it to determine the forms of socialization enabling people to express themselves within the framework of the official religion. But it is doubtful whether, even during the middle ages, there was anything approaching perfect congruence. One reason for the persistent disparity was that in every part of Europe Christianity had succeeded to earlier religious traditions. These diverse folk religions, as they have been described,[8] were partially incorporated into Christianity in many places. Holy wells or sacred feasts, for instance, were taken over and given a new, officially Christian significance. Other elements, however, were not assimilated into the universal religion. To the extent that the old social order was broken up by those who brought the universal religion to any particular area, the significance of the remaining elements of a folk religion rapidly diminished. In many places, however, the old order was left intact with only superficial political changes when the new religion was introduced. We may suggest that under these circumstances many elements of the old folk religion lived on, transformed into an unofficial religious tradition. Since it no longer bore the character of a local official religion, but was rather an underground religion of the common people, we may call it 'common' religion. If by official religion we mean beliefs and practices which are prescribed, regulated and socialized by specialized religious institutions, then common religion may be described as those beliefs and practices of an overtly religious nature which are not under the domination of a prevailing religious institution.

It must be admitted that the term 'common religion' is not altogether satisfactory, partly because the meaning it is intended to convey is not immediately apparent and partly because it has been used elsewhere with a different connotation. However, no preferable expression is available. The term 'popular religion' is really too vague to signify anything at all, other than a religion which has popular appeal, which is not necessarily a characteristic of common religion. In any case that term has already acquired something like a special meaning from its use by Louis Schneider and Stanford Dornbusch.[9] The term 'common religion' has been used by Robin Williams to denote a 'common set of ideas, rituals and symbols' which serves to create 'an overarching sense of unity, even in a society riddled with conflicts.'[10] Obviously Williams means a religion which is common to a people, whereas we are using the same expression to signify a religion of the common man. This duplication of usage, however, is a less serious impediment now that Robert Bellah has elaborated Williams's idea with particular reference to the U.S.A., using Rousseau's phrase, 'civil religion'.[11] The notion of a civil religion, consisting of belief in 'the existence of God, the life to come, the reward of virtue and the punishment of vice, and the exclusion of religious intolerance', is altogether more satisfactory than the term 'common religion' which Williams proposed, since the latter, as Bellah points out, tends to be interpreted as nothing more than 'national self-worship', as in Will Herberg's identification of the American Way of Life as the object venerated by 'American religion'.[12] It seems likely, therefore, that Bellah's idea of civil religion will supersede the notion of common religion as Williams used it, leaving the latter expression relatively free to bear the significance which we put upon it here.

In the western world common religion has generally been found in contradistinction to official religion, but this need not necessarily be so. What is important is the recognition that religion need not necessarily be found in the organized form which has characterized Christianity. The failure to appreciate this point has been remarked upon by Trevor Ling:

. . . the sociology of religion has in a sense helped to perpetuate this view of religion as fundamentally organizational; at least, it has so far done little to suggest another perspective. . . . Had there been any serious comparative or cross-cultural sociology of religion the much needed corrective might have been discovered, for example, from the study of Indian religion, which does not exhibit anything like so prominent an ecclesiastical or organizational character even after its centuries of contact with, and response to, the West.[13]

The same author also recognizes the influence upon social science of explicitly theological models of religion. Too often sociologists have blindly followed, when

Much attention is paid in theological studies to the structure of the *institutional* belief systems. What is needed . . . is investigation into the structure of the *popular* belief system, that part of the sacred cosmos which lies outside the official dogmas.[14]

The fact that popular religion, or common religion as we prefer to call it here, lies outside the confines of official religion makes it no less significant. It has greater significance, if anything, since it survives only because of its continued ability to express the transcendent element in people's experience, and to bestow meaning on what would otherwise be perplexing. In this sense the student of secularization should not be overmuch concerned with the churches. Their entrenched position in a society's institutional structure, and their persistence as organizations, will make them a deceptive indicator of religiousness in a society. Common religion has no such organizational props. If it survives it does so because it remains credible. To rule out what may be called common religion as 'mere' superstition is misguidedly to follow the prejudices of theologians. Bryan Wilson has asserted that 'religious institutions, organizations, affiliations and practices, and institutionalized belief-systems have been of more social consequence in all societies than are the contemporary private beliefs of individuals',[15] but that contains only half the truth. It can readily be granted that the beliefs of isolated individuals are generally of little importance. But institutions may assume diverse forms, and it is an entirely proper object of study to examine the institutional framework of folk and common religion, just as it is proper to explore religious institutions in primitive societies. That an institution is not clearly visible, separate, and specialized, is no reason to ignore its institutional character.

The confusion arises partly because common religion presupposes an alternative religious institution, of a diffuse and apparently unorganized nature, within a society which already possesses a sophisticated and highly developed official religion. To be confused by such a plurality of religions is further evidence that Ling is right, for it is only within the narrow confines of modern western religion that the claim to unique truth made by one particular religious system has been seriously entertained. The West presents a special case because of the unparalleled degree of institutional specialization which it has witnessed, and because of the powerful position which official religion has consequently enjoyed. In the East it is otherwise, for there the plurality of religious truth is the general rule. But even in primitive religion the same thing occurs. It might seem that religious institutions in simple societies are single and undivided symbolic systems, and yet Paul Radin found it necessary to draw a distinction between 'formulated religion' and the 'magical substratum'.[16] Indeed that distinction expresses well the relationship which is often found between magic and religion, where the difference is not a difference in kind, but only that the official religion is more authoritative, and the common religion less so. If common religion were absent from modern western societies it would provide striking evidence of an advanced 'disenchantment of the world', consonant with Weber's thesis of unilinear development: but it would be surprising to the pragmatic observer. But the confusion arises also because the 'primitive' and 'naïf' beliefs of common religion often seem utterly implausible to the academic person. That belief in luck, fate, the influence of the moon or the stars, and so on, can actually make life more meaningful to people is so far outside their experience that they assume that people who do not accept the beliefs of some variety of intellectually comprehensible official religion must, like themselves, live in a world in which ultimate explanations and ultimate satisfactions are denied them. But that is an empirical question which can be answered only after examining the beliefs people actually hold, regardless of whether or not those beliefs fall within the orthodoxy of belief and practice of the official religion.

One of the clearest examples of what is meant by common religion may help to illustrate the point. Europe in the sixteenth and seventeenth centuries saw a remarkable outbreak of accusations of witchcraft, and this dramatic efflorescence of the phenomenon points us to the existence of beliefs in magic and witchcraft throughout the middle ages and the early modern period. Belief in witches is still widespread in some western societies, but it is more significant in earlier periods of history because it was then prevalent at the same time as official religion was strong and pervasive. It demonstrates, moreover, something of the relationship between official and common religions. Until quite recently, the so-called witch-crazes had barely been touched by historians, who, like later sociologists, had preferred to restrict their attention to what was considered to be the more serious and consequential religion of the churches. As Hugh Trevor-Roper wrote recently, 'The presentation of witches is, to some, a disgusting subject, below the dignity of history. But it is also a historical fact.'[17] The lack has now been made good by the general study of religion and magic by Keith Thomas, and by Alan Macfarlane's detailed study of the accusations and trials of witches in the county of Essex.[18] What we learn from their studies is that complex beliefs in the efficacy of magic and the activities of witches and cunning men existed side by side with the official religion of the day. The two were viewed as independent and complementary spheres of belief which were in no way incompatible. The attitude of the official religion to common religion was openly hostile, but the conflict was only occasionally seen in the active form of persecution. For much of the time the two forms of religion were mutually supportive, for each provided what the other lacked, making the deficiencies of neither apparent. In some respects there was an overlap between the two, as when a priest was credited with magical powers, a phenomenon still found in the rural parts of some Catholic countries. The important fact is that none but the most committed supporters of the official religion saw any need to make a choice between them. Clearly, elements from the ancient folk religions persisted in the continuing tradition of common religion, thus making it plain that even in a period when official religion was vigorous and received wide support, it did not exhaustively account for all the religion of the period. On its own, it was unable to provide all the components of a symbolic system which were necessary to give meaning to life as people experienced it. If official religion was not the only form of religion even in the period of its greatest strength, and in those areas where its claim to unique legitimacy was pressed the hardest, it is most unlikely that exclusive concentration on official religion will provide an adequate gauge of total religiousness elsewhere and in other periods.

Many of the elements which make up common religion are very

F

ancient. In the case of belief in witches and in magic generally, they
have their roots in a folk religion which prevailed before the advent
of any official religion. This suggests that common religion forms
something like a base-line of religiousness which may change in
various ways but which maintains a continuity, and that on to it
is imposed an official religion which normally occupies a more conspicuous place. At times the common religion may come into play
as a salient feature of the religious scene, as during the time of the
witch-crazes in Europe or New England, but it will usually remain
inconspicuous. Its importance is obvious during those critical periods
when it is to the fore, but otherwise it is impossible to gauge the
extent of its significance. Geoffrey Gorer has provided some information about the frequency with which people in an English sample
admitted to a variety of superstitious beliefs and practices.[19] A paper
by Nicholas Abercrombie and others, on the basis of similar evidence,
has estimated that in England eighteen per cent of the population
may be very superstitious, twenty-four per cent fairly superstitious,
thirty per cent fairly unsuperstitious, and twenty-eight per cent very
unsuperstitious.[20] The methodological difficulties involved in this
sort of research will be discussed shortly, but for the moment these
figures may be noted with caution. The way in which magico-religious
elements of belief merge with 'scientific' elements in primitive cultures
has been noted earlier,[21] but such 'mistakes' are not restricted to
primitive peoples. Any investigation of common religion rapidly
encounters a mode of thinking which can only be described as a
modern primitive mentality, although no derogatory connotation
should be attached to the term 'primitive' either here or elsewhere.
No joke was intended by the respondent who 'appeared to have no
metaphysical belief', but who answered a series of questions thus:
' "Have you ever consulted an astrologer?" – "No". "A palmist?" –
"No". "A fortune-teller?" – "No." "Anyone else like that?" – "Only
the doctor." '[22] Witchcraft may once have been considered 'below
the dignity of history', but its investigation has proved to be very
rewarding. Research in the area of belief represented by the respondent who equated medicine with palmistry may still be beneath
the dignity of some sociologists of religion, but a thorough
study of modern primitive mentality may prove to be no less
rewarding.

Luckmann's distinction between official religion and an emergent
natural religion in one sense went too far. His attack on the assump-

tion that sociologists should confine their studies to official religion led him to turn his attention to natural religion, thus ignoring the role of the important intermediate area of common religion which, though free of the domination of official religion, yet still contains elements which refer to the supernatural. In another sense, however, he has not gone far enough. In a passage already quoted, he speaks of the modern sacred cosmos being not so much a coherent unity – as the traditional model portrays official religion as being – as 'an assortment of religious themes'.[23] His critique falls short of the mark because the assumption that a symbolic system of meaning takes the form of a systematically coherent unity is almost always invalid. Even an official religion only exhibits such a coherence in theory, and for the average believer it is in practice much more like an amalgamation of beliefs and practices held together by their common association with the church rather than by their logical relation one to another. Yet almost every piece of empirical work on contemporary religion assumes, at least implicitly, that the former assumption is valid. It is another example of the way in which social scientists have accepted unquestioningly the model of religion provided, not even by official religion, but by traditional theology, and not just by theology, but by vulgarized old-fashioned theology. Modern biblical scholarship, far from preserving the massive monolith of theology erected by the Schoolmen, has repeatedly emphasized the fragmentary nature of early Christian belief. The canon of New Testament scripture bears the marks of an earlier oral tradition which was highly thematic, and enshrines a multitude of 'credal tags' which preceded the systematic doctrinal formulations of a later generation of Christians. Given the perennial respect in theological circles for everything that can be shown to be primitive, this recognition does little to enhance the reputation of systematic theologies. The vulgar stereotype remains, however, that 'religion' is a logically coherent set of beliefs and practices; and it is this spurious model of official religion which remains the paradigm, both for the man in the street and for the average social scientist.

The persistence of this assumption is surprising when one considers how often in the past it has been decried. Peter Worsley may be correct in suggesting that this 'over-systematization of belief' is a 'natural disease of academics', something to which they are constitutionally prone, just as we have suggested that they are susceptible to the fallacy of presuming that all modern men think only in rational terms, as they believe themselves to do. But as Worsley says:

> All too often we find an exaggerated unity of belief systems, as well as the imputation of exaggerated importance to such systems, or parts of them, sometimes implicit in the very process of presenting them *in abstracto* as 'the religion' or 'the cosmology' of a given people. . . . Sequential presentation alone often implies a logic of priority *in the thought of the people*, that may be quite illegitimate, certainly as far as everyday 'operational' behaviour (as distinct from situations where people are consciously enunciating a 'philosophy') is concerned.[24]

But if we are to investigate common religion, it is imperative that this assumption should be discarded.

One of the problems connected with common religion is that of accounting for its transmission. The teachings of official religion are formally propagated as part of a person's socialization in the home, at school and at church. Luckmann's natural religion, if its existence is demonstrated empirically, is transmitted through the whole of modern culture, and its themes are articulated powerfully through all the media of mass communication. So what of common religion? Recent evidence on the beliefs of children[25] suggests that it may be handed down, at least to a significant degree, through generations of childhood peer-groups. Children's beliefs are shown to be thoroughly thematic in their structure, containing numerous elements which bear no logical relationship to one another. And yet a great number of the elements are found throughout a society and across many generations, in a profuse variety of presentations rather like the regional dialect variations within a common language. Details change from rural to urban contexts; they are modified with surprising speed to embrace contemporary technical innovations which impinge on the lives of children, but the broad outlines of beliefs remain clear and persistent. While children's beliefs are clearly caught at one stage of development, it may be suggested that they are more than merely underdeveloped religious beliefs and practices. They are also elements of common religion which persist into adult life, often only half remembered, but which in childhood appear in vigorous and un-polluted form, unaffected at that stage by the systematizing influence of official religion.

Common religion is made up of many diverse elements. There are those, for example, which refer to luck: how to avoid bad luck and enjoy good luck. An even more important element is the idea of fate and how it may be discerned in advance, including the paraphernalia of palmistry, bumps on the head, tea-leaves, crystal balls and astrology, all of which practices are chiefly important because of their implicit assumption of fate. There are other elements in common religion which are not so obviously 'superstitious', but are rather beliefs and practices which impart a sense of security in those natural situations of life which are characterized by doubt and uncertainty. Conception, birth, adolescence, courtship, marriage, menopause, failing health, sickness and death are all surrounded by beliefs and practices enshrined in a common religion, which differ only in detail from what was known in earlier centuries. Despite the informal and unorganized character of common religion, these elements persist and are widely pervasive. One of the few pieces of evidence which suggests that common religion may be transmitted as part of children's lore relates to beliefs concerning death. The beliefs about the afterlife which have been uncovered in the studies reported by Geoffrey Gorer seem to indicate that the official religion has been less responsible for forming these ideas than has the common religion which was learned in childhood.[26] Similarly a profusion of beliefs and practices surrounds the possibility of pregnancy, but recent research has shown that, at least among women who have given birth to several children, belief in the unavoidability of pregnancy is so strong that the use of contraception is dismissed as a pointless waste of time.[27] The teachings of the official religion as they relate to this kind of exigency, particularly so far as Protestant Christianity is concerned, give little comfort. All the emphasis is placed on a calm confidence in God and his beneficent will. For the common man, however, such an attitude requires a faith so heroic as to be beyond his reach, and since official religion is able to provide no immediately comforting assurance, it is sought elsewhere. Those most exposed to modern culture, who are generally members of a middle class, seek the assurance from professional advisers using scientific techniques. The working class and those whose lives are spent away from urban centres, including, perhaps, members of a residual aristocracy, resort to the beliefs of their childhood, and to other elements of common religion, for comfort and reassurance.

If patterns of common religion are transmitted, at least in part,

F*

through the lore of childhood peer-groups, it would reinforce their metaphorical description as a base-line of religiousness. Common religion then forms the first layer of a symbolic universe wherewith people give meaning and significance to their experience of life. On to it may be superimposed other aspects of a symbolic universe, such as official religion; or strictly rational systems of meaning, which render it partially or wholly inoperative. It constitutes, however, an important religious element in a society, and one which should not be ignored by empirical studies.

Two reasons have been suggested to account for the way in which common religion has been ignored by sociological research. Firstly, writers have assumed that the criteria of religiousness approved by the churches are the appropriate ones to use in social scientific research, and they have failed to recognize that these criteria are applicable only to official, organized religious institutions, and are not sensitive to other forms of religiosity. Secondly, it has been assumed that a set of beliefs, regardless of what they are, will hang together as a coherent whole. This, too, it has been argued, is an invalid assumption. Both errors have been, to some degree, a legacy from the theologians, and both need to be overcome if the religion of the theologians is not to remain the only type investigated by empirical study.

In addition to these theoretical obstacles to more adequate research into religion in contemporary society there are practical obstacles as well. The first difficulty is that religion is a highly emotive subject for many people. The investigator who does no more than merely mention the word 'religion' may unintentionally trigger off one of many emotions. For the average Englishman it may have overtones of fanaticism, dishonesty, respectability, controversy or hypocrisy, to mention just a few. Of course an emotional component may be an essential part of any comment on religious belief or practice, but having once evoked a particular emotional tone it is usually difficult to break away from it. Every subsequent remark is coloured by the initial reaction, regardless of whether or not it is appropriate. The only sure way to avoid this problem is by relying exclusively on indirect observation. Where the researcher has not himself introduced the subject of religion, he may be sure that the emotional content of any remarks on the subject he may record will be inherent and genuine aspects of the data, not artefacts of his observation. Even the most patient field worker will ask direct questions from time to time, however, and as soon as he does so, this problem will arise. For many working-class respondents, the subject is highly embarrassing. They find it easier to talk about their most intimate sexual experiences than about their religious beliefs. Often their whole manner is suffused with guilt. No reply makes sense because it is presented with an apology for the respondent's failure to do what as a child he was taught to do. Alternatively he may still be full of anger and resentment at having been forced as a child to attend Sunday School and two boring services each Sunday and for this reason he may use every reply as an occasion for protest. The middle-class respondent, on the other hand, may take each question as an opportunity to show how respectable and upright he is in being religious; or be so anxious to show himself to be an intelligent and modern agnostic that every remark will be a disquisition on the idiocy of all religion. The important point is that the moment a researcher uses the word 'religion' a ready-made set of attitudes will be thrust at him. As a rule these will be attitudes to 'the church', and any attempt to break through to the respondent's own beliefs will be impossibly hampered.

We would suggest that, short of relying on indirect observation, or unsolicited responses, the only strategy available is to make questions as unobtrusive as possible; and this means that interviews which relate explicitly and solely to religion should be avoided. Instead, questions which have been carefully worded to make them susceptible of more than one interpretation should be incorporated into interviews concerned primarily with unrelated topics, and inserted at a point when the interview is sufficiently advanced for the question to appear as being of a strictly subsidiary and unimportant nature. This would demand close co-operation between researchers, of course, which in itself might be a good thing. Where a series of questions is used, they should start by referring to religion only obliquely – for example by the mention of astrology or Jewishness or some other topic at a tangent to official religion. If an aspect of official religion is mentioned at the outset, it will define religion in those terms. Now this approach may seem 'sneaky' almost to the point of being unethical, but it is necessary if respondents are to be allowed to respond, not merely encouraged to react; and valid responses may be obtainable only by such a devious method. As Jacques Tati said recently in an interview, 'Why do you think I never show Hulot in close-up . . . ? Because I do not want to underline everything, to make things too clear. The truth is not like that at all, you know. You have to approach it stealthily, to surprise it.'[28] Religious truth, too, must be taken by surprise.

It may seem that the small-scale studies favoured by ethnomethodologists would provide an ideal method for studying in depth the ways in which people put together the elements of a symbolic universe. That may indeed be so. Only an ethnomethodological study of a religious topic will show. But all small-scale investigations run up against the problem that a phenomenon appears different when viewed against two different scales. As Henri Princoré asked, 'Would a naturalist who had never studied the elephant except through the microscope consider that he had an adequate knowledge of the creature?'[29] Too many sociological microscopists, unfortunately, are in danger of believing their observations to be the only valid ones. Yet in religion, as elsewhere, we do not find units which build neatly into a larger whole, so that the nature of the whole may be inferred from the nature of the units. This is why the phenomenon of common religion is important. It is not just the isolated beliefs and practices of isolated individuals which deserve study, but the whole irregular institution of common religion. That is why it is worth trying to devise a valid method for investigating the religious conceptions of significant numbers of people by direct interviewing, rather than by relying on entirely informal techniques.

The other practical problem in empirical studies is less intractable, but it is more complex. This is the hoary problem of how the observer is to avoid imposing his own frame of reference, or his own way of thinking about a topic, on his subjects. The sophisticated survey methods employed by Glock and Stark, whose work has been referred to earlier, are bedevilled by both of the practical problems presently being discussed. A mailed questionnaire about religious commitment evokes the whole range of emotive responses. It also sets in advance the precise definition of what shall count as religious, and the limits within which replies are acceptable. The use of exactly and inflexibly formulated questions, especially when they appear on printed questionnaires, involves a double difficulty. In the first place, precisely formulated questions assume that the respondent will understand them; and whether the respondent actually does understand a question or not is only rarely apparent, for most people who fill in a questionnaire, or agree to be interviewed, will answer the questions irrespective of whether they understand them or not. When the subject of the questions is religion this has serious implications. Respondents may never have formulated religious questions for themselves, let alone searched for answers to them. Thus Richard Hoggart has written that

> Most people in the working classes appear . . . not merely unfanatic but unidealistic; they have their principles but are disinclined to reveal them in their pure state. For the most part their approach is empirical; they are confirmed pragmatists.[30]

To ask such respondents to state or explain their beliefs in abstract terms is therefore to invite them to perform verbally in ways they feel are expected of them: it is not to elicit natural responses. It is for this reason that questions should be susceptible of several interpretations, and should clearly permit the respondent to reject them as entirely meaningless. Even the permissively open-ended method which has been employed to such good effect by Geoffrey Gorer still incorporates highly specific questions which admit of only one interpretation. These always tend to prompt a respondent to reply, rather than evoking a response. If you go up to a labourer on a building-site, gripping your data-board firmly in one hand, and ask him if he believes in any sort of after-life, you will probably get a response which, euphemistically, we may call irrelevant. It may actually signify a relevant emotional response, but supposing, for one moment, that you get a literally relevant reply, it may be the result of a train of thought running something like this: 'Do I? I've never thought about it. If the bloke's asking me, I suppose I ought to know. Do I? Tom doesn't really seem to be dead. He's probably alive somewhere.' Which yields the answer, 'Yes, I suppose I do.' While you have received a reply, it is hardly an answer to the question you asked. It is an answer to the question, 'When you stop and consider it, even though you have never done so before, do you believe in any sort of after-life?' And that is a different matter entirely. So questions should be so phrased that a respondent does not feel constrained to reply. It should be clearly implied that the respondent may well have no opinion on a question, or that it is a question which may never have occurred to him, and that either of these responses would be perfectly acceptable. Obviously such responses are not failures to respond, nor different ways of saying 'don't know': they are vitally important negative responses.

As a general rule we may say that responses should be interpreted as reactions to stimuli, and treated accordingly, not naïvely accepted as rationally thought-out answers to simple questions. Some comments by Jean Piaget on interpreting the replies of children to questions which, either in substance or in phrasing, may be foreign to their own conceptualizations, are instructive:

> We readily agree that children have never or hardly ever reflected on the matters on which they were questioned. The experiments aimed, therefore, not at examining the ideas the children had already thought out, but at seeing how their ideas are formed in response to certain questions and principally in what direction their spontaneous attitude of mind tends to lead them. In such circumstances the results can only be negative and not positive. That is to say the explanation a child gives in answer to one of our questions must not be taken as an example of 'a child's idea', but serves simply to show that the child did not seek the solution in the same direction as we should have, but presupposed certain implicit postulates different from those we should suppose.[31]

This kind of interpretative problem should occur in many empirical studies, although it is only rarely recognized. Rather than grapple with the complex problem of interpretation, the use of questions which allow for a variety of negative response is to be preferred, since few students are really interested in the spontaneous formation of religious ideas. Ironically, though, that is what many responses are, although researchers interpret them as 'people's ideas'.

The other aspect of the difficulty involved in using fixed forms of question is complementary. If, on the one hand, you get the sort of information you were not seeking, on the other hand, you lose other information of which you might have been glad. Asking whether or not a respondent believes in the resurrection of the dead may test his mental agility in coming to a decision, but it generally precludes answers of the type, 'No, but I do believe that . . .', which may contain equally religious notions, but of a different variety. Hence the more diffuse a question is, the more scope a respondent has for volunteering specific information from a wide range of relevant comments.

The foregoing remarks on method are all elementary and they contain nothing new. But familiar truths are not always put into practice and only by taking cognizance of these points will it be possible for empirical research to break out of the strait-jacket which forces it repeatedly to examine familiar material. We know that the churches are suffering a decline, and if we did not, the Archbishop of Canterbury could have told us. The sociologist, however, should be concerned with all aspects of religion and if official religion no longer serves to make most people's lives meaningful to them in some systematic way, then what does? It has been suggested that common religion fulfils this role for many people in many situations. For how many people, and in how many situations, are empirical questions. The proposition that in secular society most people experience their lives pragmatically and view them as fundamentally – ultimately – meaningless, is also an empirical proposition, and if the thesis is to be sustained, it will require positive evidence. The negative evidence supplied by the decline of official religion is manifestly inadequate.

In the concluding chapter attention will be directed to one aspect of contemporary official religion which has been variously interpreted by social scientists. At this point, however, it should be noted that by observing some of the general rules which have been sketched out for the study of religion in general we could reasonably hope to shed some new light on official religion in particular. The invalid assumptions imported from theological models of religion are equally invalid for much official religion as well. Luckmann has argued that, within official religion, those who remain faithful to the formal institutions may find that their belief in official doctrines and their fulfilment of officially prescribed practices has become a matter of routine:

> Matters of 'ultimate' significance, as defined in the *official* model, are potentially convertible into routinized and discontinuous observances (or approximate observance or non-observance) of specific religious requirements whose sacred quality may become merely nominal.[32]

Such a situation may lead in a number of directions, and I have attempted to indicate two possible lines of development elsewhere.[33] A proper hermeneutical study of contemporary Christianity would have to fulfil all the conditions which were suggested above in Chapter 1. The use of a quasi-theological model of commitment is unlikely to produce anything new because it lacks the essential quality of 'standing back' from the phenomenon, and bringing to bear on it the insight of one who has become a stranger. To undertake this task would be a lengthy enterprise, and not even the beginnings of it can be attempted here. To anyone who has even a passing familiarity with the contemporary denominations, however, it will be evident that the criterion Bryan Wilson suggests for use in distinguishing between different kinds of sect – the way in which members conceive of salvation – would be of equal value in an examination of the churches. We must ask, for instance, salvation from what? for what? by what? The answers implied in the evidence we may elicit from the churches are very varied indeed, each suggesting an entirely different hermeneutical interpretation, and each likely to have different consequences in the lives of believers. All alike recognize the lordship of Jesus, but there are different types of lordship. They overlap to some extent, but we find widely differing concepts of salvation. There is the orthodox one which sees Jesus as the Saviour who rescues men from sin and corruption; or Jesus as the one who provides the missing link in an intellectual world-view; or Jesus as the existential hero, the exemplar whom all should follow; or Jesus as the man at one with nature; Jesus as the psychologically whole man; and Jesus as the excuse for a respectable club. The theologian would claim that all, simultaneously, are profoundly true, though different theologians would emphasize different aspects. And yet heresy is only the undue emphasis put on one aspect of the truth at the expense of others, and in a pluralistic society, where the assortment of religious themes which make up the sacred cosmos is directly accessible to potential consumers, heresy is the norm. For pluralism, not secularism, is the fundamental characteristic of contemporary society. Bryan Wilson is correct in seeing the only escape from 'secular' pluralism as being in the retreat into *gemeinschaftlich* sects.

Laurence Durrell wrote that 'A state-imposed metaphysic or religion should be opposed, if necessary at pistol-point. We must fight for variety if we fight at all.' The fight, it seems, has been won, and not a shot was fired.

9. Inter-Church Relations[1]

The ecumenical movement in the Christian church has become a dominant concern of Christian leaders since the Second World War. Because of its essentially domestic nature it has attracted little attention from sociologists, who have been more interested in investigating such things as the relationship between people's formal religious affiliation and their voting behaviour, the size of family they produce, their annual income and similar matters. It may be that the cause of this neglect has been that the internal affairs of churches have been judged to be of little importance in themselves but it seems more likely that it has been due to a preoccupation with social variables more amenable to quantification, since those who have conducted surveys, either academically or commercially, have been ready enough to include items about religion in their questionnaires. If religion is to be studied seriously, however, the internal workings of a religious system must be accorded high priority, even though they appear to be of an organizational character bearing a strong resemblance to secular enterprises. And the few sociologists who have considered the ecumenical movement have in fact concluded that it is very significant for the proper understanding of the contemporary churches, though they have differed in the conclusions they have drawn from it.

The ecumenical movement is generally regarded as having originated with the first world missionary conference held at Edinburgh in 1910, although the formation of the World Alliance for International Friendship Through the Churches in 1915 and the first meeting of the International Missionary Conference in 1921 also contributed to the interest which finally took shape in the Faith and Order Conference held in Lausanne in 1927, the first gathering explicitly called to promote the cause of Christian unity. While the movement is interesting in itself, of more obvious importance is the impact which it has had in making ecumenism a popular ideal in most Christian churches. Ecumenism itself, i.e. the attempt to reunite churches, predates the movement by many centuries as may readily be seen, for example, from the attempted *rapprochement* between the Latin and the Orthodox churches at the Council of Florence in 1439 or from the various realignments within Methodism.[2] Ecumenism is interesting to the sociologist because it represents a reversal of the more readily understood phenomenon of the fragmentation of churches, and when, as at present, it becomes a dominant concern, it represents an entirely new development well worth close attention. The principal concern of sociologists, therefore, has been to discover why the desire for the reunion of churches, sporadic for many centuries, should have become a major interest in the twentieth century.

The account of ecumenism most commonly given by sociologists represents it as a response by churches to the diminishing number of their members and as an attempt to recover their strength by organizing mergers to form a larger body. It is therefore taken to be a sign of religious decline and when, as at present, it occurs on a large scale it is taken as evidence of secularization. It is proposed that in a period of religious strength a church will recruit new members and will retain the loyalty of children born to old members, and that the organization will consequently grow in size. Being vigorous, any disputes which arise amongst the members will be argued fiercely and the protagonists will have no difficulty in finding support. Disagreements are likely, therefore, to result in small groups of dissidents splitting away to pursue their ideals independently. While the churches remain vigorous, each splinter group will continue to grow, and to develop in its own particular direction, becoming more differentiated from the others as an increased emphasis is placed on the particular aspect of belief or order which originally caused the rupture. The only circumstances in which a church will renege on its own distinctive doctrine will be either when the reasons for it have been forgotten, or else when a decline in numbers renders the church no longer viable as an independent organization. In either case the original vitality has been lost, and readiness to compromise on principles which had once been the *raison d'être* of the church indicates that all hope of renewed strength has been abandoned. Robert Currie expresses this view at the end of his study of ecumenism in the British Methodist churches:

> Ecumenism develops as conflict declines and as religion declines. Failing to recruit, flourishing communities become sluggish,

ageing and dispirited. . . . As tolerance of persistent decline fails, the organization seeks to replace missing 'frontal' growth from recruitment with 'lateral' growth from amalgamation . . . close examination of the process of reunion shows that in advanced societies ecumenicalism is the product of an ageing religion. It arises out of decline and secularization, but fails to deal with either.[3]

In the context of Methodism, for which Currie is able to list four-teen *major* divisions and unions,[4] the proposition has a certain validity although other factors besides the failure of recruitment might have led to the same result even for Methodism. When the same proposi-tion is applied more generally, however, and without a detailed exami-nation of the processes at work, it is unacceptable. There are two major objections to this seriously over-simplified account.

In the first place its logic is inadequate. It is one thing to show that churches which are declining in numerical strength, even to show that only and all such churches, manifest an interest in reunion; it is another thing altogether to show that the ecumenical interest has been caused by numerical decline. It would be just as reasonable to suppose that some third factor was causing both the decline and also the interest in ecumenism. Currie at least examines the relationship in some depth, even though he does not investigate alternative explanations. It is commoner to find some vague general principle invoked in support of the proposed explanation, as when Jacques Ellul breezily says that 'it is the tendency of all groups threatened by an external enemy to gather together, to hush up internal divisions'.[5] In the second place this common account is usually presented with a disregard for the explanations given by ecumenists themselves worthy of a nineteenth-century anthropologist, and it will not do to treat an actor's own account as mere delusion even if a more cogent alternative can be provided. An ideology as strong and pervasive as ecumenism deserves careful study. If Currie is right when he says, 'much empha-sis is placed on enthusiastic international conferences, while the practicalities of everyday church life are overlooked',[6] then the way in which the usurping ideas fit into a new pattern of religious thought should be seriously explored. Since the idea of reunion does indeed represent a *volte face* for the members of many denominations, we must give due attention to the way in which ideas which were pre-viously unthinkable gained currency, rather than rest content with a general account of the causes. A cynically detached explanation will fail to convince unless it is based on an understanding of how and why people come to see things in so new a way.

The attitude which people adopt to religious organizations other than their own is dependent, to a large degree, on the nature of their own religious commitment. It is not the strength of their commitment which is significant so much as the way in which they are committed. For the purpose of distinguishing the different ways in which people may conceive of their church membership, it will be useful to consider the types of answer one might receive to the hypothetical question, 'Which church do you belong to?' The point of interest will be not so much the answers themselves, as what the answers tell us about how the question was understood, since church membership is susceptible of several interpretations. The first type of reply might be the mention of a particular congregation: 'St Mary's', or 'London Road Baptist' or 'the parish church'. To the person giving this kind of answer, 'his' church is local, 'even down to stone and lime, hassock and hymn books, gowns and surplices' as a recent church report put it,[7] and his commitment can accurately be described as a *local* type of commitment. What matters to him is the integrity and identity of the local unit in all its particularity, for his sense of religious belonging is mediated through it. The fabric and decorations of the church, its forms of service, its associated organizations and clubs, these and all the other familiar details are facets of the religious universe which surrounds him, and without which the doctrine and beliefs taught in that church would be insubstantial and difficult to grasp. They are not, for him, mere objects or arbitrarily chosen ways of doing things, but symbols which have an importance and a significance in enabling him to feel at home in familiar surroundings when he confronts the uncomfortable things with which his religion is sometimes concerned: guilt, pain, bereavement, loneliness and so on. Indeed the reality of these experiences and the belief that they will not overcome him are associated so intimately with these tangible and mundane symbols that they provide reassurance enough for most of the time. This kind of religious commitment presupposes, of course, the stability of a congregation. It occurs in its strongest form when a person is born into a congregation, when he goes to the church with his parents as a child, when he is married there and his children are baptized there, when he and his family go there Sunday by Sunday, and so on throughout the whole cycle of his life. Stability such as this is becoming less and less common, but it is still true of the experience of a substantial proportion of the older church-going population; indeed it carries, if anything, added significance for them, since the church remains as one of the few elements of continuity in a world stripped of most of the features familiar from childhood and in which most other rituals of social life have either died or been transformed out of recognition. It is worth noting that this is a form of religious belonging known to only a small minority of the clergy of any denomination. Since the time they spend at any one church tends to be limited they are more aware of the elements shared in common by the various churches they have served than of the characteristic features of any particular church, and this may make them insensitive to the experience of their congregation and unsympathetic and impatient with what appears to them to be a narrow vision of the church centring round the parish pump. The desire of someone to give to the church a new stained-glass window or to pay for the organ to be restored may appear to the minister ill-conceived in the light of world poverty, whereas to the person concerned it has a symbolic meaning which puts it in a different category from a donation to Oxfam, a meaning of which the minister may be largely unaware.

To the person with this local type of religious commitment, ecumenism appears in a particular light. Recognizing as a member of his own church someone from a different denomination is as unobjectionable as it is meaningless, since members of the same denomination who belong to different congregations are strangers anyway. A visitor is a visitor, regardless of which church he comes from. The introduction of bishops into a non-episcopal church is of little greater significance. The imposition of a new form of service is a more serious matter, but it is a change which may be accepted in time. To close the church building, however, or to share a minister with another church in the name of efficiency, are different matters altogether. To lose one's church building is to lose one's church. To join another congregation is to become a permanent visitor but never to be at home; to have another congregation join with one's own church is little better, since it is permanently to have a group of visitors, which is a contradiction in terms. To the person with a local religious commitment, the closure of church buildings on the grounds of rationalization and efficiency is as meaningless as the advocacy of working for Oxfam instead of cleaning church brasses, since alternatives are being proposed which are drawn from a different order of

reality. The church is the church is the church, and that's an end to it.
Currie quotes a calm and unemotional letter written to the *Methodist
Recorder* in 1926 which illustrates the view in a very practical way:

> On the one side of our Chapel within a hundred yards is a Free
> Methodist Chapel; on the other side is a Primitive Methodist
> Chapel about the same distance away. In each of these chapels are
> a band of eager, enthusiastic officials who have had a life-long
> connection with their Chapel, and sphere of work. Supposing,
> through Union, you close two of these chapels, what is going to
> become of these various officials?[8]

To the man with this type of religious commitment, the apparently
weighty matters of compromise – or *rapprochement*, according to
the view taken – over church doctrine and polity are of very limited
interest. He will be undisturbed by such changes and will not oppose
them; but by the same token he will not lend them his wholehearted
support. He is ecumenically minded already in that he has always
welcomed strangers to his church with genuine warmth. He is in-
stinctively in favour of intercommunion between churches since it
is only a fancy name for what is, to him, a simple act of friendship
and hospitality. If ecumenism means closing his church, however,
or encouraging others to close theirs, it violates his basic notion of
what belonging to the church is all about and he can be counted upon
to oppose it to the last ditch.

To the same hypothetical question, 'What church do you belong
to?' other people might say 'Church of England' or 'Catholic' or
'Free Kirk'. They have understood the question in a radically different way and we may infer that their sense of religious belonging is
different. Readily to identify oneself with a denomination implies
stability, but the stability is attached to the boundaries between
religious denominations rather than the boundaries of a specific
religious community. If clergy and ministers can be unsympathetic
to local commitment they are much less so towards denominational
commitment since it is more characteristic of their own sense of
religious belonging. For the person with this *party* type of commitment what is especially significant is not the particularity of any one
congregation, but the more general ethos common to all churches of
the denomination, and this is frequently seen in contrast with other
denominations. For the Catholic, what is significant is belief in the
Mass and going to Mass every Sunday, belief in the importance of

the Virgin Mary, in the authority of the Pope, the practice of going to confession and much else besides. They may or may not be things of importance in themselves, but they have an added significance as symbols of religious belonging. As the locally committed man feels at home in the familiar surroundings of a particular place, so the Catholic derives an equivalent sense of security from a set relationship with his priests, from invoking the help of the Mother of God, from the familiar ritual of attendance at Sunday Mass. They are all parts of a symbolic world which is warm and known, and within which the Catholic has grown up and lived, has buried his mother and married his wife, has been sorry for getting drunk and hoped for a life beyond death. It is the institution of the Catholic Church, rather than the surroundings of a particular congregation, which forms the religious context which he knows as his own. The beliefs which he holds and the things he does in the name of religion are important not so much in themselves as because they are characteristically Catholic. To fail to go to Mass on Sunday may be a sin for the Catholic, but it is also to alienate himself from the Catholic Church and to withdraw from a world in which his mundane experiences have a special meaning which they cannot be given in any other way.

The Catholic Church is chosen merely as an example, of course, and not every Catholic has this type of religious commitment. In countries where Catholicism is virtually the only religion, such as Spain or Malta, another model of religious commitment applies, but in such areas the problem of ecumenism and inter-church relations does not arise. The party type of commitment is found in other denominations, and the very different example of the Free Church of Scotland might have been elaborated as an equally good illustration. This type of commitment has its own appropriate response to ecumenism. The man thus committed is untroubled by the closure of particular churches, even if it involves closing the church which he normally attends. Although less easy to accept, he will not be unduly shaken by alterations, even substantial ones, in the sphere of the religious symbols with which he is familiar; Catholics accommodated themselves quite rapidly to the recent removal of a host of saints from the Calendar, to the introduction of the vernacular Mass and to the abolition of Friday abstinence from meat. Mary Douglas, it is true, has questioned this ready accommodation to change,[9] and it may be that alterations to the traditional familiar practices in other churches, besides the Catholic Church, have had consequences which are yet to become fully evident. Indeed we should expect rapid and extensive changes to an established religious tradition to be difficult for the man with a party type of commitment to accept. This does not apply to changes introduced slowly over a number of years: what is anathema is for an important symbol to be lost in a compromise as a result of ecumenical bargaining with another church. Faced with a scheme for reunion with the Methodist Church, some members of the Church of England, many of them clergymen, could countenance the closure of churches and the amalgamation of parishes, but they could not accept the idea of accepting as their fellow ministers men who had not been ordained by bishops. To repeat, then, the party type of religious commitment involves a sense of belonging through attachment to the symbolic significance of an institution such as traditional beliefs, customary practices and principles of authority. The symbols are not concrete objects or particular places, but a complex institution and ideology.

Yet a third type of commitment is implied when a person answers the question 'Which church do you belong to?' by saying something like, 'Well, I go to the Methodist church.' What is implied is a provisional and qualified attitude to a particular congregation or denomination which suggests a *pragmatic* type of commitment. Although the ecumenical consequences of this type of commitment are less positive, it would be a mistake to overlook it since it characterizes a significant proportion of the church-going population; a proportion which, moreover, is unlikely to diminish. It may arise in at least two distinct ways. It may be, for example, that in some area a devoted group of Congregationalists, with a local type of commitment, has shrunk in numbers to such an extent that their church has had to be closed or demolished. The remaining members then go to the neighbouring Baptist church, say, as the one which is least dissimilar. While becoming formal members of that congregation, they continue to think of themselves, either singly or corporately, as perpetual visitors, and are thought of as such by members of the other congregation. Their sense of religious belonging remains unchanged, probably because of a lifelong connection with their Congregational chapel, but they are permanent exiles in a friendly church which none the less cannot be home. The same situation can arise when a person moves to another area, as when a member of the Scottish Free Church moves to England and has to accept membership of a Nonconformist church there, foreign and uncongenial though it may be, as better than nothing at all.[10] For a person thus placed his pragmatic commitment has no ecumenical consequences; since his principal feeling is one of homesickness, he will be detached from any ecumenical proposals.

An identical type of commitment, which is likely to become increasingly common, can occur in quite different circumstances. In some recent research a woman respondent, when asked, 'Do you have any religion?' replied by saying:

> 'No religion really. Tend to go to Catholic because my husband is, but mother's Protestant and father's Jewish. I was brought up in Jewish religion.'[11]

Had the woman said that she was a member of the Catholic Church her membership would have implied a pragmatic commitment, and the same applies to those who attend a particular church because of a spouse's commitment, because it happens to be the nearest to home, or for any other extraneous reason. As before, the attitude to ecumenical proposals is one of detachment and non-involvement since it is a matter of no consequence.

It has been necessary to summarize these different types of religious commitment because without some prior knowledge of what church membership means to different people, it is impossible to understand how the present widespread interest in church unity has arisen. Such notions as 'compromise' have no meaning unless one first knows what church people regard as sufficiently significant to warrant the use of the word. For some people it is the integrity of the local church which is of vital concern, for others it is the integrity of the denomination as a wider institution, while for still others ecumenism matters little. Clearly, many of those who support various schemes of reunion must be prepared to set aside certain things which matter to them deeply and be willing to acquiesce in the loss of some symbol which previously had a profound significance for them. Writing about the u.s.a., David Moberg suggested that there are three ways in which this can happen:

> One is the *dogmatic* argument that divine authority has revealed an unchanging pattern; all churches ought to accept and enter into this sole authentic version of unity. Roman Catholics, many Anglo-Catholics, and the Eastern Orthodox hold this view, each

claiming to be the only valid centre for the reunion of Christendom. The second is *pragmatic*, emphasizing the practical need for churches to unite and exert a stronger influence. The rank and file of Protestantism tends to take this view. There are many *idealistic* interpretations. Some, like the Protestant Episcopal Church, find a strong sanction for unity in the ideal of continuity. Others are convinced that division, which is the alternative to union, involves weakness, waste and more seriously, an inherently divisive spirit and unkind deeds.[12]

The first reason for reunion which Moberg mentions can hardly be said to lead to genuinely ecumenical relations, but it is an accurate statement of one possible stance. As a Vatican document of 1928 put it, 'There is but one way in which the unity of Christ may be fostered, and that is by furthering the return to the one true Church of Christ of those who are separated from it.'[13] That remains the formal position of the Roman Catholic Church although it has been greatly modified, in a manner characteristic of that church, by the promulgation of other statements which, when taken together, constitute a much less dogmatic position, without actually revoking any earlier statement. Both the second and the third of Moberg's motivations amount to the acknowledgement by the parties to an ecumenical adventure of an ideal or a value to which they are willing to accord supreme importance. Each party to any such agreement must be willing to accept some new, common pattern of belief, and to alter their former doctrine and polity so that it becomes consonant with it. In this way no church is required to say that it was wrong and another was right, but all agree together that they were partially wrong and that the newly agreed formula is a better statement of the truth. This device saves any church from losing face by making concessions to another.

This process is carried on at two different levels. It is obvious in working documents used in negotiations and in finally agreed formulae; the ideals which are shared by those who initiate ecumenical discussions are rarely articulated in any formal way, however, and while they are often difficult to discover they are of much greater significance for an understanding of the process. Given the difference between independent religious traditions, the practical problem is to discover the way in which contact is established, the occasions of contact and the persons who established it. But all the time the effective constraints which are operative must be borne in mind, whether they be the importance of a denominational tradition or the sacredness of local churches.

There have been a number of factors which have promoted ecumenical contacts, some of them specific and easy to document, others more general and difficult to disentangle from wider social processes. Four factors will be considered briefly here as being of particular importance, in order of increasing generality. In the first place, the clergy and ministers in all churches have played a key role in ecumenism; it is they who have led the ecumenical movement and who have been mainly responsible for negotiating the terms on which reunions have been attempted. Bryan Wilson has argued very forcibly that their role has been crucial in the propagation of ecumensim.[14] He points out that the clergy have often been more than mere leaders of such movements: they have been the movement's rank and file as well. Clerical enthusiasm has indeed been important, and he is probably correct in supposing that ministers enthuse because they are ministers, rather than because they are motivated by the same feelings and attitudes which they share with their lay people but experience more strongly. It is a mistake, however, to begin by asking why clergy are so enthusiastic about ecumenism, for reasons are usually the last things to emerge from a sociological analysis. Rather, we should start by asking what situations have led clergy to think in terms of co-operation with other churches. The layman normally meets only those who are committed to the same religious group as he is himself so far as any matters of religious significance are concerned. In his day-to-day secular occupations he spends time with people who do not share his religious commitment, and his interaction with these people is conducted on the basis of shared secular values and ideas. If a situation arises which, for him, has religious implications, it will remain a private experience, for to interpose his religious perspective would be to violate the perceptions he shares with his fellows, which are secular. Violations take place, of course, but they are attended by sanctions and the offender will be branded as a religious fanatic or a Bible-thumper and thereafter treated accordingly. It should be noted that the imputed fanaticism consists not in the offender's religious commitment but in his breach of shared values by introducing his alien perception.[15] Religion for the layman is a private matter for most of the time, and it becomes a shared, public way of experiencing and communicating only within the religious group, or some sub-group such as a man's own family.

Exceptions to this general rule exist which would be worthy of micro-sociological analysis such as, for example, the place of a recognized religious department within an otherwise secular organization such as a television company. The minister's religion, by contrast, is a matter of public knowledge, unless he deliberately mixes in society *incognito*, but much of his time is spent within the religious group. The minister who serves a group of people who are locally committed will spend much more time than they do with members of the same denomination who belong to different churches, and this, as well as his periodic movement from congregation to congregation, will help to engender a sense of commitment to the denomination rather than to the local church. In addition to this most clergy now come into contact with clergy of other denominations. When communications were less rapid such contacts were infrequent, particularly in England where the clergy of the established church were isolated by social barriers from nonconformist ministers, who were of lower social status, and from Catholic priests, who were Irish immigrants or eccentric aristocrats or – worst of all – converts.

In certain special situations, however, contact with clergy of other churches was not unusual, especially for those working abroad in foreign missions. When two ministers of different churches met the mere fact of their meeting was in itself an ecumenical event. It could not avoid being so, for since both lived in publicly religious worlds their respective worlds could only be kept apart by playing a kind of charade. Furthermore, the clergy of all the churches were abroad for the same ostensible purpose of rescuing the natives from the darkness of the heathen night and failure to co-operate in a common endeavour meant that their shared purpose was to that extent less effectively prosecuted. It was at these informal meetings, which could be called ecumenical only in the purely descriptive sense that more than one church was represented, but not in the sense that any ideas of church unity were involved, which led eventually to the Edinburgh conference of 1910. From the ecumenical activities of missionaries grew the self-conscious desire for reunion which we describe as ecumenism.

In England some contact between clergy of different churches has for some time been inevitable. Since the late nineteenth century chaplains to the armed forces have been of different denominations, as also have chaplains to hospitals and then, gradually, to many other types of institution. Such chaplaincies are not unlike missionary situations, in which some contact is inevitable and the aims of the churches are held in common. Finally the renewed concern in the post-war period with such issues as world poverty, disarmament and race relations has led to the formation of groups and organizations to articulate these concerns which from the beginning have been unselfconsciously ecumenical. Currie alleges that 'ecumenical projects are interpreted in lofty terms of "mission", with little reference to their specific motivation and origin'.[16] The specific motivation and origin of much that was to become ecumenical in fact lay in other concerns, of which 'mission' was one of the earliest and most important.

The concerns which brought the clergy of different churches together did not override the importance of their separate religious commitments, but they were occasions on which contact was made between overtly religious persons, and therefore between different religious worlds, where no such contact had formerly existed. Often, the result was that they discovered that the differences which divided them were much less wide when they discussed them together than they had supposed when they only imagined or read about them. Wilson suggests that ecumenism has become a concern because clergy are anxious to improve their collective status. The part played by the clergy in increased ecumenical co-operation seems to have been more fortuitous than that, for the motives which have led them to pursue ecumenism with such an obsessive concern have been diverse. Some take part in ecumenical talks convinced that no reunion will come about and determined to prevent any; others take part in the hope, often expressed in grandiloquent language, of helping to solve the problems of a divided world; yet others, no doubt, take part with an eye to their own career prospects. When some clergy in England are drawing benefits from the Ministry of Social Security there is as much concern with subsistence as with status. The concern for reunion between churches is nevertheless a predominantly clerical phenomenon, and something, moreover, with which the lay members of their churches often disagree. Those clergy whose congregations are opposed to ecumenism because it would close local churches often have a radically different idea of what church membership means than have their laity, to whose wishes and feelings they can be sadly, sometimes cruelly indifferent. Division of opinion between ministers and laity of this kind has been well illustrated in the Methodist Church, both in the past, as shown by

G

Currie, and in the present also.[17] Those clergy whose congregations are opposed to ecumenism because it would deprive them of the church which they feel to be distinctively theirs often fail to realize that their own contact with clergy of other churches has reduced their exclusive loyalty to their own church, with the result that they become insensitive to the honest loyalty of their laity, which they often despise. From all this it is clear that it is the clergy and church leaders who have been largely responsible for the ecumenical movement, and that while there have been many reasons for this, it has often expressed a simple desire to create a formal organizational unity where practical ecumenical co-operation has already been experienced.

A second factor favouring the growth of ecumenism is seen in the changes in theological thought which have recently been taking place at an accelerating pace. Rodney Stark and Charles Glock have written that:

> In part, the ecumenical dream rests on the assumption that Christians are reaching a common theological outlook that the old differences have lost much of their force. In this view contemporary denominationalism is an organizational rather than a theological affair.[18]

From the data they have gathered in surveys in the U.S.A. they have drawn an analysis which suggests that 'such a view is superficial'. What has happened, rather, is that old theological disputes over such questions as predestination, infant baptism and prayers for the dead, which once divided denominations, have become much less important. In their place new disputes have arisen, which have split denominations and even congregations into partisan groups, and thereby made established church divisions appear comparatively unimportant to those who are concerned with these new issues. Such evidence as we have from survey research conducted in the U.S.A., although it is far from satisfactory, suggests that the new disputes often divide 'clergy and laity within a denomination',[19] thus aggravating further the separation which has just been noted. The short-term effect of these new disputes is to polarize people into radicals and conservatives depending on whether they sympathize with this questioning and re-evaluation of traditional beliefs or whether they react by reasserting more vehemently than ever the truth of the traditional religious symbols which they have received. This polarization has immediate ecumenical repercussions. On the one hand the radicals read writers with whose ideas they sympathize without reference to denominational affiliation and become generally careless of established religious boundaries. Conservatives, on the other hand, whom one would expect to retreat more defensively than ever within their own churches and denominations, appear to be distressed and anxious, sometimes to the point of panic. Far from defending their religious world passively, in many places they have adopted attack as the best method of defence. The absolute and unchanging truth of religious and moral ideas emerges as having higher priority than particular embodiments of that truth, and we find support coming from otherwise quietly unassuming people for such movements as the Billy Graham Evangelistic Crusades and the Festival of Light,[20] which are not so much evangelizing movements as movements to express solidarity in the old revivalist tradition.[21]

Changes in theological thought, then, tend to promote ecumenism both directly through fostering interdenominational theological debate, and indirectly through ecumenical reassertion of the threatened traditional religion and morality. In the long term this latter response will probably be seen as a very transitory phenomenon, and the radical theology itself will either be overtaken by the fulfilment of its own prophecies, or will meet an alternative fate which Peter Berger has foreseen:

> The probable fate of secular theology, once its appeal as the *dernier cri* in religion has passed, would then be its absorption into the legitimating apparatus of the institution (which, incidentally, is exactly what happened with classical liberalism). We strongly suspect that this process of neutralization is already taking place as these 'challenging new insights' are integrated in various ecclesiastical programs. In this process, there is nothing to prevent the 'death of God' from becoming but another program emphasis, which, if properly administered, need not result in undue disturbance in the ongoing life of the institution.[22]

Although it would obviously be wrong to suppose that theological thought is simply the product of the society in which it emerges, it is equally wrong to ignore completely the social context of any intellectual trend. Perhaps the most significant aspect of the wider social changes for recent religious developments has been the declining importance of some traditional secular divisions within society. The possibility of interaction across social boundaries which were formerly sacrosanct, whether national, ethnic or class boundaries played a vital role in promoting both the meeting of clergy from different denominations and also the exchange of theological ideas, both of which, as we have tried to show, have had implications for the development of ecumenism.

This decline in the importance of traditional social distinctions of a purely secular kind must itself be considered as the third factor contributing directly to the growth of ecumenism, although the effects have often been felt in a complex variety of ways. In his analysis of the origins of denominational fragmentation in the u.s.a., Richard Niebuhr wrote of the 'churches of the disinherited', pointing to the way in which many churches had grown out of a working-class milieu, for the lower social strata had been effectively excluded from the established churches of the affluent.[23] It has been argued that if religious differentiation had its origins in social differentiation, then the relative homogeneity of contemporary society will have the reverse effect, and promote ecumenism.[24] But even if it were possible to accept that today's society is more homogeneous than it was in the past (which it is not) the process would still require a good deal of explication. The process may be seen at work in a number of different ways. Where a religious group grew up in a particular social context some of the elements of its religious symbolism will have been appropriate to that context, speaking with special force to that particular social condition. Thus the experience of chronic material deprivation may find a religious response in an emphasis on the rewards which may be expected in the kingdom of heaven by those who have been poor on earth. The example is crude, but actual religious traditions have evolved in which the complexes of symbols are subtly appropriate to the conditions of their adherents. Once established, religious traditions acquire their own dynamic, and symbols persist long after the experiences of life to which they were appropriate have passed away. Whereas once these symbols had embodied the experience of a group of people and expressed in a uniquely real way their hopes and fears and aspirations, they end up as disembodied shells. In a living tradition the religion alters to express the different experiences of subsequent generations of be-lievers. But religious evolution is slow. It may often be overtaken by history, and when this happens a religion may become an empty set of symbols in its native land.

The same thing can happen even more readily when a religion is exported to a foreign land.[25] In the past there have been remarkable groups like the native Indian members of the Scottish Original Seceders in the Central Provinces of India, who had 'never been in Scotland, were in no sense original and knew nothing about secession'.[26] But it is the less spectacular examples which best illustrate the disembodiment of religious traditions in foreign lands. The Baptist Church in the U.S.A. was split into separate denominations in the northern and southern states of the east coast states, and each sent its respective missionaries to the frontier states in the west. There they both met the Disciples of Christ, a denomination indigenous to the frontier. In the course of time the Northern Baptists and the Southern Baptists met in the west and found they had much in common, while their brethren back east remained separated; on the other hand the Northern Baptists and Southern Baptists in the east both thought themselves similar to the Disciples of Christ, whom their respective brethren in the west thought entirely different.[27] Disembodiment, which can occur in a native situation when a religious tradition fails to evolve as rapidly as the secular environment, becomes almost inevitable when a new religion arrives in a foreign land and the change in environment is instantaneous.

Disembodied religious traditions may persist for many generations through sheer inertia. They may even persist long enough to find new groups of adherents for whom the symbols will again come to life. While they survive, however, they remain weak and there will be little opposition to ecumenical co-operation or reunion. With clerical leadership, the rank-and-file members will resist ecumenism only out of stubbornness or independence, and not because of any religious convictions.

Unlike the contact between clergy of different churches and the changes in theological thought, both of which positively encourage ecumenism, the changes in secular society which render religious differences obsolete do no more than remove barriers to it. To portray this third factor in anything but negative terms would be misleading. The writers who argue that ecumenism springs directly from religious weakness assume too easily that the positive factors arise in response to this weakness, whereas it seems nearer the truth to say that it is the simultaneous but independent occurrence of certain factors encouraging ecumenical activity, and of others making it less objectionable, which together promote ecumenism. Peter Berger's analysis of 'ecumenicity' provides an elegant and attractive account of the movement towards reunion, but he, too, assumes that an explanation of what makes ecumenism possible can also serve as an explanation of why reunions take place.[28] Berger introduces the notion of pluralism as a key variable in his analysis to describe a situation in which many religious traditions co-exist in a single society without any one of them being accorded a pre-eminent position. In a pluralist society no religion remains profoundly true for people, in the sense that it is related to their total experience of life – in Berger's terms each religion lacks a 'plausibility structure'. Each religious tradition alike offers something which is less than totally convincing and credible to any of its adherents. Religious pluralism, particularly as found in North America, is part of a wider pluralism which characterizes the whole social structure. In western capitalist societies the movement towards pluralism is an integral part of advancing industrialism, for it arises out of the 'free' movement of population.[29] If resources are to be exploited in the most economical way then industry must be sited conveniently and the labour force move continually. The constant movement which results has the effect of breaking down the old structures, both in local communities and also in wider communities based on social class and ethnicity, within which religious traditions had previously flourished. Continuing modernization in the West is thus responsible for the erosion of traditional social boundaries which had been of religious as well as of secular significance. The positive consequences, which are important for an understanding of ecumenism and which constitute the fourth factor, are no less obvious, for something which might be very loosely termed a 'world civilization' begins to emerge. As Roger Mehl has written, contrasting traditional science and modern technology:

> Particular societies owe their existence to the great diversity of technology and to the beliefs which support and reinforce it. Although science has been universal for centuries, the awareness of this universality was the possession of a few élites, which, moreover, were concentrated in a very limited part of the world. Technology, on the contrary, has given birth to the means of its own universalization. By creating extremely rapid modes of transportation and communication, by giving birth to techniques of information that permit every man always to be the contemporary of his fellow men, technology has opened the paths of penetration through the diversity of cultures.[30]

Such a development is incompatible with the continuing life of religious traditions whose diversity has in large part been made possible by the diversity of experience of discrete groups of people within society. The experiences which have become universal throughout what used to be called Christendom, such as exposure to the same newsreel films of men on the moon, are doubly universal since they are no longer mediated through traditional religious communities, each of which might have provided its own interpretation. Hence the unique experiences which gave life to correspondingly unique traditions of religious symbols are undermined by experiences which are increasingly universal. The process is halted only where a religious group, by forbidding the use of such things as television and 'heathen' newspapers, is able to preserve that interpretation of experience which is mediated through itself. At the same time as religious traditions thus become less compellingly real they also move closer together, since widespread contact is unavoidable. As Moberg has said:

> As the world 'shrinks' through improved transportation, religious organizations are brought closer to one another, and co-operation is thrust upon them. The ecumenical movement can be explained partly as an outgrowth of the same forces that brought the United Nations into being.[31]

This explanation is very incomplete, of course, but the general context of technology in the West is essential to an understanding of how a plurality of disembodied religious traditions has come into existence. Disembodiment is entailed in the much wider process of modernization.

Modernization, which is a shorthand term for the social effects of scientific and technical innovations, has had two independent consequences for the religious traditions of the West. By breaking down established social groups it has resulted both in the decline of the real credibility of discrete traditions of religious symbolism, and also in the blurring of the traditional boundaries between religio-social groups. The first result may be termed secularization, and the second ecumenism; but they are independent results and neither can be adduced as the cause of the other. Ecumenism develops when a variety of religions cease to be distinctively credible and, as Berger said, there would have been a 'crisis in credibility brought on by pluralism as a social-structural phenomenon, quite apart from its linkage with the "carriers" of secularization'.[32] Only by using the expression 'secularization' to mean one aspect of the process of modernization, rather than as a description of some of its effects, can it be accorded causal status.

Whether or not ecumenism and secularization, in this limited sense, are aspects of the final decline in the viability of religious symbolism *per se*, which would be true secularization, is an empirical question. To answer that question would lead us back to an examination of what should count as specifically *religious* symbolism. The problem of what religion really is constitutes the principal focus of interest for the social scientific study of religion and every specific problem in the analysis of religion leads back to it in the end.

Notes and References

Notes to 1. Sociology and Religion

1. The prominent position occupied by the Jews may be seen as, at least in part, a fruitful consequence of the constant encounter between their own jealously preserved culture and that of the gentile western tradition.
2. The expression, 'religion and society', which is unusual in England but familiar enough as the title of courses in American universities, may perhaps become a useful equivalent to the German *Religionswissenschaft*, for which no English translation has been found and for which 'history of religions' has been so unsatisfactory an equivalent.
3. Passim, but see especially 'A new humanism' and 'Crisis and renewal', reprinted in Mircea Eliade, *The Quest: History and Meaning in Religion* (Chicago and London: University of Chicago Press, 1969).
4. Peter L. Berger, *The Social Reality of Religion* (London, Faber and Faber, 1969), pp. 100 & 180; the phrase 'methodological atheism' is that of his former pupil Anton C. Zijderveld.
5. Eliade, op. cit., p. 62.
6. The present use is an extension of Weber's meaning, for he spoke of persons being '*differently qualified* in a religious way' and of the tendency for status stratification to form on this basis; see H. H. Gerth and C. Wright Mills (eds.), *From Max Weber* (London, Routledge and Kegan Paul, 1948), p. 287.
7. Particularly what has come to be known as the Winchian problem, q.v. articles by Winch, MacIntyre and Lukes in Bryan R. Wilson (ed.), *Rationality* (Oxford, Basil Blackwell, 1970).
8. See Ernest Gellner, 'The entry of the philosophers', *Times Literary Supplement,* 4 April 1968.
9. Robert N. Bellah, 'Review of *Love's Body* by Norman O. Brown', reprinted in Bellah, *Beyond Belief* (New York, Harper and Row, 1970), p. 234.
10. E. E. Evans-Pritchard, *Theories of Primitive Religion* (London, Oxford University Press, 1965), pp. 7 & 109.
11. Leo Steinberg, quoted by Clifford Geertz in 'Religion as a cultural

system' in Michael Banton (ed.), *Anthropological Approaches to the Study of Religion* (London, Tavistock Publications, 1966), p. 2.

12. The relationship of hermeneutics to recent methodological departures in sociology, especially ethnomethodology, is mentioned below, p. 158.

13. Kingsley Davis, *Human Society* (New York, Macmillan, 1948), pp. 536f.

14. Also variously known as pastoral studies, *Kirchliche Sozialforschung* and *sociologie religieuse*.

15. Louis Schneider (ed.), *Religion, Culture and Society* (New York, John Wiley, 1964), p. 374. Cf. the views in Michael Hill, *A Sociology of Religion* (London, Heinemann, 1973).

16. Cf. C. Wright Mills, *The Sociological Imagination* (New York, Oxford University Press, 1959), pp. 76ff.

17. Cf. John H. Goldthorpe et al., *The Affluent Worker*, Vol. 1: *Industrial Attitudes and Behaviour* (Cambridge, Cambridge University Press, 1968), pp. 150ff.

18. F. Boulard, *An Introduction to Religious Sociology* (London, Darton, Longman and Todd, 1960), p. 3.

19. Introduction to Norman Birnbaum and Gertrud Lenzer (eds), *Sociology and Religion* (Englewood Cliffs, N.J., Prentice-Hall, 1968), p. 16; see the present author's review of this volume in *Sociology*, Vol. 4, 1970, pp. 121f.

20. Gabriel le Bras, 'Problèmes de la sociologie des religions' in G. Gurvitch (ed.), *Traité de sociologie*, II, 1960, translated in Birnbaum and Lenzer, op. cit., p. 437.

21. Cf. Robert Towler, 'The role of the clergy' in Nicholas Lash and Joseph Rhymer (eds), *The Christian Priesthood* (London, Darton, Longman and Todd, 1970).

22. The 'true believer' who abandons one total world-view only to adopt another has been characterized – or, rather, caricatured – in a disagreeable book of the same title (Eric Hoffer, *The True Believer* (New York, Harper and Brothers, 1951)), said to have been favourite reading of ex-President Eisenhower (*Time*, 15 March 1963).

23. Robert Murray SJ, 'Tradition as a criterion of unity' in John Kent and Robert Murray (eds), *Church Membership and Intercommunion* (London, Darton, Longman and Todd, 1973).

24. See below, chapter 9.

25. Peter L. Berger, *A Rumor of Angels* (Garden City, N.Y., Doubleday, 1969), chapter 1.

26. These 'signals of transcendence', as Berger calls them (op. cit., pp. 65ff.), bear a certain resemblance to what I. T. Ramsey termed 'cosmic disclosures'; the objection that even a universally experienced need tells us

nothing about the necessary existence of its possible satisfaction was answered in a characteristic manner by C. S. Lewis (I. T. Ramsey, *Models and Mystery* (London, Oxford University Press, 1964), pp. 58ff.; C. S. Lewis, 'The weight of glory', in *They Asked for a Paper*, (London, Geoffrey Bles, 1962)).

27. Robert Bellah, in what has already become a celebrated paper delivered to a plenary session of a conference of the Society for the Scientific Study of Religion and the American Academy of Religion in October 1969 at Harvard, published as 'Christianity and symbolic realism', *Journal for the Scientific Study of Religion*, Vol. 9, 1970, p. 93.

28. Harmondsworth, Middlesex, Penguin Books, 1961, p. 62.

29. Bellah, loc. cit.

30. Eliade, op. cit., pp. 4ff.

31. Monica Wilson, *Religion and the Transformation of Society* (London, Cambridge University Press, 1971), especially pp. 52–75.

32. Eliade, op. cit., p. 73.

33. This is not to say that the statement could not become meaningful if it were once used and spontaneously accepted as meaningful by others, for this would be an example of religious innovation; cf. Wilson, op. cit., pp. 57ff.

34. W. Percy, 'The symbolic structure of interpersonal process', *Psychiatry*, Vol. 24, 1961, pp. 39–52.

35. Geertz, op. cit., pp. 37f.

36. Bellah, *Beyond Belief*, p. 233.

37. Ibid.

38. A tendency towards élitism is apparent elsewhere amongst contemporary religious visionaries, as in J. A. T. Robinson, *The Difference in Being a Christian Today* (London, Fontana Books, 1972).

39. G. Santayana, *The Life of Man* (London, Constable, 1905–6), quoted as an epigraph in Geertz, op. cit.

40. See, inter alia, Roland Robertson, *A Sociological Interpretation of Religion* (Oxford, Basil Blackwell, 1970), pp. 34–51; J. Milton Yinger, *The Scientific Study of Religion* (London, Collier-Macmillan, 1970), pp. 3–16.

41. Cf. Carl G. Hempel, 'Fundamentals of concept formation in empirical science', *International Encyclopedia of Unified Science*, Vol. 2, no. 7, p. 2.

42. Edward B. Tylor, *Primitive Culture* (London, John Murray, 1871); for a recent defence, see Jack Goody, 'Religion and ritual: the definitional problem', *British Journal of Sociology*, Vol. 12, 1961, pp. 142–64.

43. Melford E. Spiro, 'Religion: problems of definition and explanation' in Banton, op cit., p. 96.

44. A useful distinction, albeit an obvious one, underlined by W. G.

Runciman, 'The sociological explanation of "religious" beliefs',
European Journal of Sociology, Vol. 10, 1969, pp. 149f.

45. Talcott Parsons, *The Social System* (London, Routledge and Kegan
Paul, 1951), pp. 367ff.
46. Geertz, op. cit., p. 4.
47. Berger, *The Social Reality of Religion*, p. 39 et passim.
48. The boundary drawn by Gurvitch, who is not interested primarily in
religion, is made complex through the modification of his fundamental
notion of types of knowledge by the introduction of forms of knowledge
as a separate concept; see Georges Gurvitch, *The Social Frameworks of
Knowledge* (Oxford, Basil Blackwell, 1971), chapter 4.
49. 'We say that the granary collapsed because its supports were eaten away
by termites. That is the cause that explains the collapse of the granary.
We also say that people were sitting under it at the time because it was
in the heat of the day and they thought that it would be a comfortable
place to talk and work. This is the cause of the people being under the
granary at the time it collapsed. To our minds the only relationship
between these independently caused facts is their coincidence in time
and space. We have no explanation of why the two chains of causation
intersected at a certain time and in a certain place, for there is no inter-
dependence between them. Zande philosophy can supply the missing
link . . . Witchcraft explains the coincidence of these two happenings.'
E. E. Evans-Pritchard, *Witchcraft, Oracles and Magic among the
Azande* (Oxford, The Clarendon Press, 1937), p. 70.

Notes to 2. The First Inheritance

1. See, inter alia, Talcott Parsons, *Essays in Sociological Theory* (London,
Collier-Macmillan, rev. ed. 1954), pp. 197–211; Birnbaum and Lenzer,
op. cit., pp. 1–16.
2. Talcott Parsons, *The Structure of Social Action* (London, Collier-
Macmillan, 2nd ed. 1949), pp. 149ff.
3. F. Max Müller, *Lectures on the Origin and Growth of Religion* (The
Hibbert Lectures, 1878) (London, Longmans, Green, 1880), p. 177.
Concerning the precursor of all specific forms of divinity, Müller wrote:
'before the separation of the Aryan race, before the existence of Sanskrit,
Greek or Latin, before the gods of the Veda had been worshipped, and
before there was a sanctuary of Zeus among the sacred oaks of Dodona,
the supreme Deity had been found, had been named, had been invoked
by the ancestors of our race by a name which has never been excelled
by any other name, Dyaus, Zeus, Jupiter, Tyr, – all meaning originally
light and brightness.' (*Introduction to the Science of Religion* (London,

Longmans, Green, 1893, first published 1870)). The proposed origin of the category of deity in the word denoting 'the bright sky' is a typical example of the naturists' practice, mentioned below, of tracing back later divinities, through philology to immediately sensible things.

4. Herbert Spencer, *The Principles of Sociology* (London, Williams and Norgate, 1893–7).

5. Op. cit.

6. Evans-Pritchard, *Theories of Primitive Religion*, p. 23.

7. Op. cit., p. 24.

8. Tylor, op. cit., Vol. I, p. 428.

9. R. R. Marett, *The Threshold of Religion* (London, Methuen, 4th ed., 1929), p. xxxi.

10. James G. Frazer, *The Golden Bough* (London, Macmillan, 2nd ed. in 3 vols, 1900), Vol. III, pp. 458ff.

11. Lucien Lévy-Bruhl, *How Natives Think* (London, George Allen and Unwin, 1926), pp. 367f and 381ff.

12. Sigmund Freud, *Civilization and Its Discontents* (The International Psycho-Analytical Library, ed. Ernest Jones, No. 17) (London, The Hogarth Press, 1955) (first published 1930), p. 23.

13. Preface to Theodore Reik, *Probleme der Religionspsychologie* (1919), quoted in Ernest Jones, *Sigmund Freud* (London, The Hogarth Press, 1957), vol. III, pp. 379f.

14. J. J. Atkinson, 'Primal law', supplement to Andrew Lang, *Social Origins* (London, Longmans, 1903), cited in Evans-Pritchard, op. cit., p. 42n.

15. Jones, op. cit., p. 393.

16. Cf. Wilhelm Schmidt, *The Origin and Growth of Religion* (London, Methuen, 1931), p. 114.

17. Sigmund Freud, *The Future of an Illusion* (The International Psycho-Analytical Library, ed. John D. Sutherland, No. 15) (London, Hogarth Press, 1962) (first published 1927), p. 26.

18. Jones, loc. cit.: 'We cannot refrain from wondering how Freud when nearing his end came to be so engrossed in [religious questions] and to devote to them all his intellectual interest during the last five years of his life.'

19. Quoted, op. cit., p. 377.

20. *Civilization and Its Discontents*, pp. 23f.

21. Preface to the Hebrew edition of *Totem und Tabu*, in the English translation, *Totem and Taboo: Some Points of Agreement between the Mental Lives of Savages and Neurotics* (London, Routledge and Kegan Paul, 1950) (first published 1913), p. xi.

22. Philip Rieff, *The Mind of the Moralist* (New York, The Viking Press, 1959), p. 290.

23. Karl Marx, 'Contribution to the critique of Hegel's philosophy of right: Introduction' in T. B. Bottomore (trans. and ed.), *Karl Marx: Early Writings* (London, C. A. Watts, 1962), pp. 43f., emphases omitted.

24. 'Economic and philosophical manuscripts (1844), I' in Bottomore, op. cit., p. 121.

25. 'Contribution to the critique . . .', loc. cit.; Marx's inheritance from Hegel and Feuerbach has been discussed often and will not be rehearsed here: see, e.g., Birnbaum and Lenzer, op. cit., pp. 4f.

26. See Robert Bellah, *Beyond Belief*, pp. 3ff.

27. See Arthur O. Lovejoy, *The Great Chain of Being* (Cambridge, Mass., Harvard University Press, 1948).

28. 'Contribution to the critique . . .', loc. cit., emphases omitted.

29. 'Alienated labour' in Bottomore, op. cit., p. 125.

30. Op. cit., pp. 127ff.

31. Erich Fromm, 'The present human condition', *The American Scholar*, vol. 25, Winter 1955–6, reprinted in Fromm, *The Dogma of Christ and Other Essays on Religion, Psychology and Culture* (New York, Holt, Rinehart and Winston, 1963), pp. 95–104.

32. Mircea Eliade, *Cosmos and History* (New York, Harper and Row, 1959), p. 10 et passim.

33. 'Alienated labour', op. cit., p. 122.

34. Peter L. Berger and Thomas Luckmann, *The Social Construction of Reality* (London, Allen Lane The Penguin Press, 1967).

35. See Melvin Seeman, 'On the meaning of alienation', *American Sociological Review*, Vol. 24, 1959, pp. 783–91.

36. Friedrich Engels, letter to J. Bloch, Karl Marx and Friedrich Engels, *Selected Works* (London, Lawrence and Wishart, 1954, Vol. II), p. 443.

37. In Bottomore, op. cit., p. 5, emphases omitted.

38. See below, chapters 4 and 5.

39. Alvin W. Gouldner and Richard A. Peterson, *Notes on Technology and the Moral Order* (New York, Bobbs-Merrill, 1962).

40. P. 103.

41. 'Contribution to the critique . . .', loc. cit.

Notes to 3. Science, Magic and Religion

1. Talcott Parsons, *Essays in Sociological Theory*, p. 200.

2. Bronislaw Malinowski, *The Coral Gardens and their Magic* (London, George Allen and Unwin, 1935), Vol. II, p. 235.

3. Lucien Lévy-Bruhl, *How Natives Think* (London, George Allen and Unwin, 1926); *Primitive Mentality* (London, George Allen and Unwin, 1923).

4. Malinowski, *Magic, Science and Religion and Other Essays* (New York, Doubleday Anchor Books, 1954), p. 17 (the essay, 'Magic, science and religion', first published 1925).

5. Op. cit., pp. 30f.

6. Ibid., p. 87; cf. Parsons, op. cit., p. 203.

7. *Coral Gardens,* vol. II, p. 239.

8. Introduction to H. Ian Hogbin, *Law and Order in Polynesia* (London, Christophers, 1934).

9. *Magic, Science and Religion*, p. 32; the belief that the retraction of the penis is a cause of death, called *koro,* is cited in Ralph Linton, *Culture and Mental Disorders* (Springfield, Ill., Charles C. Thomas, 1956), pp. 67–9.

10. A. R. Radcliffe-Brown, *The Anderman Islanders* (New York, Free Press, 1964), chapter 5 (first published 1922); *Taboo* (Cambridge, Cambridge University Press, 1939).

11. *Coral Gardens,* I, p. 77.

12. Evans-Pritchard, *Witchcraft, Oracles and Magic among the Azande,* p. 464.

13. Ibid.

14. Peter Worsley, *The Trumpet Shall Sound* (London, MacGibbon and Kee, 2nd ed. 1968), p. xxvii.

15. Cf. George Herbert Mead, *Mind, Self and Society* (Chicago, University of Chicago Press, 1934).

16. Below, chapter 8.

17. *Coral Gardens,* loc. cit.

18. Evans-Pritchard, op. cit., p. 444.

19. *Magic, Science and Religion*, p. 88.

20. Op. cit., p. 90.

21. Ibid., p. 87.

22. Yinger, *The Scientific Study of Religion,* p. 71; quotation from John Middleton, *Magic, Witchcraft, and Curing* (Garden City, N.Y., The Natural History Press, 1967), p. ix.

23. William J. Goode, *Religion Among the Primitives* (New York, Free Press, 1951), pp. 50–4. As well as following the work of Malinowski, Goode draws also on Max Weber, who distinguished between magic and religion under the headings of 'cult' and 'sorcery', and who showed the distinctive roles of the priest and the magician as the respective practitioners of the two. The criticisms of Malinowski and Goode which are offered here could be extended to Weber although his work is considerably more sophisticated, as we see from his assertion that 'this contrast is fluid, as are all sociological phenomena. *Even the theoretical differentiae of these types are not unequivocally determinable.*' (Max Weber, *The Sociology of Religion,* trans. Ephraim Fischoff from the section

'Religionssoziologie' in *Wirtschaft und Gesellschaft* (Boston, Mass., The Beacon Press, 1963), p. 28, emphasis added.

24. Robin Horton, 'A definition of religion and its uses', *Journal of the Royal Anthropological Institute*, Vol. 90, 1960, pp. 201–26; for a summary of the criticisms made of Durkheim, see Imogen Seger, *Durkheim and His Critics on the Sociology of Religion* (New York, Bureau of Applied Social Research, Columbia University, 1957).

25. Cf. Worsley, op. cit., p. xxviiin.

26. See *Coral Gardens*, passim.

27. Op. cit., I, p. 95f.

28. Ibid., p. 233.

29. Revision of ritual in recent years has generally been in the direction of simpler rites. Many practices which originated as annual performances (like baptismal initiation) became weekly observances, and recent changes have attempted to revert to the customs of primitive Christianity by removing the accretions of many centuries.

30. The full complexity of the rubrics and other regulations is not material and some simplification is necessary to keep the account brief.

31. Alexander Cruden, *Complete Concordance to the Old and New Testaments* (London, Lutterworth Press, rev. ed. 1954). q.v. *salt*.

32. Genesis iii. 17f.

33. II Kings ii. 19–22.

34. John xvi. 23–7.

35. This is a free translation of the equivalent collect in the older Catholic tradition.

36. *Coral Gardens*, II, p. 253.

37. E. R. Leach (ed.), *Dialectic in Practical Religion* (Cambridge, Cambridge University Press, 1966), p. 1; cf. Robertson, *The Sociological Interpretation of Religion*, pp. 47ff.

Notes to 4. The Durkheimian Tradition

1. For the immediate influences on Durkheim's thought, see, inter alia, Robert A. Nisbet, *Emile Durkheim* (Englewood Cliffs, N.J., Prentice-Hall, 1965); and Raymond Aron, *Main Currents in Sociological Thought*, Vol. II (Harmondsworth, Middlesex, Penguin Books, 1970).

2. Emile Durkheim, *The Elementary Forms of the Religious Life* (New York, Collier Books, 1961), (first published 1912), pp. 21 and 15.

3. Ibid., p. 44; Tylor, *Primitive Culture*, I, p. 424.

4. The literature on totemism is vast, but for a recent discussion in the Durkheimian tradition and a short bibliography, see Claude Lévi-Strauss, *Totemism* (London, Merlin Press, 1964).

5. Evans-Pritchard, *Theories of Primitive Religion*, p. 58.
6. Durkheim, op. cit., pp. 126ff.
7. Ibid., p. 166, quoting L. Fison and A. W. Howitt, *Kamilaroi and Kurnai* (Melbourne, G. Robertson, 1880), p. 170.
8. Ibid., p. 236.
9. Ibid., p. 469.
10. Ibid., p. 471.
11. Ibid., p. 297; cf. Berger, *The Social Reality of Religion*, chapter 1.
12. Durkheim, op. cit., p. 62.
13. Cf. Evans-Pritchard, op. cit., p. 54.
14. Ibid., p. 57.
15. '*Les phénomènes dits religieux consistent en croyances obligatoires, connexes de pratiques définies qui se rapportent à des objets donnés dans ces croyances. – Quant à la religion, c'est un ensemble, plus ou moins organisé et systématisé, de phénomènes de ce genre.*' *L'Année sociologique*, Vol. 2, 1899, pp. 22f.
16. Ibid., p. 21 n2; *Elementary Forms*, Book 1, chapter 1, § 4.
17. Ibid., p. 58nn.
18. Ibid., p. 59.
19. Ibid., Book 2, chapter 7, § 3.
20. One of the central rites is to encourage the proliferation of the totemic animal or plant; see Book 3, chapter 2; cf. Book 3, chapter 4, § 2.
21. Ibid., pp. 251f.
22. Cf. ibid., Book 2, chapter 7, § 2; Edward Shils and Michael Young, 'The meaning of the coronation', *Sociological Review*, Vol. 1–2, 1953, pp. 63–81; Norman Birnbaum, 'Monarchs and sociologists: a reply to Professor Shils and Mr Young', *Sociological Review*, Vol. 3–4, 1955, pp. 5–23; Morris R. Cohen, *The Faith of a Liberal* (New York, Henry Holt, 1946), pp. 334ff.
23. Goody, 'Religion and ritual', p. 157.
24. Alexander A. Goldenweiser, 'Religion and society: a critique of Emile Durkheim's theory of the origin and nature of religion', *Journal of Philosophy, Psychology and Scientific Methods*, Vol. 12, 1917, cited in Evans-Pritchard, op. cit., p. 67.
25. Malinowski, *Magic, Science and Religion*, pp. 55–60.
26. Evans-Pritchard, op. cit., pp. 67f.
27. Parsons, *The Structure of Social Action*, pp. 436ff.
28. Evans-Pritchard, op. cit., p. 66.
29. *Elementary Forms*, p. 16.
30. Ibid., p. 332, emphases added.
31. For a contemporary application of this problem, see below, chapter 9.
32. Berger, op. cit., p. 45 et seq.
33. Guy E. Swanson, *The Birth of the Gods* (Ann Arbor, The University of Michigan Press, 1960).

34. Op. cit., pp. 3–6.
35. Monica Wilson, 'Witch beliefs and social structure', *American Journal of Sociology*, Vol. 56, 1951, p. 313, quoted in Swanson, op. cit., p. 138; cf. Wilson, *Religion and the Transformation of Society*, passim.
36. Clyde Kluckhohn, 'Navaho witchcraft', *Papers of the Peabody Museum of American Archeology and Ethnology*, Vol. 22, no. 2 (Harvard University), 1944, cited in Swanson, op. cit., p. 239, quoted, pp. 139–43.
37. Swanson, op. cit., p. 126.
38. Ibid., chapter 2.
39. Ibid., p. 147.
40. He uses thirty-nine in all: 24 social variables and 15 religious ones; see ibid., Appendix I, pp. 194–213.
41. Ibid., p. 65.
42. Cf. the review by Elizabeth Nottingham, *American Sociological Review*, Vol. 26, 1961, pp. 488f.
43. Cf. Evans-Pritchard's dictum, 'generalizations about "religion" are discreditable', quoted in Swanson, op. cit., p. viii.
44. Guy E. Swanson, *Religion and Regime* (Ann Arbor, The University of Michigan Press, 1967).
45. Mary Douglas, *Natural Symbols* (London, Barrie and Rockliffe, The Cresset Press, 1970); see also her *Purity and Danger* (London, Routledge and Kegan Paul, 1966).
46. *Natural Symbols*, p. x.
47. Ibid., p. 15; see Colin M. Turnbull, *Wayward Servants: the two worlds of the African pygmies* (London, Eyre and Spottiswood, 1965).
48. Basil Bernstein, 'A socio-linguistic approach to stratification' in Julius Gould (ed.), *Penguin Survey of the Social Sciences* (Harmondsworth, Middlesex, Penguin Books, 1966). While these categories are derived from Bernstein with ingenuity, it would be inaccurate to say, as did a reviewer, that they are *combined* with Bernstein's categories: *The Times Literary Supplement*, 14 May 1970.
49. *Natural Symbols*, p. 57; the dissimilarity from 'sovereign groups' is clear.
50. Based on Diagrams 5 and 6, op. cit., 59f.
51. Ibid., p. 57.
52. Below, chapter 7.
53. See *Natural Symbols*, pp. 62f.
54. Ibid., p. 64.

Notes to 5. Religion and Social Change

1. Max Weber, *The Religion of China, Confucianism and Taoism, Ancient Judaism, The Religion of India* (London, Collier-Macmillan, 1951, 1952,

1958) (first published, 1921); see also *The Sociology of Religion* (first published, 1922).

2. Reinhard Bendix, *Max Weber: An Intellectual Portrait* (London, Heinemann, 1960), p. 85, Max Weber, *The Protestant Ethic and the Spirit of Capitalism* (London, George Allen and Unwin, 1930) (first published, 1904–5).

3. *The Protestant Ethic*, chapter 5, note 119 (added for the 1920 edition).

4. 'Contribution to the critique . . .' in Bottomore, *Karl Marx: Early Writings*, p. 43.

5. Ibid., pp. 52f., emphases omitted; the confusion which usually results if Marx's grand prose is interpreted literally is apparent, since the German Reformation appears as a phenomenon affecting 'man'. For a recent discussion of Marx's writing which is relevant at this point see Arend Th. van Leeuwen, *Critique of Heaven* (London, Lutterworth Press, 1972).

6. *The Protestant Ethic*, pp. 90f.

7. 'In spite of this and the following remarks, which in my opinion are clear enough, and have never been changed, I have again and again been accused of this.' Ibid., chapter 3, note 91.

8. Monica Wilson, *Religion and the Transformation of Society*, p. 55.

9. *The Protestant Ethic*, p. 78.

10. See John M. Mecklin, 'The passing of the saint', *American Journal of Sociology*, Vol. 24, 1919, reprinted in the supplement to Vol. 60, 1954–5, pp. 34–53.

11. *The Protestant Ethic*, p. 181.

12. 'Though I may be sent to Hell for it, such a God will never command my respect' was Milton's comment on the doctrine (ibid., p. 101).

13. *Westminster Confession*, chapter 3, no. 5, quoted, ibid., p. 100.

14. Ibid., pp. 114f.

15. Ibid., p. 91; cf. Durkheim's use of the phrase with the same connotation of reciprocity, *Elementary Forms*, p. 174.

16. Bendix, op. cit., p. 84, and further, p. 85 n. 27.

17. See *The Protestant Ethic*, p. 86.

18. Ibid., chapter 3, note 8.

19. Max Thurian, *Marriage and Celibacy* (London, SCM Press, 1959), pp. 57ff.

20. Weber later added the qualification that he meant places of 'only Diaspora Calvinism' – see H. R. Trevor-Roper, *Religion, the Reformation and Social Change* (London, Macmillan, 1967), p. 20, n. 1.

21. See *The Protestant Ethic*, chapter 1, note 1; R. W. Green (ed.), *Protestantism and Capitalism: The Weber Thesis and Its Critics* (Boston, Mass., Heath, 1959); David Little, *Religion, Order, and Law* (Oxford, Basil Blackwell, 1970), Bibliographical essay A, pp. 226–37.

22. R. H. Tawney, *Religion and the Rise of Capitalism* (Harmondsworth, Middlesex, Pelican Books, 1972) (first edition 1926), especially chapter 4, note 32.

23. Tawney, Foreword to *The Protestant Ethic*, p. 10.

24. Ibid., p. 7.

25. Trevor-Roper, op. cit.

26. Ibid., p. 13.

27. Ibid., p. 19.

28. Ibid., pp. 19f.

29. Ibid., p. 25.

30. Ibid., p. 41.

31. Ibid., p. 27.

32. Robertson, *The Sociological Interpretation of Religion*, p. 178.

33. See Parsons, *The Structure of Social Action*, pp. 529ff. and 575ff. for a further discussion.

34. Trevor-Roper, op. cit., p. 24.

35. Michael Walzer, *The Revolution of the Saints* (London, Weidenfeld and Nicolson, 1966), p. 306.

36. Ibid., p. 20.

37. An important way in which Puritanism was spread was through magistracy: ibid., pp. 306f. et passim.

38. Quoted, ibid., pp. 310fn.

39. Ibid., pp. 308f.

40. John H. Randell, *The Making of the Modern Mind* (Boston, Mass., Houghton Mifflin, 1926), p. 36, quoted in Mecklin, *The Passing of the Saint* (Chicago, The University of Chicago Press, 1941), p. 147; cf. Arthur O. Lovejoy, *The Great Chain of Being* (Cambridge, Harvard University Press, 1936).

41. Johan Huizinga, *The Waning of the Middle Ages* (Harmondsworth, Middlesex, Pelican Books, 1972) (first edition 1924), p. 28.

42. For a discussion of some lower-class social movements of the Middle Ages and their significance, see Norman Cohn, *The Pursuit of the Millenium* (London, Secker and Warburg, 1957).

43. Norman O. Brown, in *Life Against Death* (London, Routledge and Kegan Paul, 1959), chapter 14, provides a valuable psychoanalytically informed account of Puritanism's appeal.

44. Little, op. cit., p. 127.

45. Ibid., p. 14.

46. *The Protestant Ethic*, p. 51.

47. Walzer, op. cit., p. 316; cf. *The Protestant Ethic*, pp. 181f.

48. Walzer, loc. cit.

49. Parsons, op. cit., p. 501.

50. Swanson, *Religion and Regime*, p. 44.

51. Ibid., p. 32; David Easton, 'An approach to the analysis of political systems', *World Politics*, Vol. 9, 1957, pp. 383–400.

52. Cf. Swanson's notion of sovereignty: above, p. 75.

53. Swanson, op. cit., p. 33.

54. Termed *gubernaculum*, after the medieval usage, and contrasted with *jurisdictio*.

55. See Swanson, op. cit., pp. 39f. and 198f.

56. Ibid., p. 231.

57. Loc. cit.

58. Ibid., p. 232.

59. David C. McClelland, *The Achieving Society* (Princeton, N. J., Van Nostrand, 1961).

60. Ibid., p. 45.

61. Loc. cit. for the results.

62. Ibid., pp. 340ff.; Marian Winterbottom, 'The relation of need for achievement to learning experiences in independence and mastery', in J. W. Atkinson (ed.), *Motives in Fantasy, Action, and Society* (Princeton, N.J., Van Nostrand, 1958), pp. 453–78.

63. McClelland, op. cit., p. 46.

64. Ibid., p. 47.

65. Ibid., p. 334.

66. Friedrich Nietzsche, *The Birth of Tragedy and the Genealogy of Morals*, trans. Francis Golffing (Garden City, N.Y., Doubleday Anchor Books, 1956). Cf. the provocative discussion of Nietzsche's types in Brown, op. cit., pp. 157ff. and 269–81.

67. Gouldner and Peterson, *Notes on Technology and the Moral Order*, p. 36.

68. Ibid., p. 33.

69. E.g., the steam engine.

70. Op. cit., p. 50; Swanson, *The Birth of the Gods*, pp. 153–72.

71. Gouldner and Peterson, op. cit., pp. 52f.

72. Robert A. Nisbet, *The Sociological Tradition* (London, Heinemann, 1967), p. 221.

Notes to 6. Religious Orientations

1. Max Weber, 'The social psychology of the world religions' in Gerth and Mills, *From Max Weber*, p. 287.

2. Weber, op. cit., pp. 287f.; the following quotations are from the same place.

3. Ernst Troeltsch, *The Social Teaching of the Christian Churches*, trans. Olive Wyon, 2 vols (London, Allen & Unwin, 1931).

4. Parsons, *The Structure of Social Action*, p. 603.
5. Robert K. Merton, *Social Theory and Social Structure* (Glencoe, Ill., Free Press, rev. ed. 1957), chapter 4.
6. H. Richard Niebuhr, *The Social Sources of Denominationalism* (New York, The World Publishing Company, 1929).
7. Quoted in Weber, *The Protestant Ethic*, p. 175.
8. Liston Pope, *Millhands and Preachers* (New Haven, Conn., Yale University Press, 1942), especially pp. 121ff.
9. David A. Martin, 'The denomination', *British Journal of Sociology*, Vol. 13, 1962, pp. 1–14.
10. Howard Becker, *Systematic Sociology on the Basis of the Beʒeitungslehre and Gebidelehre of L. von Wiese* (New York, Wiley, 1932), pp. 624–43.
11. Harold W. Pfautz, 'The sociology of secularization: religious groups', *American Journal of Sociology*, Vol. 61, 1955, pp. 121–8.
12. J. Milton Yinger, *Religion, Society and the Individual* (New York, Macmillan, 1957), pp. 144–55.
13. See *Journal for the Scientific Study of Religion*, Vol. 6, no. 1, 1967, especially the articles by Allan W. Eister and Paul Gustafson.
14. Yinger, *The Scientific Study of Religion*, p. 260.
15. Robertson, *The Sociological Interpretation of Religion*, pp. 122–8.
16. Ibid., p. 123.
17. For an illustration, see ibid., p. 128; it is confusing that both dimensions are inverted in the illustration.
18. Bryan R. Wilson, *Religious Sects* (London, Weidenfeld and Nicolson, 1970), p. 24; this volume contains a general discussion of sects.
19. See Wilson, 'An analysis of sect development', *American Sociological Review*, Vol. 24, 1959, reprinted in Wilson (ed.), *Patterns of Sectarianism* (London, Heinemann, 1967), pp. 22–45; the following paragraph closely follows Wilson's discussion.
20. Robert C. Towler, *A Sociological Analysis of the Professional Socialiʒation of Anglican Ordinands*, unpublished Ph.D. thesis, The University of Leeds, 1970, pp. 397f.
21. E.g., see Charles Y. Glock, 'The role of deprivation in the origin and evolution of religious groups' in Robert Lee and Martin E. Marty (eds.), *Religion and Social Conflict* (New York, Oxford University Press, 1964).
22. Ibid., p. 29.
23. Wilson, *Religious Sects*, pp. 36f.
24. Wilson, *Patterns of Sectarianism*, pp. 25f.
25. Towler, op. cit., p. 259.
26. As Erikson says, 'no other reported statement of Luther's has made mature men squirm more uncomfortably, or made serious scholars turn their noses higher in contemptuous disbelief', but the interpretation of 'Cl.' as meaning *cloaca* is both obvious and also in keeping with Luther's

excremental imagery: '*Dise Kunst hatt mir der Spiritus Sanctus auff diss Cl. eigeben*' (the holy spirit endowed me with this art on the Cl.). Otto Scheel, *Documente zu Luthers Entwinklung*, Tuebingen: J. C. B. Mohr, 1929, no. 238, quoted in Erik H. Erikson, *Young Man Luther* (London, Faber and Faber, 1972), q.v. pp. 198–200.

27. Wilson, *Religious Sects*, pp. 231f.
28. Wilson, *Patterns of Sectarianism*, p. 24.
29. E.g. Towler, op. cit., pp. 199–204 et passim.

Notes to 7. Dimensions of Institutional Religion

1. See, *inter alia*, Bryan R. Wilson, *Religion in Secular Society* (London, C. A. Watts, 1966).
2. A much-needed corrective to the easy assumption of secularization's factuality is provided in David A. Martin, *A Sociology of English Religion* (London, SCM Press, 1967), and *The Religious and the Secular: Studies in Secularization* (London, Routledge and Kegan Paul, 1969), especially part I.
3. Charles Y. Glock and Rodney Stark, *Religion and Society in Tension* (Chicago, Rand McNally, 1965), pp. 19f.
4. Gerhard Lenski, *The Religious Factor* (Garden City, N.Y., Doubleday Anchor Books, rev. ed. 1963), especially pp. 18–26.
5. The nature of 'the group' is different in each case, a point of which Lenski makes little, but which is taken up again below, pp. 166ff.
6. Lenski, op. cit., p. 25; a nice example of devotional commitment appeared in *The Observer* for 12 March 1972: 'The year's most sensational piece of evangelical one-upmanship seems to have passed unnoticed. The March newsletter of the Billy Graham Evangelistic Association records that on Friday 24 February, at 6.40 p.m. (Vespers, Peking time) President Nixon in China telephoned Billy Graham, the White House evangelist, at his hotel in Florida (Matins, Miami time). Dr Graham, busy preparing for his next series of crusades, said he was bowled over but they had time for a quick prayer before the pips went.'
7. Lenski, op. cit., p. 26, emphases added.
8. Ibid., p. 25, n. 30.
9. Glock and Stark, op. cit., chapter 2; we shall follow here the names of the dimensions as used in Stark and Glock, *American Piety: The Nature of Religious Commitment* (Berkeley and Los Angeles, University of California Press, 1968), chapter 1.
10. Stark and Glock op. cit., p. 16.
11. Cited in Will Herberg, *Protestant-Catholic-Jew* (Garden City, N.Y., Doubleday Anchor Books, rev. ed. 1959), pp. 91f., n. 6.

12. Ibid., p. 5, n. 6.
13. Loc. cit., n. 8.
14. E.g., see Peter Worsley, *The Trumpet Shall Sound.*
15. Emile Durkheim, *The Elementary Forms of the Religious Life,* p. 61.
16. Loc. cit., n. 62.
17. Wilson, op. cit., p. xiv.
18. Thomas Luckmann, *The Invisible Religion* (London, Collier-Macmillan, 1967), pp. 90f.
19. William James, *The Varieties of Religious Experience,* quoted as the epigraph in Luckmann, op. cit.
20. Wilson, op. cit., p. xv.
21. Luckmann, op. cit., p. 43.
22. P. 17, above.
23. Luckmann, loc. cit.
24. Ibid., p. 61.
25. Ibid., p. 62.
26. Ibid., pp. 66f.
27. Max Weber, 'The social psychology of the world religions' in Gerth and Mills, *From Max Weber,* p. 287.
28. The term 'sacred cosmos', which Luckmann uses as an equivalent to 'symbolic universe', is shared with Berger, who distinguishes between them, defining religion as 'the human enterprise by which a sacred cosmos is established', or 'cosmization in a sacred mode'; Berger parts company with Luckmann when, for the latter, 'religion is equated with symbolic self-transcendence', since Berger prefers to define religion as a system of *sacred* symbols (see Berger, *The Social Reality of Religion,* p. 26 and Appendix I). The terms involved are from Rudolf Otto and Mircea Eliade.
29. See the discussion of 'official' religion in the following chapter.
30. In missions, for instance, the general process will be referred to as 'disembodiment', below, pp. 178ff.
31. See Bellah, *Beyond Belief,* p. 233.
32. Luckmann, op. cit., p. 103.
33. See above, p. 17.
34. Mary Douglas, *Natural Symbols,* see above, pp. 79ff.
35. Johann C. Lavater, *Aphorisms on Man* (London, 1788).
36. Wilson, op. cit., p. xv.
37. Gerth and Mills, op. cit., p. 51.

Notes to 8. Common Religion

1. Some of the points raised in this chapter have been discussed briefly in a paper which also reports findings from a study which attempted to use

a relatively untried method of research, Robert Towler and Audrey Chamberlain, 'Common religion' in Michael Hill (ed.), *A Sociological Yearbook of Religion in Britain*, Vol. 6 (London, SCM Press, 1973).

2. Lenski, *The Religious Factor*, p. 331.

3. Stark and Glock, *American Piety*, p. 13.

4. Joseph E. Faulkner and Gordon F. DeJong, 'Religiosity in 5-D: an empirical analysis', *Social Forces*, Vol. 45, 1966, pp. 246–54; Morton King, 'Measuring the religious variable: nine proposed dimensions', *Journal for the Scientific Study of Religion*, Vol. 6, 1967, pp. 173–90; Andrew J. Weigert and Darwin L. Thomas, 'Religiosity in 5-D: a critical note', *Social Forces*, Vol. 48, 1969, pp. 260–3; Robert B. Tapp, 'Dimensions of religiosity in a post-traditional group', *Journal for the Scientific Study of Religion*, Vol. 10, 1971, pp. 41–7.

5. See the Manual to the British edition (revised from the 1960 American edition), by Sylvia Richardson (Slough, The National Foundation for Educational Research, 1965).

6. Richard A. Hunt, 'The interpretation of the Religious scale of the Allport-Vernon-Lindzey Study of Values', *Journal for the Scientific Study of Religion*, Vol. 7, 1968, p. 70; cf. Donald E. Super, *Appraising Vocational Fitness* (New York, Harper and Brothers, 1949), p. 466.

7. Luckmann, *The Invisible Religion*, p. 91.

8. Gustav Mensching, 'Folk and universal religion', trans. Louis Schneider in Schneider (ed.), *Religion, Culture and Society* (New York, Wiley, 1964), pp. 254–61; cf. E. Wilbur Bock, 'Symbols in conflict: official versus folk religion', *Journal for the Scientific Study of Religion*, Vol. 5, 1966, pp. 204–12.

9. Louis Schneider and Stanford Dornbusch, *Popular Religion: Inspirational Books in America* (Chicago, University of Chicago Press, 1958).

10. Robin M. Williams Jr., *American Society: A Sociological Interpretation* (New York, Knopf, 1951), p. 312.

11. Robert N. Bellah, 'Civil religion in America' in Bellah, *Beyond Belief*, pp. 168–89.

12. Ibid., p. 168.

13. Trevor O. Ling, 'Anthropology and international understanding: the role of comparative religion', paper presented to the Indian Anthropological Society, November 1971; to appear in L. P. Vidyarthi (ed.) forthcoming.

14. Ibid.

15. Bryan R. Wilson, *Religion in Secular Society*, p. xviii.

16. Paul Radin, *Primitive Religion: Its Nature and its Origin* (London, Hamish Hamilton, 1938), pp. 15–39 and 59–65.

17. Hugh Trevor-Roper, *Religion, the Reformation and Social Change*, p. xi.

18 Keith Thomas, *Religion and the Decline of Magic* (London, Weiden-

feld and Nicolson, 1971); Alan Macfarlane, *Witchcraft in Tudor and Stuart England* (London, Routledge and Kegan Paul, 1970); see also Trevor-Roper, 'The European witch craze of the sixteenth and seventeenth centuries' in Trevor-Roper, op. cit.

19. Geoffrey Gorer, *Exploring English Character* (London, Barrie and Rockliffe The Cresset Press, 1955), chapter 14.
20. Nicholas Abercrombie *et al.*, 'Superstition and religion: the god of the gaps' in David A. Martin and Michael Hill (eds), *A Sociological Yearbook of Religion in Britain*, Vol. 3 (London, SCM Press, 1970), pp. 93–129.
21. See above, pp. 44ff.
22. Abercrombie *et al.*, op. cit., p. 127.
23. Luckmann, op. cit., p. 103, cf. above p. 141.
24. Worsley, *The Trumpet Shall Sound*, p. xxiv.
25. See Iona Opie and Peter Opie, *The Lore and Language of Schoolchildren* (London, Oxford University Press, 1959), pp. 121–6; Gustav Jahoda, *The Psychology of Superstition* (London, Allen Lane The Penguin Press, 1969), pp. 105–10.
26. Gorer, op. cit., pp. 254–62; and *Grief, Death and Mourning in Contemporary Britain* (London, Barrie and Rockliffe The Cresset Press, 1965), pp. 161–68.
27. Audrey Chamberlain, *Fertility Behaviour and Attitudes among Highly Fertile Women in Leeds*, Ph.D. thesis, The University of Leeds, in progress.
28. *The Guardian*, 19 November 1971.
29. Quoted in Mircea Eliade, *Patterns in Comparative Religion* (New York, Sheed and Ward), p. xi.
30. Richard Hoggart, *The Uses of Literacy* (Harmondsworth, Middlesex, Penguin Books, 1957), p. 119.
31. Jean Piaget, *The Child's Conception of the World* (London, Routledge and Kegan Paul, 1929), p. 123.
32. Luckmann, op. cit., p. 76; see pp. 74ff.
33. 'The role of the clergy today' in C. L. Mitton (ed.), *The Social Sciences and the Churches* (Edinburgh, T. and T. Clark, 1972), pp. 151–62.

Notes to 9. Inter-Church Relations

1. This chapter has previously appeared in John Kent and Robert Murray, eds, *Church Membership and Intercommunion*, op. cit., and is reprinted by permission of the publishers.
2. Stephen Neill and Ruth Rouse, eds, *A History of the Ecumenical Movement* (Philadelphia, The Westminster Press, 1954); on Methodism, see John Kent, *The Age of Disunity* (London, Epworth Press, 1966), and

Robert Currie, *Methodism Divided: A Study in the Sociology of Ecumenicalism* (London, Faber and Faber, 1968).

3. Currie, op. cit., pp. 314 & 316.

4. Ibid., p. 54.

5. Jacques Ellul, *Fausse présence au monde moderne* (Paris, Librairie Protestante, 1963), p. 72, quoted in Roger Mehl, *The Sociology of Protestantism* (London, SCM Press, 1970) (trans. from the French edition of 1965), p. 204.

6. Currie, op. cit., p. 11.

7. Interim Report of the Multilateral Church Conversation in Scotland, *Reports to the General Assembly of the Church of Scotland*, 1972, p. 591.

8. *Methodist Recorder*, 16 September 1926, quoted in Currie, op. cit., p. 197.

9. On the abolition of Friday abstinence, see Mary Douglas, *Natural Symbols: Exploration sin Cosmology* (London, Barrie and Rockliffe, The Cresset Press, 1970), pp. 3f.

10. The example contrasts strangely with Max Weber's agnostic experience on the occasion of a visit to the Isle of Skye, when he was asked one Sunday which service he had attended, H. H. Gerth and C. Wright Mills, eds. *From Max Weber* (London, Routledge and Kegan Paul, 1948), p. 303.

11. Robert Towler and Audrey Smith, 'Common Religion' in Michael Hill (ed.), *A Sociological Yearbook of Religion in Britain*, No. 6 (London, SCM Press, 1973).

12. David O. Moberg, *The Church as a Social Institution* (Englewood Cliffs, N.J., Prentice-Hall, 1962), p. 257.

13. The encyclical *Mortalium animos* (1928).

14. Bryan R. Wilson, *Religion in Secular Society* (London, C. A. Watts, 1966), part 3, 'The religious response'.

15. In a more than trivial sense the man is treated as mad: not just as if he were mad, but as mad.

16. Currie, op. cit., p. 11.

17. See Michael Hill and Peter Wakeford, 'Disembodied ecumenicalism: a survey of the members of four Methodist churches in or near London', and Bryan S. Turner, 'Institutional persistence and ecumenicalism in Northern Methodism' in David A. Martin, ed., *A Sociological Yearbook of Religion in Britain*, No. 2 (London, SCM Press, 1969).

18. Rodney Stark and Charles Y. Glock, *American Piety* (Berkeley and Los Angeles, University of California Press, 1968), pp. 24f.

19. See Jeffery K. Hadden, *The Gathering Storm in the Churches* (New York, Doubleday, 1969), especially chapter 5.

20. On the Festival of Light in Great Britain, see Roy Wallis, 'Dilemma of a moral crusade', *New Society*, 13 July 1972, pp. 69–72, and John Capon, . . . *And There Was Light* (London, Lutterworth Press, 1972).

21. Cf. Wilson, op. cit., pp. 149f.
22. Peter L. Berger, 'The secularization of theology', *Journal for the Scientific Study of Religion,* Vol. 6, 1967, p. 15.
23. H. Richard Niebuhr, *The Social Sources of Denominationalism* (New York, Holt, 1929). Cf. K. S. Inglis, *Churches and the Working Classes in Victorian England* (London, Routledge and Kegan Paul, 1963), and E. P. Thompson, *The Making of the English Working Class* (Harmondsworth, Middlesex, Penguin 1964).
24. Robert Lee, *The Social Sources of Church Unity* (New York, Abingdon Press, 1960).
25. The useful distinction between native and foreign cases of disembodied religious traditions is drawn from P. A. J. Waddington, *The Ecumenical Movement: a study in the sociology of religion,* unpublished M.A. dissertation (The University of Leeds, 1970).
26. Cited in Bengt Sundkler, *Church of South India: The Movement Towards Union, 1900–1947* (London, Lutterworth Press, 1954), p. 36, quoted in Wilson, op. cit., p. 148.
27. Rector, 'Baptist-Disciple conversations towards unity' in Nils Ehrenstrom and Walter G. Muelder, eds, *Institutionalism and Church Unity* (London, SCM Press, 1963).
28. Peter L. Berger and Thomas Luckmann, 'Secularization and pluralism' *International Yearbook for the Sociology of Religion,* No. 2, 1966, and, Berger, 'A market model for the analysis of ecumenicity', *Social Research,* Vol. 30, 1963.
29. People are 'free' to move in accordance with the 'demands' of the economy, that is, rather than free to move where they will.
30. Mehl, op. cit., p. 196; for the effect on traditional ethics, see Robert A. Nisbet, 'The impact of technology on ethical decision-making' in Robert Lee and Martin E. Marty, eds, *Religion and Social Conflict* (New York, Oxford University Press, 1964).
31. Moberg, op. cit., p. 260.
32. Peter L. Berger, *The Social Reality of Religion* (London, Faber and Faber, 1969), p. 150.

Index